14.45
BT

THE DYNAMITE FIEND

The Chilling Tale of a Confederate Spy, Con Artist, and Mass Murderer

ANN LARABEE

palgrave
macmillan

First published 2005 by
PALGRAVE MACMILLAN™
175 Fifth Avenue, New York, N.Y. 10010 and
Houndmills, Basingstoke, Hampshire, England RG21 6XS.
Companies and representatives throughout the world.

PALGRAVE MACMILLAN is the global academic imprint of the Palgrave
Macmillan division of St. Martin's Press, LLC and of Palgrave Macmillan Ltd.
Macmillan® is a registered trademark in the United States, United Kingdom
and other countries. Palgrave is a registered trademark in the European Union
and other countries.

ISBN 1-4039-6794-6

Library of Congress Cataloging-in-Publication Data
Larabee, Ann, 1957–
    The dynamite fiend : the chilling tale of a Confederate spy, con artist, and
mass murderer / Ann Larabee.
        p. cm.
    Includes bibliographical references and index.
    ISBN 1-4039-6794-6 (alk. paper)
    1. Keith, Alexander, b. 1827. 2. Spies—Confederate States of America—
Biography. 3. Bombers (Terrorists)—Confederate States of America—
Biography. 4. United States—History—Civil War, 1861–1865—Underground
movements. 5. Swindlers and swindling—United States—Biography. 6.
Mass murderers—United States—Biography. 7. Bombers (Terrorists)—
United States—Biography. 8. Halifax (N.S.)—Biography. I. Title.
E608.K37L37 2005
303.6'25'092—dc22
[B]

                                                                    2004065033

A catalogue record for this book is available from the British Library.

Design by Letra Libre, Inc.

First edition: June 2005
10 9 8 7 6 5 4 3 2 1
Printed in the United States of America.

To my mother, Ruth Larabee, who read to me.

CONTENTS

—◄●►—

Photosection appears between pages 128 and 129.

He was the mildest manner'd man
That ever scuttled a ship or cut a throat.
—Lord Byron

INTRODUCTION

Tens of thousands of travelers crossed the ocean on the great transatlantic steamships in 1875, looking for love, for adventure, for profit, for new lives in new worlds. None yet suspected that on some of these voyages, amidst the hustle and bustle of ship life, an evil genius was in a first class cabin plotting to blow all his innocent fellow passengers to atoms. It was still an age of innocence that could not yet conceive of malevolent designs to destroy thousands of unwitting human beings in a single horrific stroke. But that innocence was about to come to an abrupt end.

The train from Bremen, Germany, was packed with travelers, making the forty-five minute journey out to the docks where they would board the *Mosel*, one of the nineteenth century's elegant transatlantic steamships. Mostly emigrants to the New World, they were full of high emotion as they sat close to their loved ones, murmuring their sad farewells or chatting excitedly about their destinations in America. Many dreaded the ocean crossing, as they fearfully imagined seasickness, gales, icebergs, exploding steam boilers, and the occasional vessel that simply disappeared without a trace. Just a few days before, the steamer *Deutschland* had run aground on a shoal, and forty people had died in the rough waves and freezing winds before a rescue ship could arrive. Seated next to a group of nervous, inexperienced travelers was a bespectacled, portly man radiating expansive friendliness and calm. He called himself William King Thomas. From his neatly trimmed reddish-brown whiskers to the showy gold watch fob lying on his great belly, he appeared the respectable Victorian businessman. With a soothing, confident tone, he spoke expertly of his forty transatlantic crossings. It was all perfectly safe, he said.

When the train reached the dock in Bremerhaven, an eager young passenger, Fritz Zumann, detrained and made his way to the *Mosel*, accompanied by his aunt, his uncle, and his brother. It was a cold, sunny morning in December 1875, and passengers shivered as they waited to embark, standing on the snow-covered dock, tearfully hugging and kissing their friends and loved ones. In his exuberance for his ocean adventure, undeterred by tales of shipwreck and the misery of passage, Fritz forged ahead of his family and boarded the massive ship. Behind him, a few workers stood near a baggage cart, drawn by a horse and holding a very heavy wooden barrel. They were attaching it to a winch when it slipped and hit the dock.

At that moment, as Fritz stood on the gangway next to the ship's kitchen, the ordinary world suddenly exploded and surrounded him with flying wooden splinters and shards of glass and pottery. Shocked and deafened by the noise, which was like a bullet boring through his ears, he found that he had miraculously survived the furious blast, but was now trapped beneath the debris. Terrified that the ship would sink at any minute, he desperately clawed a hole and crawled for safety through a slick of blood and over remains of the unlucky ones. Outside, he found his aunt and uncle, lying in an embrace, stripped naked by the force of the explosion but still alive. And with joy he saw his brother, safe and unharmed, and they fell into each other's arms.

Producing a great shockwave, the explosion had caved the bow of the *Mosel* and buckled the deck of its tug, the *Simson*. Cabins and decks were covered with sand, broken glass, and pieces of wood and twisted iron. On the cobbled loading area of the dock, the explosion had produced a black, smoking hole six feet deep and seven feet wide. The sound of the blast reached even to Hamburg, where it was perceived as a low rumble. In retrospect, the citizens of that city imagined that they had heard the moans of the dying. Traumatized witnesses would forever remember the scene as indescribable carnage, an apocalyptic battlefield, everything besmirched with blood and human flesh. The injured lay vulnerably naked and terribly maimed; whole families had been lost or severely injured. Soldiers were called in from a nearby drill ground to aid the Bremen police; four men were assigned to collect body parts from the dock, place them in a basket, and take them to the lighthouse. Others carried the wounded to the baggage hall, where they awaited medical personnel who had been rushed in by train.

In the midst of the chaos, the man called William King Thomas, who had already settled into his first class cabin, rushed onto the promenade deck and stared down at the scene. Others who stood witnessing the horror noticed him pull out a schnapps flask and take several deep swigs. With other dazed survivors, he moved about the wreckage, and engaged the *Mosel's* captain in a brief conversation. Then he disappeared back into his cabin.

Baffled police officials, ship personnel, and witnesses struggled to make sense of the catastrophe. They immediately guessed it to be an accident. Zumann and many other survivors first thought that a ship's boiler had exploded, an understandable conclusion given the still precarious nature of steam engines. Dozens of ships and thousands of lives were lost on rivers and oceans because of faulty boilers. But it was soon realized that only dynamite could have created such an explosion, dynamite packed in the luggage of a passenger. Over the next few days, a horrific scenario unfolded, an insurance swindle so innovative and cold-blooded that it could hardly be believed. Eighty-one people had died and some fifty were injured in a plan gone awry. And if the plan had been carried out as intended, several hundred more would have perished on the sea, the *Mosel* disappearing without a trace.

The perpetrator of this awful crime was the friendly, affable William King Thomas, much to the shock of his friends, who remembered him as an upstanding, prosperous burgher, a kind and loving father to his four small children. A big, friendly bear of a man, Thomas had always inspired the greatest confidence. Everywhere he went on his international travels he was admired for his gregariousness and his generosity toward everyone, including ordinary working people and the poor. He moved in the *beau monde*, among Saxon generals and American socialites, lavishly entertaining them and impressing them with his wealth, Victorian manliness, good humor, and charismatic charm. But William King Thomas was not what he seemed. Behind this respectable Dr. Jekyll hid a vicious Mr. Hyde who had spent many months perfecting an elaborate time bomb for the deed that the *London Times* called the "most diabolical that human wickedness could ever devise." Newspaper editors across the Western world proclaimed

Thomas the "Dynamite Fiend," a man who thought nothing of destroying entire passenger ships and all onboard for personal gain. He seemed to distill the worst of the new Gilded Age with its exuberant capitalism and unmitigated greed. Travelers feared that they, too, could be taken in by a pleasant, cosmopolitan stranger who, undetected, was planting bombs in the holds of ships.

The Mr. Hyde that the amiable Thomas so carefully disguised was his real identity, Alexander Keith, Jr., whose violence lay deep in a hidden past. Keith had once served as a Confederate secret service agent during the Civil War, and from his base in Halifax, Nova Scotia, had helped organized some of the most infamous terrorist plots of that war. He was part of a little-known underworld, a web of Confederate covert operatives and terrorists, mostly social malcontents and misfits, who often confused their political cause with lust for profit. In their greed, rage, and desperation, they had no compunction about targeting innocent civilians if they thought they could gain wealth and glory by making a satisfactory psychological blow against the North. Toward the end of the war, betraying the trust of his nefarious colleagues, Keith had gone on the run, attempting to distance himself from his crimes, finally landing in Germany, where he lived a thoroughly respectable life. But Keith himself was a ticking time bomb that would eventually go off, to the grief of a nation and the stunned horror of the Western world.

My fascination with Alexander Keith, Jr., alias William King Thomas, began in the summer of 2002 when I braved a flight to Germany with the historian Mark Roseman, who was on a book tour for *The Past in Hiding,* his brilliant biography of Holocaust survivor Marianne Strauss. With his help, I was planning to take a brief side trip to the Bremen State Archive in the hope that I could clear up a small mystery. Researching Confederate terrorists, I had become deeply curious about a fleeting reference that linked the elusive Alexander Keith, Jr., and the bomber William King Thomas. I had no other aim than simply to establish that they were one and the same man, though neither of them appeared to be more than an obscure historical footnote. My pursuit of what would turn out to be fact was really just a whim.

Less than a year after the September 11 attacks, Mark and I still felt insecure on a plane and many of our colleagues and loved ones were choosing to stay home rather than risk travel abroad. After all, in the next seat might be an ordinary looking stranger concealing a box cutter under his sweater or plastique packed in his running shoes. We were constantly reminded of our vulnerability by the elaborate new search procedures as we practically disrobed at the security check-points, stripping off our belts and shoes, my laptop on one occasion setting off the explosives detector for completely mysterious reasons. The airports suddenly were filled with a visibly armed presence of guards and soldiers. I felt suspicious eyes on me, and I felt suspicious of others. The atmosphere was tense and panicky.

Therefore, I was in a susceptible frame of mind when Mark and I arrived in the small, fluorescent conference room of the Bremen State Archive and booted up our laptops, expecting to have our work done in an hour or two. Much to my surprise, the archivist lugged in eight huge file folders, most of them over five inches thick, overflowing with ragged, yellowing documents from the police investigation of the "Thomas-Katastrophe." We looked in excitement and then despair, since the documents were all written in *Suetterlin*, an archaic German running hand, which even native Germans can no longer read. The project suddenly seemed immense even for Mark, who had translated Marianne's diaries, written in meticulous *Suetterlin* while she was on the run from the Nazis. We decided to skim through the documents for any immediate clues, and I turned page after page of an impenetrable cipher, finding small clues such as corroded metal bits of Keith's bomb concealed in a folded piece of brown paper. But I had no idea what I was seeing.

Then I had the moment historians dream of. Buried in the middle of one of the folders was a long report from the Pinkerton Detective Agency, a journal of an investigation, written in English on legal paper. Relieved to see script I could instantly recognize, I perused the document, slowly realizing that I had found one of the most amazing true stories I had ever read. As I followed the gumshoes on their pursuit of an elusive quarry, finally discovering the real identity of their man after dozens of false leads, I was gripped by the eerie familiarity of Keith, the mass murderer who faded into every society like a chameleon and then compulsively traveled back and forth on passenger ships with his dynamite bomb, waiting for his moment to strike. The detectives interviewed people who had traveled with him, and I wondered what they must have felt upon discovering that this affable Victorian gentleman who ate with gusto and often strolled the decks had all the while been planning to kill them, that he had been a terrorist who still harbored war in his deepest thoughts. I could think of no case prior to Keith's when the international transportation system had been targeted for a bombing. With astonishing ruthlessness, he was the first to introduce this concept to the modern world: that murderous energies could be focused on the innocent, unwitting masses of human beings crossing the Atlantic together. The story resonated with the insecurities of my own time, the fears that beneath the ordinary-seeming world was a volcanic rage. When Mark and I packed up, having only scratched the surface of the files, I knew this was a story I had to tell.

I would return to Bremen, where I would find more clues to Keith's life, including his personal letters and photographs. But my quest took me further as I tracked him through four countries, my research finally ending in the far northern corner of Scotland where he was born. I bumped along in a reconditioned school bus to Halkirk, where I was deposited on one of only ten streets in that tiny rural town. Then, with the sun beating down on my head, unusual weather for that part of the world, I walked four miles past the slate quarries and fields full of bleating Cheviot sheep to arrive at the ruins of Brawlbin at the southern tip of Loch Calder. Traces of the old tenant farms were still there, but this once populous place had an unruffled quietude that hid its history of suffering. In the late eighteenth century, avaricious landlords had violently forced their tenants off this land to make way for the large-scale agribusiness of sheep ranching. Many of these farmers, like the Keiths, made their way across the ocean for a new life. Sitting at the edge of peaceful Loch Calder, I wondered whether Keith's rage had begun at that moment of childhood dislocation, when the arrogant, ruthless landlords, who valued profit over people, had forced him from this place to Halifax, Nova Scotia. Dispossession and war: how many others have they twisted and driven to violent desperation over the centuries? I hoped that through one man's life I could begin to understand how our modern fears took shape at that moment of catastrophe in Bremerhaven.

ONE

THE CLAN KEITH

On a hot night in August as the annual Perseid meteor shower streaked across the sky, a huge explosion shook the citizens of Halifax, Nova Scotia from their beds. It had been a quiet year, 1857, with no great wars of empire to fill the British garrison on the top of the hill. With its bristling cannons and bombproof casements, the four-bastioned Citadel had never once engaged in any real battle and never would. Thus, the secure, complacent citizens of Halifax were shocked to find their houses reverberating from a great blast, as if a long-anticipated war had begun, and they rushed outside to the acrid smell of gunpowder and a sky fill with fiery debris, the most brilliant display of pyrotechnics they had ever seen. Thinking that a meteor had struck, some raced down to the harbor where they found the powder magazine leveled to the ground, the nearby houses shattered, and their residents crushed and broken, one dead. Only the poorest families lived in the north suburb down by the harbor, in the perilous vicinity of the magazine. Why the powder magazine should suddenly blow up by itself seemed a mystery, and as soon as the smoke cleared the townspeople demanded an explanation.

The town's aldermen gathered to investigate the cause of this very expensive and ruinous accident. At first glance, with no apparent evidence of human tampering, the aldermen must have thought the explosion was an act of God. On further consideration, they decided to call on two learned men, the former mayor Andrew McKinlay and the local chemist Robert Fraser, to investigate the incident in greater depth. They put an end to speculation that the heat lightning shimmering in the sky that night somehow ignited the gunpowder. Nor had either of them heard of gunpowder spontaneously combusting. Had a fiery shooting star then crashed into the magazine? McKinlay noted that the meteors were flying too high and in the wrong direction. Finding no natural reason for the catastrophe, the committee concluded that the blast had been no accident. Someone, either through chance or design, had blown up the magazine.

A criminal investigation ensued. Suspicion immediately fell on the victims, the neighbors who had been loitering around the magazine, smoking their pipes. Yet evidence quickly surfaced that a carelessly tossed match was not the culprit. In a field adjacent to the explosion site, a yeoman farmer came across a stone buried ten inches deep from the force of the blast. It was coated with gunpowder, but even more curiously, it held a lump of candle wax and a three-inch wick. It would have been an act of insanity for anyone to carry a lit candle into a gunpowder magazine unless he had some malevolent design. A candle with a long wick, carefully and surreptitiously placed, could have timed the explosion, taking minutes or hours to burn down to its fatal end, allowing the villain to escape before the blast. It was a primitive but effective means of causing mayhem.

The motivation for such a deed was difficult to imagine. The constables tried criminal profiling, rounding up the usual suspects, who could sign their depositions only with an X. An Irish spinster, Honora Walsh, had walked down to the water the afternoon prior to the explosion to take a bath. Some neighborhood boys had been throwing rocks on the beach and had struck her in the head as she emerged from the water. She had raised her fist and threatened them, "By God, you will not rest in your bed tonight without I get satisfaction!" Then there was the farmer on a rum-drinking binge who had slept in the Victorian gardens the night of the explosion. For the next few nights, Patrick Crockwell had slept wherever he fell in various parts of town, including the woods, and investigators suspected he might have been hiding. But there was no other evidence or apparent motive to connect him to a complicated arson attempt.

Suspicion also fell on the regular visitors to the magazine, including Alexander Keith, Jr., nicknamed Sandy for his reddish-brown hair. An agent for civil engineering projects around the province, he was the last person to have the key to the public magazine. He was, in fact, the only gunpowder customer that the magazine's keeper, who had been sick in bed for six weeks, had entrusted with the key. But even if the investigators suspected Sandy, they were not about to humiliate one of the most powerful men in town. Sandy's uncle was Alexander Keith: a prosperous brewer, private banker, three-time mayor, and paterfamilias of the town's many Scottish immigrants. Loyalties and reputations were involved in the tight-knit world of Haligonian business and politics.

Sandy Keith was called in to testify, but the interrogators' questions cautiously revolved not around his possible guilt or innocence, but around the tidiness of the magazine. Though several witnesses testified that the place was well kept and the floor neatly swept with a hair broom, Sandy Keith complained that he had "seen a very slovenly state of things" and that loose gunpowder was piled against the copper shutters. He presented himself as the most safety conscious of all the various people who frequented the magazine, for, as he said, he had often scraped powder off the floor with his own hand or a wooden hoop. He cast further aspersions on the keeper, Samuel Marshall, complaining of having had to chase Marshall all over town to get the key. When the keeper was ill, he said, the key had been placed in a public shop, available to anyone who happened by. His testimony was all deflection, for Sandy Keith was the only suspect to have a real motive, one that was tacitly known but which would never be pursued or openly spoken — better meteors, lightning bolts, angry spinsters, and drunks than the town's favorite son. The committee decided that the evidence was inconclusive and offered £500 reward for any further information, a reward that no one would ever claim.

It was only some twenty years later that folks around Halifax admitted that they always thought Sandy Keith was the villain, but even then these witnesses insisted on anonymity, unwilling to openly challenge powerful Haligonian families. A government contractor later revealed that he had lost $2,000 in the powder magazine explosion and was convinced Sandy Keith had done it. But he could never find conclusive evidence. More tellingly, a "prominent banker of Halifax" told

Pinkerton detectives this story. Sandy Keith worked as a clerk in his Uncle Alexander's business, a highly trusted position managing not only the brewery, but also all of his uncle's diverse financial affairs. As one of the investors and organizers for the notoriously mismanaged Halifax-to-Windsor railroad project, Alexander Keith had given his nephew the important task of looking after his contracts and contractors. The railway construction used huge quantities of gunpowder to blast through rocks, stumps, and dirt, and Sandy was a primary distributor. He therefore would often take a wagon down to the magazine supposedly to pick up the powder and then distribute it along the rail. Suspicion grew among the railway investors that he was taking money from them to buy gunpowder at twenty-five cents per pound from the Halifax magazine, but actually buying it at half that price from contractors elsewhere in the province. The investors guessed that Sandy was secretly keeping the twelve and a half cents as profit, and since he was not taking enough powder from the Halifax magazine, to which he had relatively free access, he had to cover up the discrepancy. Before any investigation could be made, he apparently blew up the magazine, erasing the evidence of his swindle without a thought to its poor neighbors, who ended up dead, disabled, or homeless.

Haligonian businessmen involved in the railroad believed Sandy had done it, but the matter was settled privately. Judges, newspaper editors, and church leaders railed against violent crime concentrated in the poor neighborhood to the east of Citadel Hill, where the prostitutes, thieves, and drunken rowdies lived. But surely such base impulses could not exist among the wealthy chiefs or their heirs. At least one merchant, who had lost $50,000 due to the explosion, demanded satisfaction of Sandy Keith and was given his money, the equivalent of about a million dollars today. A brewery clerk like Sandy, even a cheating one, could not have amassed such a fortune; the family had rescued him behind closed doors. Sandy came to rely on business being done this way in Victorian Halifax.

Sandy Keith's relationship with the powerful uncle who protected him was a psychologically complicated one. Sandy admired and emulated him, but on occasion demonstrated a violent jealousy toward him. Alexander Keith and his brother, Sandy's father John, were both brewers who began their trade in the farthest northern part of Scotland, in a quiet river valley full of heather and marsh grass, surrounded by low hills slanting down to the River Thurso and Loch Calder. The residents of this place, as a local Presbyterian minister characterized them, were "industrious, temperate, economical, and very hospitable," as well as "intelligent, moral, and religious."

The Keith patriarch, Donald, was a well-to-do tacksman holding a coveted long-term lease on a large farm, wrested from wild land to raise skinny black cattle and fine-wooled indigenous sheep and to cultivate corn, oats, barley, potatoes, and turnips. In the hierarchy of the Scottish agricultural system, the tacksman was a gentleman farmer who served as a middleman between the tenants, with whom he often had family ties, and his landlord, for whom he administered leases, collected rents, and maintained social order. In the early eighteenth century, the clan chiefs bestowed the socially exalted position of tacksman upon loyal clan warriors who were then obligated to oversee the chief's lands, watch over his tenants and laborers, and organize and train them into a fighting force.

After many Highland clans sided with James VII and his heir, Prince Charles Edward Stuart, during the failed Jacobite rebellion ending in 1746, the clan chiefs, as well as their tacksmen, lost much of their power in the severe repression, economic distress, and social disintegration that followed. Keeping their hold on the British Crown, the Hanoverian dynasty attempted to crush Highland clan spirit and identity by banning the tartan and the bagpipe. Furthermore, in the interest of efficiency, profit, and their own luxury, landlords across Scotland began raising rents beyond anyone's ability to pay, dividing or consolidating the old farms, and, more ruthlessly, removing whole communities and dumping them on hard, uncultivated ground or on rocky shores to retrain as fishermen.

By the end of the eighteenth century, most of the tacksmen, who had once been considered minor chiefs, had been phased out. Replacing them, as well as their subtenants and laborers, were flocks of hardy Cheviot sheep, the latest development in eighteenth-century agribusiness. The greatly lamented Clearances of Highland communities were moving ever closer to Halkirk and the Keiths' peaceful lands around the loch. From his base in the small town of Halkirk, overlooked by a Presbyterian church and the ruined Braal Castle, Donald Keith could see the great changes coming toward him—the decline of his power and the old ways of the Highland clans—and some of his family grew restless to change. These included his youngest sons, Alexander and John, who had witnessed the substantial benefits of the fading order, but could not take up their father's path.

In a region known for the healing quality of its mineral waters, the other great trade in Halkirk parish was brewing and distilling, with, at one time, thirteen establishments within a population of somewhat less than 3,000 people. The four inns in the tiny town did a thriving business, causing the Presbyterian ministers to rail against the corruption of the parish's youth, whose only other wild behavior was poaching game. For many years, the reverends preached against their congregation's zeal for brewing and distilling, complaining that the barley was not being exported, but rather used for the production of alcoholic beverages. With the ready availability of fine barley and the import of light, aromatic English hops, Scottish brewers produced a unique, mellow, balsamic amber ale. Resisting the temperance-minded pressures of the churches, the younger Keith brothers both cast their fortunes on this craft, yet only one would die a wealthy man.

Lured by the prospects of the princely fortunes made by commercial brewers, the more adventurous and ambitious Alexander went off for training in the modernized scientific breweries of northern England. When he was only twenty-two, he sailed for Halifax, where he took a job as a business manager in Charles Boggs' brewery. Within a few years he earned enough to buy the brewery, supplying porter, ale, ginger wine, and spruce beer to thirsty, homesick soldiers on their two-year stint in the British garrison at the Citadel, so crowded that an escape to the pub was the only relief. The liquor trade boomed in Halifax, which one temperance reformer ruefully designated "a great big Rum shop." From there, Alexander Keith began to consolidate his wealth and power, diversifying into banking and insurance, sitting on boards of trade, and running for public office. He was a practical and forceful man, successfully bringing the old tacksman's role to the New World, overseeing the fortunes of other Scottish immigrants. Like many of them, his memory of home became fanciful, nostalgic, and grandiose.

Although he had no real claim to the title, Alexander set himself up as the "chief of the Clan Keith," purloining the lineage and the mythology of the ancient Grand Marischals of Scotland. In traditional accounts of the Scottish nobility, the fortunes of the titled Keiths, the

Marischals, fluctuated wildly. Under the banner of the three red stags' heads, three red stripes, and the motto "Veritas vincit" (Truth conquers), the various holders of the title were famous for their military exploits. The Keiths received their red stripes when their primogenitor, the first Sir Robert Keith, slew the leader of the invading Danes and his grateful king wiped three bloody fingers across his shield. Immortalized by Sir Walter Scott, another of the many Sir Robert Keiths rallied his cavalry with the cry, "Mount, ye gallants free!" and routed the English archers at the Battle of Bannockburn in 1314 for Scottish independence. Known for his soldierly prowess, William Keith of Galston went off to the Holy Land in 1330, following the dessicated heart of Robert Bruce, a talisman kept in a small lead casket carried by the crusaders. In Caithness, where Sandy spent his earliest years, the Keiths were legendary for their endless feud with their mortal enemies, the Gunns. In these tales, the Keiths often took the role of base and brutal deceivers of their nobler enemy. An especially beloved horror tale involved Big Keith, who carried on his shoulder the devil disguised as a raven that would swoop down to peck out the eyes of the Gunns.

During the Jacobite rebellion, the Keiths were one of the clans that made the ill-fated decision to lend diplomatic and military support to the Old Pretender and Bonnie Prince Charlie on their abortive quests to regain the throne of England. For this, the Keiths lost their vast wealth and landholdings, including the dreary, wind-swept castle, Dunnottar, where the gloomy earl, William Keith, secluded himself, presiding over a clanking dungeon where political prisoners begged for merciful deaths. Exiled to the Continent, the last Earl Marischal, George Keith, as a full-grown adult played toy soldiers with Frederick the Great of Prussia while squandering whatever was left of the family fortune. The Keiths' tragic fall resulted in a famous poem, "Lady Keith's Lament," in which the aged matriarch pines for the return of her title and the "guid auld day, the day o' pride and chieftain's glory." Noble but tragic warriors, bloody battlefields, and a nostalgic sense of entitlement were part of the Keiths' fanciful psychic legacy that came across the ocean with them.

By taking on the title of clan chief, Alexander Keith proved how selective and opportunistic memory could be in the New World. His brewing finesse, which led to his social success, roundly proved Shakespeare's adage, "A quart of Ale is a dish for a King." Enamored of pomp and circumstance, this local chieftain took as his proud personal symbol the red stag's head from the Keiths' coat of arms. He stamped it onto his ale casks, carved it into his dining room table, and set it in stained glass at the top of his hall stairs. Even today, the red stag, as the logo of Keith's Brewery, rides around town emblazoned on Halifax's green city buses, as familiar as the Canadian flag. Like many of the New World's upper-class gentlemen, Alexander Keith named his Georgian mansion after a home he knew from his childhood: Keith Hall. However, the original Keith Hall, located in Edinburgh, never belonged to Alexander's family but rather was the seat of the real clan chief, the Earl of Kintore. Still, in remote Halifax, Alexander could live as whomever he pleased. The motto "Veritas vincit" gave way to an imaginative performance of nostalgic faux nobility, costumed in the old blue, green, and black tartan. Like Alexander Keith himself, only the façade of Halifax's Keith Hall is made from elegant, elaborately carved buff sandstone while the bulk of the building is solid, plain red brick.

With the authority of a full beard, an imposing countenance, a substantial girth, and the props and decorations of office, Chief Alexander Keith watched over other Scottish immigrants who came over the sea to Halifax, arranged their affairs, lent them money, and gained their undying loyalty and support. His social fêtes were legendary. As chief of the Caledonian Club, he presided over the transplanted Highland celebrations, which included bagpipes and elaborate costumes, awards for great leaps and feats of strength, and performances of the gillie callum, in which dancers leapt over swords, and the Highland fling, in which they mimicked a stag's prancing. Grand Masonic parades began and ended at Keith Hall, with cheers and toasts to the chief, music by Highland pipers, specially commissioned decorations of gaslights flickering behind metal cutouts, and great feasts of roast beef and plum pudding. Keith's old-world sociality, along with his considerable modern business acumen and solid Presbyterianism, raised him from a farmer's son to an enormously successful town leader.

His younger brother John, on the other hand, remained for several more years in Halkirk parish, working at Donald Sutherland's liquor business in Brawlbin, a tiny place on the south shore of Loch Calder that boasted three commercial whiskey distilleries by 1821. John married Sutherland's daughter, Christian, in 1827, and Sandy was born ten months later on November 13, followed by a brother and a sister.

(There would eventually be ten children in all.) In the early 1830s, the family, along with many others who were feeling economic distress, decided to emigrate. At about this time, an amusing story was related in the local *John O'Groats* newspaper that gives a sense of what emigration meant to the residents of Halkirk and a glimpse into the culture that produced the manipulative disguises and trickster nature of Sandy Keith. On a late spring day, an apparition came to Halkirk wearing a full military uniform complete with a cocked hat, a sash, a sword, and a pair of elegantly-worked pistols. He told the townspeople that he was an agent of the "New Zealand Immigration Company" and that he had come to take everyone to a land of gold. Enticing them with the future of their greatest dreams, he offered them various prestigious civil and military appointments in the new government and thousands of acres of their own land. In those days, when a few powerful landlords owned huge acreages and all the people on them, land was the most precious commodity imaginable, always desired and never gained. Preying on these deep wants, the alleged travel agent promised to hold a town meeting at Mrs. Stewart's Inn where he would give each man £15 and each woman £10 start-up money in return for a promise to come with him. On the appointed day, dozens of hopeful utopianists arrived to find no agent and no money, and rushed from inn to inn trying to find their Pied Piper. Eventually, he appeared to announce that the whole thing had been a huge joke, much to the hilarity of the neighboring county whence he came. This hoax was in its turn based on the real exploits of another fake clan chief, the infamous Sir Gregor Macgregor, who in 1823 lured gullible Scottish immigrants to the mythical land of "Poyais" only to abandon them on the uninhabitable Mosquito Coast. The fantasy of leaving the hard life of the tenant farmer for a more dignified, sustainable existence lured many Scots across the sea, and some of them, like Alexander Keith, found their real "Poyais," inspiring others to join them.

With somewhat lesser goals than a seat in an illusory parliament, John Keith made the rocky, cramped six-week voyage with his family, including the imaginative nine-year-old Sandy, to Halifax. Alexander Keith's prosperous brewery could be clearly seen from the busy harbor. On Citadel Hill stood the lonely clock tower, showing the time in all four directions, built by the Duke of Kent to raise the rough provincial townspeople into an orderly and punctual way of life. From their lofty positions, the clock tower and the garrison dominated the town, as they did the psyche of young Sandy Keith, who would become obsessed with time and war. He would now also come under the sway of his uncle, for the family settled just around the corner from Alexander Keith's brewery. Most of the big events of Sandy Keith's life in Halifax took place in that claustrophobic space of a few city blocks, under the constant light of his uncle's wealth and power, illuminating his father's own chronic lack of means.

Eleven years after his arrival, the first public trace of John Keith in Halifax is an odd one, hinting of the strange relationship between the two brothers. With partner Angus McLean, he announced the opening of their new business, the Caledonia Brewery, on Lower Water Street, a mere block away from his brother's concern: "The undersigned, from long experience in the business feel confident of being able to compete with any in the trade, and now humbly solicit public patronage." Contending with dozens of other brewers, distillers, and sellers, they offered to supply ale and porter "of superior quality" to public houses and private families. By now, Alexander Keith was running the biggest and most successful brewery in Halifax, a massive ironstone building, bustling with teamsters, coopers, brewers, and clerks. In a hard-drinking port town with hundreds of saloons, John must have seen his opportunity to emerge from the shadow of his powerful older brother; it called to him, even though it meant putting himself in direct competition with Alexander. But whatever success over other brewers, including his brother, that John imagined, the Caledonia Brewery began and ended in a ramshackle wooden structure and would rise no higher. John would always circulate in far humbler social spheres than Alexander.

As John's eldest son, Sandy Keith would have been expected to follow in his father's business, but that role fell to his much younger brother, George. Instead, when he came of age, Sandy moved up the street to work for and live with his uncle. His hand was severely cut while he was bottling beer in the brewery, leaving a ragged tell-tale scar, but he worked his way into a comfortable clerk's job, eventually acquiring a share in the business, a sign of the trust he had earned from his uncle. His dreams were grandiose. Distancing himself from his father, he presented himself as though he were his uncle's son, tacking "Jr." or "the Younger" to his name. But irksomely, he was not his uncle's heir. That was his ineffectual young cousin Donald, admitted to partnership when he was only fifteen. Donald would never marry, never do well at business, never escape Keith Hall and his spinster sisters. Sandy was not to this manor born, though he had convinced himself he was the rightful heir and deserved all of an heir's rights and privileges.

In the house of his uncle, who was the Grand Provincial Master of the local Masonic lodges, Keith became familiar with the workings and trappings of this secret society, and he was eventually initiated into it. Membership in the Masons was a way of cementing the social networks of Britain's empire building and maintaining ties to the Old World and to the Queen. As a young queen, Queen Victoria had been the first British monarch to travel to the Highlands in two centuries, and was so enamored of its natural beauty that she built a retreat there, Balmoral Castle, with walls and floors covered in specially designed royal tartans. During her reign, she suffused the Highlands with a nostalgic glow that hid the continuing crisis of displacement and poverty in her northern lands, including more Clearances of her subjects. The Queen's romantic image of proud, rustic Highlanders, who now held a place as kilted soldiers in Britain's empire, was appealing to ambitious Scottish immigrants who comprised the majority of lodge membership. At its renowned, festive dinners, the Virgin Lodge of Nova Scotia stood for many ceremonial toasts to the Queen and the Craft. Loyalty and trust were ensured through the Masons' mysterious initiation and membership rituals, which included ciphers, passwords, and conspiratorial handshakes. This potent brew of secrecy, camaraderie, ambition, and social hierarchy contributed to Sandy's view of the world and his place in it, still a lowly apprentice.

Eventually, with even greater appetite for power, Sandy began to pretend he was his uncle, encouraging the confusion caused by their same names. He began to resemble his uncle, growing more and more rotund. Through the model of his uncle, he learned how flexible identity could be, how easy it was to play the role of an important man, a distinguished member of the community. Sandy astutely observed how his uncle managed to disguise his humble origins. If his uncle was a self-made man, in the fullest sense of it, then Sandy could be such a man too. It was possible, he had learned, that if one habitually pretends to be what one is not, then eventually one becomes that thing. As he walked through the underground passage from the basement of his uncle's house to his clerk's desk in the brewery, Sandy schemed to become as rich and popular as his uncle, to be even greater than his uncle, and finally to escape the old stag's suffocating authority.

His efforts began in small, easily hidden ways, exploiting his uncle's reputation and business networks. To the family's secret embarrassment, he took full advantage of his highly trusted position, using his uncle's influence to gain the faith of his dupes. He expressed his jealous hatred in devious ways, forging his uncle's signature on phony bills of exchange (roughly the nineteenth-century equivalent of passing bad checks). He worked in league with at least one other corrupt Halifax business owner, the grocery and liquor dealer John McDougall, who, under suspicion of endorsing the phony bills himself, absconded to Ohio. These small swindles were only tiny pricks at his grandiose uncle, easily brushed off. Then came the railway scheme and the powder magazine explosion, the first release of Sandy Keith's violent impulses, his greed and hatred made visible. At that moment, like all bombers, he felt drunk with his own power. But no matter what they knew, the close-knit familial, business, and social networks of Halifax closed protectively around Sandy Keith, as they always would even through his worse crimes.

To have caused an explosion, and thus a possible fire, was one of the worst offenses possible in a nineteenth-century city, with its highly flammable wooden buildings. And this the Keiths knew well. In 1834, Alexander Keith had been briefly suspected of an arson attempt, a crime that would have eerie echoes in the life of his villainous nephew who had just arrived in town. Alexander Keith had extended business credit to David Sinclair Sutherland, a recent immigrant from Scotland. However, the newcomer decided he did not much like his new home, and so he turned his warehouse over to Keith, who was to settle with Sutherland's other creditors. Suffering from what the town believed to be delirium, Sutherland sneaked away, hidden in a horse-drawn sleigh, in the middle of a snowy January night. Needless to say, his abandoned wife, Esther Ann, who ran a small dressmaking shop with her partner Eleanor Smith, was furious. She raged and cursed at a boarding house proprietor, Mr. Paul, whom she suspected of aiding and abetting the getaway. She also blamed Alexander Keith, who had taken their property and would give her no satisfaction. Women had few property rights anyway, and she had come away with nothing from the absconding cad.

One night, under cloak of darkness, someone threw a turpentine-soaked muslin bag filled with combustibles through a window of the repossessed warehouse, over which Mr. Paul kept his boarding house. Only a smoldering hole was burned in the spruce floorboards, but the thought of an arsonist on the loose was terrifying enough to the town. Esther Ann Sutherland and Eleanor Smith fell under immediate suspicion, as did Alexander Keith, who held the insurance claim on the building. The bag contained charcoal, wood shavings, some wadding with the marks of a hot iron, and a piece of fine blue cotton with a scalloped edge. The women had recently sent their apprentice to buy turpentine, the muslin matched a bolt of cloth in their shop, and the serrations in the cotton exactly matched those in the lining of a silk cloak they were stitching. The constables also compared the cotton to material in Alexander Keith's general store, but though it was of the same color, it was deemed not so finely woven. The two dressmakers were arrested and given a sensational public trial.

Despite the paltry outcome of the arson attempt, the prosecuting attorney called for the death penalty and evoked witchcraft, reminding the jury that under Saxon law arsonists were burned at the stake. Arson was worse than theft or murder because it indiscriminately endangered the innocent lives and property of a whole community. Had the "infernal machine," as he called the muslin sack, performed its evil deed, a "night of desolation and death would have ensued, that one must shudder to contemplate." Mr. Paul and all of his lodgers would have been consumed, as might the entire church square where the warehouse stood. Only a "wicked, depraved, and malignant spirit" could have designed such a horror. Despite this emotional, apocalyptic argument, the jury took only eleven minutes to acquit the women, whether because the evidence was entirely circumstantial or because their sympathies lay with the abandoned Esther Ann Sutherland.

This was a big event in the public life of the Haligonian Keiths, buzzing in the small town gossip and covered in good detail by the local newspaper. At the time Sandy Keith blew up the powder magazine, they would have forgotten neither their former embarrassment nor the apocalyptic preaching of the prosecution against the most vicious crime against humanity. They now suspected another malignant spirit among them, one of their own kin, who would someday make a truly infernal machine. But they did not seek to stop or control him. Instead, Sandy Keith continued to expand his social influence and remained, amazingly enough, one of the most popular, beloved, and respected figures in the town.

Keith made all the right friends and moved in all the right circles. His popularity, especially with the fast young men of Halifax, owed much to his extravagant generosity, for he was always throwing parties and bailing them out of their financial predicaments, laughing off their debts. All the while, he was creating a network of trust and obligation that he would fully exploit when the time came. In 1859, when the British Crown called for all able-bodied Canadian men to help provide for their own defense, he joined the most prestigious volunteer militia corps, the Chebucto Greys, made up entirely of the sons of gentlemen, and became its quartermaster. They cemented their comradeship by abusing and scapegoating their less well-clad rivals: the Victoria Rifles, comprised of men from Nova Scotia's black settlements, dating back to the American Revolutionary War when black Loyalists fled to Canada to escape slavery and war. The Chebucto Greys were an arrogant, splendiferous, and often wild group of fellows who impressed the whole town, especially its patriotic women. Halifax adored a military regiment, for it was a boom-and-bust town that prospered most during Britain's wars of empire and its showy saber rattlings against the Yanks. Described by the London journalist George Augustus Sala as "a brawny, firm race on the masculine side," the townspeople loved nothing more than a parade, especially to sounds of cannon and rifle fire. When Albert Edward, Prince of Wales, sailed with his grand royal squadron to Nova Scotia in July of 1860, huge crowds made the trip to greet him and the Provincial Governments put up a million dollars to fête him. People crowded every window to hear the thundering cannons and catch the first glimpse of the naval officers' black cocked hats, white pants, and crimson jackets as they stood on the decks, peering into their spy glasses. The children sang and threw flowers, and civil engineers produced a great underwater gunpowder blast to salute jolly Prince Bertie. In Halifax, he passed through twenty-seven evergreen-bedecked wooden arches and solemnly reviewed the troops, including the Victoria Rifles and the Chebucto Greys, who marched proudly through their drills and evolutions. At the end, as one of the

Prince's companions related, they stood at the end in "a long line of up-lifted bayonets glittering in the sun, and on the points of these the uni-form caps of every man of the battalion, the variegated plumes of which enhanced the picturesque effect." Though some hungry, high-spirited militia members later brawled in the streets, angry that they hadn't been invited to a complimentary breakfast, the Chebucto Greys received a commendation from the Prince.

In that same summer of 1860, the thirty-three-year-old Keith, who had had some experience with ocean travel on his childhood trip from Scotland and a more recent trip to Bermuda, took a group of his young friends to visit New York and tour the *Great Eastern*, also called *Leviathan*, the huge 700-foot-long steamship built by the great trans-portation engineer, Isambard Kingdom Brunel. With its awesome ma-chinery, two monstrous paddle wheels, and stupendous shafts and pistons, the *Great Eastern* was considered the greatest wonder of naval architecture, the only ship big enough to lay the transatlantic cable. On her first trip across the Atlantic, breathless dispatches went ahead of her. At the hefty admission price of a dollar, thousands of tourists poured down to the New York dock to take official tours of the mon-ster, and even more when the price was slashed to fifty cents. Visitors could view most of the ship. In their white gloves and stockings, the ladies would tour only the clean upper decks, while hundreds of men descended into the bowels of the ship to view the mammoth cylinders and boilers and to crawl along the screw. The great transatlantic steamship of the age had arrived in full force with its gargantuan size and tremendous speed, and its seemingly unlimited power. It was a Tom-Swiftean adventure for the young scions of Halifax, some who had sneaked away from home for the opportunity to take in such an awesome machine. They would never forget it. When they got home, they were all in hot water, but Keith smoothed it over. He offered, after all, to pay for everything.

So, like his uncle, Sandy Keith rose swiftly in the little world of Halifax, his vulgar manners and his felonies quickly forgotten under the sway of charm and money. If his gain was ill gotten, nobody much cared, especially since Keith appeared so willing to lavish it on every-one around him. Like every seaport town, Halifax had always had its share of pirates, smugglers, and profiteers, and a certain tolerance for people not taking the more respectable paths towards wealth. And like all towns, it had a way of keeping its dirty dealings hidden behind its grandly carved sandstone facades. Numerous Haligonians other than Keith had connived their way into the fur-blanketed sleighs of the wealthy, which looked to Charles Dickens, who described Halifax in his travel notes, like "triumphal cars in a melodrama." So, at the dawn of the American Civil War, when the most arrogant, devious, and ruthless villains of all came to town, dressed as noble, endangered aristocrats, they were welcomed into the best society with cheers and champagne. Nearly everyone saw profit, especially Sandy Keith, who now imagined playing his role on a much bigger stage than little Halifax.

TWO

THE CONFEDERATE CONSUL

As civil war loomed to the south, Haligonians were susceptible to waves of panic about their Yankee neighbors, imagining their harbor suddenly filled with gunboats, their snug wooden houses shattered by bombardment from the enemy's cannons. They envisioned their proud, well-drilled young men marching like chivalrous knights to defend their hearths from the aggressor. Haligonians heard rumors that the United States government was about to "wag the dog," attacking Canada to deflect attention from its own internal problems. Then, they heard that the U.S. war sloop *San Jacinto*, commanded by the polar explorer and audacious defender of the Union, Captain Charles Wilkes, had swept down on the British vessel *Trent*, sailing along past Cuba, and fired a shot over her bow. The *San Jacinto* came alongside, and its officers boarded the *Trent*, taking into custody two Confederate ambassadors to England, John Slidell and James Mason, both ardent defenders of a renewed African slave trade. Poor Miss Rosina Slidell, Haligonians read, bravely slapped a nasty Federal lieutenant three times as he tore her father from her arms. Spoiling for a fight, full of outrage at the insult to England, not to mention genteel young ladies, most Haligonians declared themselves on the side of the Southern rebels. Five thousand British troops flooded into Halifax, swelling the saloons, thirsty for Keith's pale ale.

Smart and calculating, Sandy Keith instantly tasted the profits of war. As a member of the Chebucto Greys, he had played the tin soldier with his rifle and his plumed hat. Now the proximity of the great conflict swept him up in its excitement, and he declared himself for the Confederates, idealized in Halifax as gentlemen freedom fighters under the yoke of the Yankee oppressor. He did not volunteer to join the fight; his was always the way of the sneak in an underground of secret handshakes and clandestine exchanges. Just as his chameleon-like abilities allowed him to move freely in the business world of Halifax, it would prove even more valuable in the Confederate network of entrepreneurs, secret agents, and opportunists who began busily making their base in Canada. Sandy Keith always sought out friends who would gratify both his ego and his greed, and he changed his skin to fit the new crowd of disgruntled Southern gentlemen who were deeply flattered by his imitation. Tearing apart and reshaping entire communities, the Civil War, like any war, allowed many weak men to suddenly reinvent themselves in their own benighted images of swashbucklers and daredevils, martyrs and princes, nation builders and heroes. Keith liked to imagine himself as an adventurer and a warrior in a great romantic conflict, but he became little more than a messenger and a broker of opportunistic and cowardly deeds.

Two events allowed Keith to fully reinvent himself in this new environment, to be his own man at last, at the age of thirty-six. In late July 1863, his father had died after a severe, lingering illness, receiving only a one-line obituary in the local paper. Around that time, Keith left Keith Hall and the employ of his wealthy uncle. In one version he gave of his life, he said that his uncle had exercised a very intimate control over him, pressuring him to marry his first cousin, one of the Keith Hall spinsters. But he had refused, and thus had been forced to leave. Glossing over his own cheating and thieving, he also said that he'd had a falling out with his uncle's business manager, though he did not say why. But Sandy Keith had reason to hide the truth of his bad relations with his uncle, and his abrupt departure from Keith Hall and his work at the brewery suggests that he was forced out. Now holding a seat in the legislative council of the provincial government, the politically ambitious Alexander Keith was one of the few townspeople who did not sympathize with the Confederacy and became deeply mortified by his nephew's notoriety. Perhaps Sandy Keith's political allegiance was the last straw in a long stream of his abuses of Alexander's trust and honor. If the family was angry, it was never a matter for public knowledge or rebuke. For whatever reason, Sandy had fallen from the grace of Keith Hall and left quietly. He started his own business as a broker for various Southern blockade-running enterprises, set up an office on Hollis Street, a few blocks from his uncle's house, and hung out his sign: A. Keith, Jr.

He worked in partnership with Benjamin Wier, a pugnacious import-export merchant who lived right next door to Keith Hall in his own imposing sandstone mansion overlooking the harbor. Like Keith, Wier was a member of the gentlemen's militia, the arrogant and racist Chebucto Greys, many of whom sided with the Confederacy. Both Wier and Keith were part of a nucleus of hard-core sympathizers. Most were very prominent, distinguished members of the community: lawyers and doctors, loyal subjects of the British Empire who hated the Yanks, and therefore concluded that the enemy of their enemy was their friend. For some Haligonians, like Dr. William Almon and former U.S. Consul Albert Pilsbury, support of the Southern cause was deeply felt, and whole families openly espoused their loyalties. Their sons went off to serve in the Confederate armies, while their debutante daughters held charity auctions to aid prisoners of war. Other Haligonians felt a homeland connection to the blockade-runners when they first came to port. Flying British colors, nearly all of the officers onboard these ships were English or Scots, sailing from Glasgow and Liverpool. They were avidly and unabashedly pursuing profit. When Southerners began to take greater command of these operations, many Haligonians welcomed them for the same reason: money, and lots of it. "Bohemian," a sailor on the notorious Confederate raider *Tallahassee*, observed: "The people [of Halifax] generally are very friendly to the South, but in many instances I can but think it an interested friendship." Infamous for flying false colors and ramming ships full of bewildered European immigrants, the *Tallahassee* was fueled and refitted by Wier and Keith, who supplied it with coal, a compass, and other necessities. "Bohemian" singled out Sandy Keith, among a handful of others, for having shown "sympathy in something else besides empty words."

Wier and Keith helped blockade-runners through the red tape of invoices and bills of lading, connecting them with buyers and suppliers in town. They also prepared ships for duty. The first blockade-runner they fitted out was the *General Banks*, later called *Fanny and Jenny* after two women in town. It was a thoroughly corrupt business from the start. The primary investor, who had previously been in desperate financial straits, made a hefty profit by securing advances on the promised wares, and then shipping second-hand goods in their place. Learning new ways to cheat and steal, Keith, too, became notorious for shipping seconds while realizing on firsts at the bank. Indeed, weary of their diet of hominy and cassina tea and craving luxuries like brandy, oranges, and real coffee, Southerners in port towns rushed down to greet the white sails of the blockade-running ships only to find them full of bad bacon and other worthless stores. But there was little recourse and enough desperation to keep the Halifax suppliers doing landmark business. The *Fanny and Jenny* made several trips through the Bermudas to North Carolina before a Union gunboat ran her aground near Cape Fear in February 1864. Before they burned her, her captors found a jewel-encrusted gold sword in her cargo inscribed: "To General Robert E. Lee, from his British sympathizers." Certainly one of the reasons Britain's Canadian colony sympathized with the South was the tremendous wealth it received from the trade in cotton and other goods. British capitalists were dependent on ever more precious Southern cotton for their textile mills, and, during the war, cotton flowed there through the blockade-running center of Halifax. The war produced a literal mountain of gold. Keith and Wier continued to fit out blockade-runners, handling the huge wealth in the kegs of gold and cargoes of cotton that arrived in town.

Keith's rooms in the Halifax Hotel became the rollicking headquarters of blockade-runners who came in and out of port. These sailors had lived ordinary lives before the war, making very modest incomes. In peacetime, sea captains typically made about seventy-five dollars a month, but now they had the heady experience of making ten thousand dollars in gold on a single run. Running a thousand bales of cotton through the blockade could net investors a quarter of a million dollars. Ordinary sailors saw their lot improve to monthly wages of one hundred gold dollars, and fifty more upon successful completion of a trip. Blockade-running ships also carried prosperous Southern merchants and their families, army and navy supply clerks, inquisitive journalists, English gentry out on a lark, Confederate prisoners escaped from Northern jails, and disgruntled exiles and spies. Although blockade running was not, in truth, a particularly dangerous side of war, it had a romantic aura, with tales of exciting chases and near escapes in the silence and pitch-black darkness of a moonless night.

With their fabulous profits and sudden popularity, privateers and blockade-runners arrogantly felt they owned the world. They thought of themselves as gallant young fellows and young Hotspurs full of derring-do. The worst of their natures was rewarded, fêted, and celebrated in song. From Britain to Canada to Bermuda to the Confederate States to Havana, they swaggered about the ports like South Seas pirates, brandishing their big Colt revolvers, rowdily eating and drinking with their suddenly expensive taste, and abusing the locals, especially if they were black. Later, as they recounted their adventures with racist depictions of brutal, lazy, or drunken savages, they could advise their listeners, as Captain Augustus Charles Hobart-Hampden did, that "the only vulnerable part of a nigger" was his shins. Robbery, murder, and mayhem came to port with the Jacks, who, in rum-besotted deliriums, made target practice on their fellows or the locals. Insufferable braggarts, many had stories to tell about their bold encounters with the Union blockaders, the admonitions to extinguish all lights, the sounds of bullets whizzing over the decks, the hair-raising cannon fire, and the thrilling speed of the chases. After the war, one of Keith's old associates, Mike Usina, who captained the *Atalanta*, nostalgically told a rapt audience: "An ordinarily brave man had no business on a blockade runner. He who made a success of it was obliged to have the cunning of a fox, the patience of a Job, and the bravery of a Spartan warrior." He did not add the greed of Midas and the pride of Lucifer. Despite such self-aggrandizing fictions, the more sedate citizens and court judges of Halifax shook their heads sternly at the drunkenness, rowdiness, and loose morals of this new, floating population of adventurers and traders, but did little to curtail them.

Others, like Sandy Keith, were busy wining and dining the sea captains, their pursers, and other traders and supply agents, a hefty investment since such men had very expensive tastes. He was frequently invited onboard their ships, like the *Lilian*, the *Ad-vance*, and the *Old Dominion*, just back from their long voyages, loaded with bales of cotton. The successful captain of the *Robert E. Lee*, a ship notorious for its thieving, brawling, and rowdy crew, John Wilkinson, in safe hindsight, remembered Keith as a "coarse, ill-bred vulgarian," who managed to woo

every visiting Southerner through his "brazen assurance, a most oblig-
ing manner, and the lavish expenditure of money." In the clamorous,
smoky common rooms of the Halifax Hotel, the manager could not
keep up with the orders for his finest champagne to accompany the
endless toasts, brags, vows of friendship, and curses for the villainous
tyrant Lincoln. Sandy Keith was at the center of the merriment, hosting his many new friends in his rooms, which were conveniently on the
first floor near a private entrance.

Because of his obsequious approaches to all Southerners, who
were only too glad to be treated as exiled aristocrats, Keith became
known as the "Confederate Consul." One of his clients was Dr.
Thomas J. Boykin, owner of the steamer *Ad-vance*, sent from North
Carolina to arrange for blankets, shoes, and other army supplies to be
shipped through the blockade. He and his clerk, Wilkes Morris, both
remembered that they could never account for the deep interest, beyond the usual trade relationship, that Keith seemed to have in them.
But like all his compatriots, Boykin was completely taken in by
Keith, depositing thousands of dollars with him to invest in blockade
goods.

To further his interests, Keith had developed a sales spiel and was
able to talk like a military man, a lover of the sea, and a Southern gentleman. Southerners, many of whom were Scots themselves, greatly
admired Highland warriors like the Jacobite Keiths, who had fought
to the end in the lost cause of preserving their democratic rights as a
people against the divine rights of the Stuart kings. They romantically
named their plantations Waverly, Montrose, and Dunleith after place
names in Sir Walter Scott's novels, the bloom of magnolias disguising
the far more sordid, violent realities of slavery. Many of Keith's new
friends were the sons of Southern cotton and tobacco merchants who
aspired to the roles of gentleman gallant, romantic outlaw, knightly defender of the "guid auld day, the day o' pride and chieftain's glory," as
in Lady Keith's lament. They were all supreme fantasists. With them,
Keith created a slanted mirror of his uncle's world, with its aspirations
to wealth and gentility, clannish camaraderie, and ritual secrecy. He
embraced his role as "Confederate Consul" with great seriousness, and
all his life he would gravitate toward wealthy diplomats, desperate for
the station occupied by his uncle. But Keith's violence, anger, and envy
always self-destructively burst through his fantasies of popularity and

power, and he would eventually take full advantage of his new friends' deluded grandiosity and blind faith in noblesse oblige.

Typical of the adventurous men who passed through Sandy Keith's hands was young James Sprunt. Possessed of a romantic view of the old South, which he imagined as a bucolic Acadia full of well-dressed belles and beaux, the studious Sprunt had emigrated from Scotland and was raised in a family of modest means, despite his father's prestigious appointment as British Vice Consul in Wilmington, North Carolina. Like many children growing up near a harbor, their heads full of the popular sea adventure stories of Masterman Ready and the jolly, infinitely brave Jack Tar, Sprunt had dreams of the sea. "As a boy," he later wrote, "I delighted to wander along the wharves where the sailing ships were moored with their graceful spars and rigging in relief against the sky-line, with men aloft whose uncouth cries and unknown tongues inspired me with a longing for the sea, which I afterwards followed, and for the far-away countries whence they had come." When he was sixteen, the handsome, red-haired Sprunt fulfilled his fantasy, taking the position of purser aboard various blockade-runners, including the *Lilian*, whose agent in Halifax was Sandy Keith.

In July 1864, on its third run out of Wilmington, the *Lilian* encountered heavy fire as Sprunt and all his mates, including several mutinous firemen, quivered in fear. A great stream of water suddenly gushed through the starboard side of the ship, struck by a shell. The men tried to claw their way through bales of damp cotton stuffed tight in the hold, but were unable to reach the leak. The ship veered and teetered, the water rose to the level of the deck, and the captain sullenly surrendered. He defiantly turned his back to the Federal officers as they boarded and captured the dejected crew. Imprisoned in a dark, rat-infested prison, Fort Macon, lying on an island in the outer banks of North Carolina, Sprunt managed to escape with his shipmate, Jim Billy, who had some gold coins hidden in the waistband of his pants. Traveling all the way from North Carolina, they chose Halifax as the place to go for aid and safety. There they knew that Sandy Keith and other friends of the South would help them get back home to "dear Dixie Land, the haven of our dreams." Keith so earned Sprunt's trust that the young purser, soon back at sea, gave him $1,600 to invest. Sprunt never saw his money again.

Although in hindsight many of the blockade-runners would rue the day they ever met Keith, at the time they found him amiable enough. Whether the blue-eyed, medium-tall, and pudgy Keith was a handsome man or not lay entirely in the eye of the beholder. Some thought he was piggy-eyed and repulsive; others found him ruddy, strong, and manly, admiring his thick reddish hair. Those who found him most attractive were those who were most taken by his displays of wealth. He was still not married at the age of thirty-six; it was customary among the soldiers in the garrison to give their emotional loyalties only to the other lads. It was a rowdy, boisterous, and violent man's world in which Keith felt most comfortable. But in the Halifax Hotel he settled down with Mary Clifton. At their feasts of oysters, terrapin soup, imported truffles, and pâtés, and an endless flow of champagne, Keith and the other jolly good fellows were served by the hotel servants known as "the two Marys." One, whose last name is lost, was a lovely dark-eyed, dark-haired young Irishwoman, the other a "rosy and robust Nova Scotia girl, with a handsome face and a splendidly developed form, a perfect type, in fact, of physical beauty." As a hotel servant, the young Mary Clifton had a very hard life. Mark Twain once sardonically described what such a job entailed in the nineteenth century: "A hotel chambermaid has nothing to do but make beds and fires in fifty or sixty rooms, bring towels and candles, and fetch several tons of water up several flights of stairs, a hundred pounds at a time, in prodigious metal pitchers. She does not have to work more than eighteen or twenty hours a day, and she can always get down on her knees and scrub the floors of halls and closets when she is tired and needs a rest." In the interested person of Keith, Mary got a glimpse of a better life, a life of excitement and adventure, of luxury and ease, without hard calluses, chilblains, and housemaid's knee. Like many women throughout history, Mary saw love and opportunity on the fringes of war. What she did not know was that Keith possessed a cold and arrogant heart that would bring her nothing but misery.

Through flattery and indulgence, Keith became the man to know in Halifax for all Southerners with any business, and that included swaggering privateers and raiders who managed to entirely confuse their political cause with lust for profit. The idea, actively promoted by the Confederate government, was to do whatever damage possible to the property of a superior enemy, encouraging terrorist deeds with substantial rewards. A host of social malcontents and misfits, cowards who could not face real battle, were attracted to this kind of indirect action. Living on the fringes of war in Canada, they, too, came naturally into Sandy Keith's orbit, where he served as their organizer and supplier.

One of these was the restless, excitable Patrick Martin, who was Keith's counterpart in Montreal, arranging blockade-running shipments for the Confederacy. Martin would eventually achieve infamy for his involvement with John Wilkes Booth and the Lincoln conspirators. A wine merchant and experienced sailor, Martin had been living in Baltimore when he was swept up in the early secessionist fever of the city, throwing himself immediately into privateering and blockade running. He was involved in the celebrated pirating of the Baltimore-based steamer, *St. Nicholas:* One night, the sailors of the *St. Nicholas* were shocked to see the heavily veiled French lady they had welcomed aboard suddenly burst from her stateroom as a brawny man in a Zouave uniform—Colonel Zarvona Thomas. With several other burly men (apparently including Martin) hiding in the lady's cabin, Thomas pulled out his cutlass, seized the ship, and went off on a raiding party. Some of the raiders were later caught and imprisoned, but Martin slipped away to Montreal, where he continued his career as a broker and a blockade-runner, and, with the help of his wife, as a courier and a spy. With their common interests, Keith and Martin naturally formed a business relationship smuggling goods through the Great Lakes.

In late 1863, Martin, along with another refugee, former Baltimore police chief George Kane, conceived of a plan to raid Johnson's Island, a Federal prison that stood on a small wooded island in Lake Erie, an emotional locus for many bitter Confederates who dreamed of liberating their mates. In October, the low, sleek *Robert E. Lee* arrived in Halifax, carrying twenty-two men, armed and ready for action, and a load of cotton. Sandy Keith sold the cotton to fund the expedition, and dispatched the men to Montreal where they were joined by a handful of other glory seekers, a far smaller number than Kane and Martin had expected. Disguised as workmen on their way to Chicago, the conspirators were supposed to seize a passenger vessel using Colt revolvers and two small cannons. Then they were to ram the vessel into a Federal gunboat, capture it, and use it to subdue the heavy forces guarding the island. An attractive feature of this plan was that the plotters would seize a safe, filled with bonds, and divide the profits. Milling suspiciously about the Welland Canal waiting for orders, they received word that the plot had been betrayed, and they then straggled away home to the South as best they could. It had been a costly, disorganized, and ramshackle affair, but Keith and Martin remained business associates, eventually investing in two ships together. This relationship would eventually have profound consequences for both men.

Keith also aided and abetted the pirating of a passenger steamship, the *Chesapeake*, which regularly plied the route between New York and Portland, Maine. On the afternoon of December 5, 1863, with a crew of seventeen, the *Chesapeake* took on board twenty-two passengers, among them John Brain, an Englishman, braggart, jailbird, and brief resident of Halifax. Before he took up the romantic role of swashbuckling pirate, the sallow, weak-chinned Brain was a flimflam man who had wandered into town that summer. He announced himself as "J. C. Brain, Publisher." With the plodding demeanor of a salesman, strangely carrying a lady's portmanteau, he went around to various businesses with legal-looking contracts, taking orders for subscriptions and advertisements for *Brain's Mercantile and Statistical Work, and Business Directory of Canada and the Provinces.* Local business owners put up much as twenty-five dollars, in advance, for the privilege of appearing in the phony directory. But Brain had even bigger game in mind. Like many ineffectual men of his time, the self-styled colonel coveted the adventurous roles of pirate and spy, and he believed that stealing the *Chesapeake* would bring him fame and profit.

He worked in league with Vernon Locke, from a notorious family of traders and smugglers who lived near St. John, New Brunswick. Before returning home to Canada, Locke had lived for a spell in South Carolina and become an energetic blockade-runner known as John Parker. "He is said to be a great scamp," another war profiteer said of him, "and a very plausible one." Locke was to provide official papers to prove legitimate ownership of the *Chesapeake*. He waited in New Brunswick while Brain went to do the dirty work of stealing her. Pretending to be a British steamboat agent — for he was very good at such disguises — Brain finagled a free ticket on the wooden steamer, taking a group of local toughs he had enlisted in St. John.

The *Chesapeake* sailed from port and spent two uneventful days on the open sea, despite the threat of privateering ships cruising for prey fat with cargoes of sugar and cotton. Then, in the early hours of the morning on December 7, Brain and fifteen other passengers, all pirates, rose up to take the ship in the name of the Confederacy. Four of them smashed down the door of the second mate, ordered him to get dressed, pronounced him a Confederate prisoner and handcuffed him. A gun battle ensued, leaving the second engineer dead, shot in the head, his big body dangling over the gangway. The captain rushed out of his cabin, but was peppered with fire and captured on his way to the pilothouse. He was clapped hard in irons and thrown back into his cabin, soon joined by the first mate and chief engineer, both wounded. The body of the second engineer was unceremoniously tossed overboard. The chief engineer, with a bullet lodged in his chin, was forced below to stoke the furnace and tend the boilers. Fortunately for the crew, all the pirates were terrible shots and only the second engineer died in the melee. The stewardess, announcing that she was not afraid, was treated with respect and courtesy. Under Brain's command, the *Chesapeake* sailed on as the new crew painted over the name of the ship, polished up the brass, generously tended the wounds of their victims, and helped themselves to the kitchen and the cargo of port wine.

When they reached the Bay of Fundy, the pirates picked up Vernon Locke near St. John. They then extracted their original ticket money, eighty-seven dollars, from the captain, and dumped him on the cobble beach of Partridge Island, along with his charts, his clock, and his sextant. With him were the stewardess, the cabin boys, and some of the other sailors and passengers. The rest of the crew was kept as forced labor. With Locke now in command, the *Chesapeake* steamed up the southern coast of Nova Scotia, stopping at various small ports, selling goods for a song, and merrily dispensing three hundred gallons of wine, considerably lessened by the pirates' prodigious drinking. It was one big party all along the way. A large bell was also onboard, ultimately destined for a congregation in Maine. The pirates gave it away to some pious deacons who afterwards refused to return it to its rightful owners. Finally, the *Chesapeake* ran out of coal and laid anchor at Sambro, a small fishing community. The pirates planned to sail on and commit depredations against Northern shipping, foreseeing a lucrative enterprise that they hoped could make them all rich and famous. Locke walked fourteen miles to Halifax to acquire coal, a quadrant, and two Scottish engineers, William and John Henry. He already knew who would help him arrange these matters: a Confederate agent in Halifax named Sandy Keith, who was happy to oblige. But before the *Chesapeake* could sail on, it was confiscated by the Union.

Rumors arrived in Halifax that armed men from the Federal gunboat *Ella and Annie* had boarded the purloined *Chesapeake* in Canadian waters and manacled the local lads, two brothers of the Henry clan. Consternation and outrage ensued at the U.S. Navy's brute force and arrogant incursion into Canadian waters. The pirates of the *Chesapeake*, including John Brain and Vernon Locke, had all escaped at the first signs of trouble, fading into the forests and villages of Nova Scotia and New Brunswick. They left only their uneaten breakfasts, the Henrys, and one of their own: the skinny, nervous George Wade, sleeping in his berth under a buffalo robe. A dozen of the pirates soon appeared near the town of Sambro, where they boldly walked about together in plain sight, randomly firing their revolvers as three reluctant constables tried and failed to arrest them. For his mythical fearlessness and defiance of authority, the supposedly gallant Brain became a folk legend, fêted in toasts and songs, having transcended his inglorious past. On the fringes of the Civil War, there were many men like these, exploiting the chaos for their own bizarre, often abortive schemes that provided an easy road to glory.

The recaptured *Chesapeake*'s new destination was Halifax, and its arrival was the most exciting event of its kind since several notorious pirates had been hanged in the public square twenty years before. All the townspeople were following the news closely as the *Ella and Annie*, accompanied by the gunboat *Dacotah*, towed the *Chesapeake*, with the three prisoners still clamped tightly in irons. Canadian authorities pursued the release of the hapless trio through circuitous diplomatic channels, complicated by contests over jurisdictions and neutrality agreements and debate over whether the *Chesapeake* was a legitimate war prize that belonged to the Confederacy or a pirated vessel that must be returned to its lawful owners in the North. When the ships reached the harbor on a Saturday afternoon, hundreds of people climbed up to the Citadel or down to the shore to watch the spectacle. At Queen's Wharf, the officer of the guard refused to admit anyone who was not respectably dressed. Thus, only about forty of the town's leading citizens were allowed on the dock. One of the distinguished gentlemen standing there unobtrusively was Sandy Keith, the secret

Confederate Consul. As the *Chesapeake*'s supplier, unknown to the Canadian or U.S. authorities, he had a particular interest in the ship.

The plan of key government officials was to free the prisoners from Federal custody and then have Wade arrested by provincial police on the wharf. The Henrys were considered unwitting accomplices and were to be released. Carrying the men in chains, a skiff moved towards the slip. The three men were ordered out, and their manacles removed. Clutching a warrant in his left hand, an officer, Lewis Hutt, dressed in a drab civilian coat and a broad-brimmed, wide-awake hat, began to push through the crowd toward Wade. But the scrawny Wade, to the great pleasure of the wildly cheering spectators, leapt into another boat that had come up to the slip, rowed by two muscular oarsmen. Wade's boots thumped on the bottom of the boat, and the oarsmen pulled away as Hutt ran towards them, waving the warrant and loudly demanding that they return. The crowd cried, "No! No!" Hutt drew his revolver. Sandy Keith, usually a covert operator, now made the only truly bold move of his life. He rushed toward the policeman and tried to wrest the pistol out of his hand, aiding two of the town doctors, Peleg Smith and William Almon, who had already grabbed hold around Hutt's waist. The crowd hurrahed, the oarsmen heaved away, and Wade made good his escape. It had been a most exciting and satisfying spectacle.

The scowling lions and stern old magistrates that stared from the sandstone façade of the brand new Provincial Courthouse belied the jocular mood that prevailed inside during the preliminary examination of Keith and his fellows, Smith and Almon, accused of obstructing justice. The courtroom was packed. The examining alderman, sea captain William Roche, amused the crowd with his droll observations and wisecracks. Even the generally unsympathetic mayor occasionally chuckled. The testimony of the witnesses suggested that the three men had only acted out of a desire for public safety. Despite the uniform buttons glinting under his coat, Hutt had not been recognized as a police officer, and his flagrant waving of a gun in a crowd obviously had to be stopped. The three men were heroes, not criminals. When the accused were allowed to speak in their own defense, Almon launched an impassioned, crowd-pleasing diatribe against the damned lawless Yankees invading their waters, flagrantly abusing British subjects, interfering with the telegraph, and unfairly hounding poor Brain and his men about the provinces. Keith and Smith spoke briefly, downplaying the whole affair as trivial. In the end, the mayor, unmoved, ruled that the actions of the accused were indictable, and bound the men over on £200 bail apiece. But it was all show, and the charges were eventually dismissed.

The only physical combat Keith ever faced was the tussle on the dock during the *Chesapeake* uproar, for he always sought to avoid any real danger. Trying to be as indistinct as possible, Keith's light treatment of his involvement in the event hid far more devious machinations. Through his increasing contacts with violent, nakedly avaricious men, he was fast becoming an important figure in a murky network of Confederate covert agents who used Canada as their base of operations. The *Chesapeake* affair cemented their trust in him, for he had proven himself helpful and discrete. A jack-of-all-trades, he eventually had his hand in every aspect of the South's business in Halifax. He acted as a private broker, helping Confederate blockade runners exchange their goods and navigate the complex financial systems of Halifax, based on commissions, loans, and gentlemen's agreements. He helped steal and fit out ships to run the blockade or prowl the Union shipping lanes. He fielded coded messages from the central Confederate government to its covert satellites: spies and terrorists planning acts of mass destruction across the border. Thus, he became an important operator in a corrupt and violent world of white supremacists, adventurers, and profiteers who imagined themselves as much finer and nobler beings.

By the end of 1863, Keith had solidified his popularity and was living the high life. As the black vomit and jaundice of the dreaded yellow fever swept across Bermuda and Nassau, the tar barrels of Wilmington pitching out thick black smoke believed to ward off sickness, the Confederate government's blockade running operations shifted more to the clean winds of Halifax and to official agent Sandy Keith. The war grew ever more desperate for the South. Sea captains, pursers, clerks, and quartermasters—all trying to supply a beleaguered government and its army—entrusted Keith with their goods and their gold. Investors all along the triangle from Wilmington to Bermuda to Halifax were shoving gold dollars into his hands to buy cotton, pork, ships, and even locomotive engines. In the midst of this attention, Sandy Keith seemed to fit right in, flattering his new friends, glorifying their cause and celebrating their stories of war and adventure. But as much as he seemed to admire them, he also loathed them, knowing that defeat and disgrace could befall even the most honored warrior clans weakened by self-delusion and arrogance. His hidden thoughts were unromantic, callous, even ruthless, as he carefully calculated the options best suited to his self-interest. Yet none of his friends, old or new, saw behind his congenial mask. As Confederate Consul, Keith acquired a taste for champagne and fine cigars that would last for the rest of his life. But as he secretly swindled many a hot-blooded man, he also gained another habit: sleeping with his revolver.

THREE

THE SECRET AGENT

Behind the loud, boisterous parties of the hotheaded Jacks, wannabe raiders, and grandiose pirates lay a cool shadow world of fierce, discrete Confederate agents, a world of codes, disguises, and apocalyptic fantasies. For their schemes to wound the Union from the north, these agents needed ships to get their men, weapons, and secret messages across borders and blockades. The man to trust in the key port of Halifax was Sandy Keith, possessed of just the right combination of geniality and furtiveness. To the Halifax Hotel came well-dressed, genteel, soft-spoken men who flattered Keith as much as he flattered them. They promised him great rewards for carrying out deeds beyond the scope of even his dark imaginings. These were not the usual boisterous ship captains, rough provincial privateers, and adventurous boys with a taste for the sea. These were angry men—doctors, ministers, wealthy businessmen, and former U.S. congressmen and cabinet officials— driven by visions of losing their wealth and power and their control over land and people. They had grown desperate enough to wage a clandestine war, with approval from the highest levels of the Confederate government. A secretly ruthless man himself, Keith had found a closed society in which his darkest obsessions, his unique blend of greed and violence, were welcomed as great virtues.

As he went in and out of the Halifax Hotel, busily arranging the movements of goods, money, and men, Keith was being carefully watched by one of his uncle's close neighbors, U.S. Consul Mortimer Melville Jackson. Jackson had been given the unenviable task of looking after his country's interests in Halifax, a town almost Southern in its hatred and ill will toward the Union. With its tedious rounds of ceremonial dinners, public inaugurations, and badly danced provincial balls, the life of a diplomat was not always an interesting one, especially in a small garrison town like Halifax. But war and strife tended to liven up the job. In the nineteenth century, no CIA or Interpol existed, and bored diplomats were the principal international spymasters. This aspect of the job alleviated the interminable socializing and paper shuffling, but usually did not lend itself to very efficient intelligence gathering. An eloquent abolitionist, educational reformer, and highly polished gentleman of open and pleasant disposition, Jackson was not especially equipped for spying, but war transformed him. Watching ships go in and out of the busy harbor, he delivered enough information about blockade-runners to cost the Confederacy $3 million in seized war munitions.

Living within eyeshot of Keith Hall and Benjamin Wier's warehouse, he also listened to rumors and observed the movements of Sandy Keith who, of all the shady figures in town, became a particular object of his fascination. He believed that the *Chesapeake* tussle had been a premeditated plan, revealing a wider conspiracy of Southerners and Haligonians, and that Keith was at the center of it. It was bad enough that Canadians were aiding the slave-holding rebels, interfering with the Union's attempt to squeeze the South into submission, but now they were actively supporting hijackings and raids. In December 1863, Jackson reported to his superiors that Keith was the hub of this activity in Halifax, associating with rebels and acting as their courier.

Despite his suspicions, Jackson never fully grasped the full extent of what he was seeing, for the abortive hijacking of the *Chesapeake* by a few roughnecks was nothing compared to other plots and schemes being busily cooked up in the Halifax Hotel. The hotel was one node in a network of spies and terrorists, held together by couriers disguised as Union laborers and soldiers, connecting Toronto, Montreal, Halifax, Chicago, St. Louis, New York, and Richmond. Keith's activities stretched in many underground directions that were difficult to detect, for he maintained, with others of his kind, a Masonic secrecy, ringed round with ciphers and pledges of silence. The Federal government, as well as later historians of the period, always sensed that they were seeing only the surface of these complex, yet often disorganized Confederate operations. With his closely guarded inner life, Keith was especially adept in this environment. And he was protected by the reluctance of the U.S. government to open another front with Britain and its hostile colony. Federal consuls and spies could track the movements of these Confederate sympathizers, but what could they do to stop them? They could only report the information, hoping that it would lead to seizures of blockade-runners and arrests of raiders when they actually crossed the border.

The War Department took Jackson's suspicions seriously and circulated Keith's name as a potential enemy. On December 18, 1863, an alert New York postmaster intercepted a message addressed to Sandy Keith from J. H. Cammack. A known rebel agent, "Cam" had arrived in New York in August to visit another agent, his good friend "Trow": Nelson Trowbridge. Extremely nervous that he might be arrested, Cam

Figure 3.1: Intercepted letter from J. H. Cammack
Source: *Harper's New Monthly Magazine*, 1898

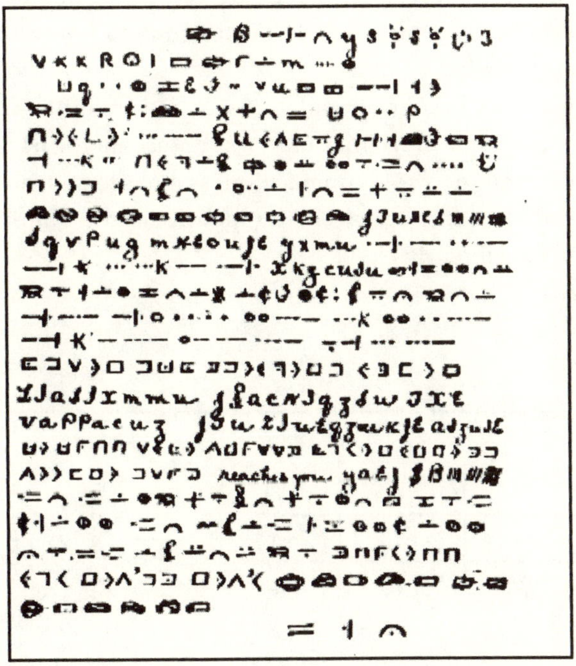

had another motivation for taking the risk of visibility in the city: He was rendezvousing with a beautiful widow, a member of one of the F.F.V., the First Families of Virginia, dynasties established before the Revolutionary War. Trow was suspicious of his friend's ladylove, and wrote, "Of course he [Cammack] thinks her virtuous, and as it will do him no good to inform him to the contrary, I keep shady on the subject."

When Cam was not wining and dining his girlfriend, chaperoned by her sister, at Delmonico's, he was busy crafting ciphers, and it was one of these that was intercepted by the postmaster. The letter was a tangled jumble of letters, squiggles, squares, dots, and triangles that the clerks in the War Department struggled to decode.

After two days of intensive study, they threw up their hands in defeat. It was then delivered to the tiny U.S. Military Telegraph Corps, situated in the War Department across the lawn from the White House. The Corps was made up of three enthusiastic code-breaking wizards, David Homer Bates, Charles Tinker, and Albert Chandler, whom their boss jokingly referred to as "the Sacred Three." Bates later recalled that Cammack's cipher "was unlike any we had ever been called upon to translate, and the 'Sacred Three' puzzled their brains for hours before they succeeded in making full sense out of the jargon, while the President hovered about us, anxious to know the sequel of our united cogitations."

Bates was the first to crack it. As a boy in Pittsburgh, he had worked as a clerk in a store that used a cryptogram for its price marks, and line fourteen of the Cammack message seemed similar. Bates worked out that in line fourteen, Cammack used a simple system of substitution, based on this key:

Figure 3.2: Cipher key
(drawn by author)

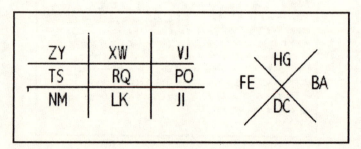

Each letter corresponded to the shape framing it, with the second letter given a dot to distinguish it, so that Z = ⌐ , Y = •⌐, X = ⌐⌐, W = ⌐•

Figure 3.3: Cipher key
(drawn by author)

and so on. Line fourteen of the code was translated thus:

The Sacred Three guessed that the next word must be "pro-gramme," giving them clues to another line of code, and in this way were able to finally unravel the ten distinct codes used in the letter.

N.Y., Dec 18, 1863.
Hon. J. P. Benjamin, Secretary of State, Richmond, Va.:

Willis is here. The two steamers will leave here about Christ-mas. Lamar and Bowers left here via Bermuda two weeks ago. 12,000 rifled muskets came duly to hand and were shipped to Halifax as instructed. We will be able to seize the other two steamers as per programme. Trowbridge has followed the President's orders. We will have Briggs under arrest before this reaches you. Cost $2,000. We want more money. How shall we draw. Bills all forwarded to Slidell and rects. recd. Write as before. J.H.C.

The Sacred Three also decoded a second message from Cammack to Keith dated three days later. It revealed an extensive network of Confederate operatives in New York, in the very heart of the Union, working directly for the rebel government in Richmond.

The ring had two major plots in the works. Much worse than the *Chesapeake* piracy, the operatives and their men planned to board two ships in Halifax with their luggage: innocuous-looking hogsheads, purported to be full of provisions, that actually disguised their hoard of 12,000 rifled muskets as mentioned in the dispatch. They would then rise up and seize the ships, and proceed to wreak havoc on Northern shipping. Given the light treatment of the *Chesapeake* pirates, the plan appeared to hold little danger and the possibility of great success. With the authorization of the Confederate Secretary of the Treasury, Christopher Memminger, the agents were also printing $5, $50, and $100 Confederate notes along with treasury bonds. The South lacked the resources for this kind of printing and had to organize it in the North as a covert operation. Promised a cut of the notes and bonds as compensation for their work, the plotters had commissioned an excellent printer, Winthrop Hilton, who was busily cranking out the currency in a room above a saloon. Cam was supposed to take the notes and the perfected machinery, including two finely worked steel plates and a geometric lathe, to Sandy Keith in Halifax. In turn, Keith would help Cam run them through the blockade to Florida. This was a lucrative and prestigious role for Keith, directly involving him in plans sanctioned at the highest level of the Confederate government.

Within days of the Sacred Three's successful efforts to decode Cammack's message, the Federal marshal, with the help of New York City detectives, began trailing the suspects around Manhattan. On New Year's Eve, 1863, they raided Hilton's workshop above the saloon, but met disappointment. They found Hilton, one of his helpers, and several lithographic stones, but essential parts of the printing apparatus were missing. Interrogating the suspects, they learned the whereabouts of the missing machinery. At two o'clock in the morning, they broke down the door of another room on Park Row, netting six million dollars worth of newly minted Confederate bonds, one million in treasury bills, and the lathe. The plates were found the next day. Cammack managed to escape to Havana and the 12,000 muskets shipped to Sandy Keith mysteriously disappeared. Safe in neutral Canada, Keith himself was never touched or even questioned, though he would eventually detect that he was being watched and followed.

How had Keith become involved in these distant New York operations? His connection came through his shipping interests with one of the plotters, Charles Augustus Lafayette Lamar, son of a wealthy Georgia capitalist and substantial slave owner, Gazaway Bugg Lamar. Father and son had a long history with ships, and had once suffered a terrible trauma together. On a family trip to Baltimore aboard the steamer *Pulaski*, the boiler had exploded, killing over a hundred passengers and tearing the ship into pieces. Gazaway and his son survived by clinging to the remaining planks of the deck, but his wife and three other children were lost. Charley, who was only fourteen at the time, could never remember the ordeal without the greatest emotion, but the tragedy did not put him off ships or make him a better man. Named after a family friend, the famous French supporter of the American Revolution, the Marquis de Lafayette, the red-haired Charley became a monomaniacal fanatic and profiteer, cold to any human suffering other than his own. A dandy who spent much of his time betting on horses, his one true passion was to resurrect the slave trade with Africa, from which the United States had withdrawn in 1808. He so ardently defended his right to trade in human beings that he frequently threatened to stand at fifteen paces and blast at anyone who contradicted his view.

The most infamous of his crimes involved the *Wanderer,* a fast pleasure yacht that he converted into a slave ship in 1858, bringing four hundred blacks from the Congo whom he planned to sneak past the authorities and sell for $650 each back in Georgia. Packed into a filthy space designed to fit fifty, without sanitation or adequate food and water, the slaves sweltered in the heat, many dying of thirst while the crew above drank champagne. The venture did not turn out as expected, but Charles Lamar saw these kinds of losses as the necessary cost of learning a new business. He wrote to one of his many friends, "You are aware that this is a risky business. I lost two out of three. To be sure, at first I knew nothing of the business. I have learned something since, and I hope I can put my information to some account. I have been in it for 'grandeur,' and been fighting for a principle. Now I am in for the dollars." At the onset of the war, Charley turned his interest from the slave trade and began acquiring ships to be used in the more lucrative business of blockade running and privateering. His business partner in all these endeavors was his old friend, Nelson Trowbridge, who wrote to Charley of the sartorial splendor made possible by Charley's new wealth: "There are devilish few rebels nowadays that come rigged out in your style."

When the war began, the rapacious Charley and his father Gazaway saw the potential for profit, as they did in everyone and everything, and took up blockade running. In the summer of 1863, with the help of investors in England and France, they began building a multinational company, the Importing and Exporting Company of the State of Georgia, also called the Phinizy Line for one of their primary investors. They promised their stockholders that the new enterprise would have the fastest boats and the best pilots, including a former arctic explorer. In their sales pitches to nervous "men of capital," they argued: "As the risks increase, the profits do also." Hearing of heavy losses at Gettysburg and the surrender at Vicksburg, Gazaway Lamar contemplated the soaring exchange rate for gold and blithely assured his son that "with Mexico, France, and the Confederacy in alliance, and free trade, we should eclipse the world."

Convinced that France and England were going to rally to help the Confederacy and sneering at any suggestion of a Southern defeat, Charley Lamar surely envisioned a legal, thriving international slave trade once the war was over. The arrest of his friend Trow, who was tossed into Fort Warren for his role in the currency caper, did not deter him. The most self-deluded of men, Lamar was finally felled by a stray bullet as he pranced about on his horse in Columbus, Georgia, after the town had surrendered. He was rumored to have been the last man killed in the Civil War. Perhaps in a reference to his overblown masculinity, the inscription on his tombstone reads, "In the morning it flourisheth and groweth up; in the evening it is cut down and withereth." Despite Charley Lamar's arrogance, the *Wanderer*'s voyage was to be one of the last in the African slave trade.

For their official agent in Halifax in their grandiose endeavors, the Lamars chose the now firmly-established Sandy Keith, trusted by blockade-running captains and Southern investors. The Lamars had helped Keith and his associate Patrick Martin acquire two blockade-running ships. With Keith's prime location at a major neutral port, he was a natural choice to help Charley and his good friends Trow and Cam in their ill-fated side business as would-be currency brokers, gunrunners, and privateers. Keith undoubtedly met with Charley on his visit to Halifax in August 1863, but Keith was never welcomed into the innermost sanctum of Charley and his fellow rebel agents who had been staunch friends before the war. They depended on Keith solely as a courier and middleman in their network of operations. These schemes shared a hatred for the Northern tyrant with an unparalleled lust for financial speculation. Such motives and utter contempt for human life resonated with Keith's own rage, jealousy, and avariciousness, giving his dark side a larger meaning and purpose.

If all of his prior deeds for the Confederacy could somehow be justified as adventurous larks or the necessities of business and war, his complicity with Luke Blackburn left no doubt of Keith's underlying maliciousness. In August 1863, around the time Charley Lamar and Colonel Brain came to town, Blackburn arrived from New Orleans with his charming wife, Julia, and took a room at the Halifax Hotel, as was natural for any Southern visitor. The elegant couple must have made quite an impression on Keith, because he later imitated them in his disguise of a Southern gentleman with a wife from New Orleans. Blackburn had a veneer as smooth as polished mahogany, but he was the most bizarre schemer to ever emerge from the backwoods of Kentucky. He seemed the perfect gentleman, elegant and genteel, with strong features that attracted admiration. He was also a Mason, which gave him a special kind of connection to Sandy Keith. Blackburn's plan, for which he needed the help of an agent, was to buy a ship on the Great Lakes, load it with ice, run it through the blockade to Wilmington, and trade the ice for cotton. Ice, which Southern towns had to import from the North, was desperately needed as the only truly effective remedy for yellow fever, striking its victims especially hard in the summer months with violent black vomiting, boiling fevers, profuse sweating, and convulsions. In Richmond, ice could only be legally obtained by medical prescription because of its scarcity. After this philanthropic deed, Blackburn planned to make for Havana, where he would trade cotton for gold, guns, and ammunition.

When Blackburn presented the scheme to the governor of Mississippi, he was appointed the state's military supply agent in Canada. All the Confederate supply agents and their clerks worked through Sandy Keith, who, with Patrick Martin, probably helped Blackburn arrange the purchase of his ship and his ice in Montreal. Blackburn then sailed for Wilmington as supercargo: the crewman, often the investor, who oversaw the transport and sale of goods. His plan was all going well until, after loading his fifty cotton bales and sailing from port, the North Atlantic Blockading Squadron ran him down in the Wilmington harbor and confiscated his cargo. But because he looked and acted the part of a respectable doctor rather than a profiteer and a gunrunner, his captors were fooled into letting him go.

Blackburn returned to Halifax, where he began cultivating relationships with Confederate sympathizers. When three of the *Chesapeake*'s minor pirates were arrested, having doggedly and stupidly lingered around the childhood home of escapist George Wade, Blackburn testified at their hearing for extradition. Keith's good friend, William Turlington, a North Carolina corn merchant who married a young Canadian lass, helped organize the pirates' legal representation. Blackburn was enlisted as a witness for the defense, impressing some three hundred spectators with his distinguished and gentlemanly manner. His role was simply to verify, on a commission letter, the handwriting of Jefferson Davis and the authenticity of the Great Confederate Seal with its motto, *Deo Vindice* (God Will Vindicate). This letter was supposed to prove that the *Chesapeake* pirates had acted lawfully under official orders, a strategy that failed when the prisoners were ordered back to jail to await extradition.

Traveling between Toronto and Montreal, Blackburn was among a cadre of powerful men who harbored plans for the first acts of a truly modern system of terrorism. In the desperation of the times, as the South began to feel its end, fantasies of total war and mass murder—burning down cities and destroying entire populations—became ever more acceptable. Hair neatly oiled and combed, dressed in elegant long coats and starched white shirts, conspirators huddled in hotel rooms in Montreal, Toronto, and Halifax, drinking fine wine and angostura bitters as they talked of their childhood days in the sunny old South, their way of life threatened by raping, burning, and pillaging invaders. Their brainstorming was desperate, intense, and apocalyptic. They plotted to make raids across the border, liberate Confederate prisoners, burn down cities, poison reservoirs, destroy dams, use biological weapons against urban populations, kidnap or assassinate the president, and blow up the White House with hidden barrels of gunpowder. In sharp contrast to their bucolic dreams of the South, these cigar-smoking armchair gladiators fantasized about scientific warfare, secret weapons that could kill at a distance, booby traps and time bombs, chemicals that combusted fifteen minutes after the terrorist escaped, and viruses that did their dirty work only after contact with unsuspecting victims. They were not especially proficient terrorists, and most of these schemes curled off with their cigar smoke or floundered against the sheer ineptitude of their gullible, troubled recruits who had more moxie than brains, discretion, and common sense.

Sandy Keith was certainly one of the better sort, a well-connected gentleman like them and he shared their mindset that the loss of wealth and power must be avoided at any cost, even that of innocent lives. Later, a similar sense of individual desperation and loss of power would drive Keith to the same compulsive fantasies of mass murder, and he was no doubt chosen for his role in helping organize Confederate terrorist acts because he was already susceptible. Among his many involvements with raids across the border, he was trusted with part of a major operation, unprecedented in its ruthlessness and utterly senseless in its design. Luke Blackburn was its mastermind. The two villains had much in common, their portly, respectable figures disguising thoroughly deviant minds.

As a young man in Natchez, Mississippi, Blackburn had made his reputation as an untiring, altruistic doctor, specializing in the treatment of epidemics, selflessly treating the sick ravaged by yellow fever. During the war, Blackburn put this knowledge of infectious disease to far more malicious use, plotting to wipe out urban populations with biological warfare, a deep violation of traditional military ethics that forbade, for example, the dumping of rotten animal carcasses into the enemy's wells. In his brainstorming sessions with like-minded Confederate leaders, whom Jefferson Davis had given a million dollars for waging terrorist warfare from their base in Canada, Blackburn presented a plan, based on faulty medical science, to send clothing infected with yellow fever to Northern cities. Like many of the Confederate's attempts at scientific terrorism, it would fail. In this instance, what Blackburn did not know was that mosquitoes, rather than miasmic air or infected surfaces, are the primary disease vectors for yellow fever.

In Toronto, Blackburn looked around for a man gullible and reckless enough to handle his Pandora's boxes, which the good doctor claimed would kill everyone within sixty yards when opened, and he finally found a willing dupe: Godfrey Hyams, an itinerant shoemaker, a ten-pound weakling originally from London, and a former resident of war-torn Arkansas. Hyams later testified that Blackburn had taken him to his room in the Queen's Hotel in Toronto and asked if he were a member of the Masonic Craft. Though Hyams said no, Blackburn offered his hand and pledged his friendship as a Mason. Blackburn offered Hyams glory, greatness, and $100,000 if he would carry the soiled clothes that the doctor would collect from his sweating, vomiting patients in Bermuda. Hyams felt honored by his association with the esteemed doctor. He saw himself raised from his humble lot, and he sat patiently in Toronto awaiting further orders. In January 1864, Blackburn went to Bermuda, where he collected rank bed linens, soiled poultices, and stained pajamas and underwear. A hospital nurse observed him piling blankets on his patients, making them sweat even more profusely. Over the next few months, he packed five trunks and a valise with his prizes, wrapping the dirty fabric in new fancy woolen shirts, satin dresses, and coats, making sure, to his mind, that all was ripe with fever.

In May, he wrote to Hyams and ordered him to Halifax where his handler would be Sandy Keith. Keith was often assigned to shepherd Confederate couriers, agents, and escaped prisoners through Halifax, sending them on to their missions in Canada or back home to Dixie. He welcomed them into the warmth of the Halifax Hotel, fed them well, and listened closely to their adventures and troubles. He would steal their stories and later make them part of his own false identities. Arriving in town, Hyams went to Keith's rooms in the Halifax Hotel and pulled out a letter from Blackburn. They discussed what they called "the expedition." Keith pronounced it "all right" and they went over the details of the plan. The destitute shoemaker stayed in the Halifax Hotel for two nights before Keith moved him out to the Farmer's Hotel. This was Keith's standard procedure with the more troubled men who arrived. After a couple of days he would send them off, keeping an eye on them from a distance.

Meanwhile, Blackburn was smuggling his supposedly toxic cargo through Havana, and then finally on to Halifax. When he arrived, he checked in to the Halifax Hotel and sent for Hyams, ordering him to go and fetch the roped green trunks and one very special leather valise packed with elegant silk shirts and a black suit. Blackburn had taken the most care with these, for they were destined for Lincoln, and he had treated them with both yellow fever and smallpox. In a bizarre twist, Hyams, with his English accent, was supposed to personally take the valise to Lincoln as a present from "the working men of Manchester," but he spooked at the task and declined. He did agree to take the trunk that Blackburn had fondly named "Big No. 2" and distribute its contents in Washington. He bribed a steamer captain with a twenty-dollar gold piece to smuggle Big No. 2 and the remaining trunks to Boston, but they were detained for five days. For mysterious reasons,

Hyams asked that the trunks be shipped to Philadelphia and waited for them there. Using his alias, "A. K. Thompson," Keith also traveled to Philadelphia at the same time on other business and perhaps to coordinate the shipments. Then, Hyams traveled to Baltimore where he donned gloves, smoked the Havana cigars Blackburn had cordially provided him, and chewed pungent, bitter camphor to ward off infection. He neatly smoothed and refolded the clothes, preparing them for auction. Through various unwitting commission agents, he dispersed the trunks to Washington, D.C.; Norfolk, Virginia; and New Bern, North Carolina, where they were supposed to do their dirty work.

Puffed up with his success, Hyams went back to Canada where Confederate leaders told him he would now be a gentleman instead of a poor, humble laborer. But he was never given enough to even pay for his expenses. Suddenly a finicky accountant, Blackburn insisted on seeing Hyams' receipts from the commission agents, and then refused to pay him. Blackburn had, by now, begun other arrangements for dispensing more trunks, and had some stored at Nassau awaiting transport. Later, in the public hysteria that followed the Lincoln assassination, the angry and spiteful Hyams finally ratted on Blackburn. In his statement to the Toronto police court and later at the trial of the Lincoln assassination conspirators, Hyams briefly mentioned Keith's role in the plot but he was far more interested in inflating his own importance to demonstrate how badly he'd been cheated. He would have little satisfaction. Blackburn was tried in Canada, but never convicted of any crime. After the war, the good doctor resumed his medical practice and successfully ran for the governorship of Kentucky, while Hyams slunk away into obscurity, disbelieved and reviled.

As the disgruntled Hyams chased Blackburn through Canada, besieging him for money with telegraphs and letters, another one of Keith's charges, the rebel courier Francis X. Jones, had grown disenchanted with his adventurous role. On a mission from Montreal in the spring of 1864, Jones sailed to Halifax where Keith received him and placed him out of sight in St. John. There, as Jones waited a long seven weeks for orders, something compelled him to write to President Lincoln, begging for amnesty and a pardon for his youthful folly. He explained that he had been forced into the Confederate secret service by "the cajolery of those who know how to entrap the unsuspecting." All he wanted, he said, was to return home and live in peace, working on his mother's farm. Some weeks later, after Jones participated in an abortive raid on the town of Calais, across the border in Maine, he was arrested and hauled off to prison, where he continued to beg for asylum, ever more paranoid about a "powerful conspiracy" of "wicked and designing men" who had lured him from the path of honor. He finally wrote down statements detailing vast and elaborate plots to wage war across the Northern border, naming, among many others, Sandy Keith and Benjamin Wier. Inflating the capacity of disorganized Confederate operatives, he warned that he would be relentlessly sought and assaulted by secret agents sent by his Confederate adversaries. His letters finally reached Secretary of War Edwin Stanton who ordered an investigation. One of the Sacred Three, Charles Tinker, was sent on a secret mission to Halifax, after which "it was generally concluded that Keith was capable of any crime in the calendar." But no one at all suspected whom Keith's next target would be.

FOUR

THE SWINDLER

During the long siege of the South in the summer of 1864, barefoot Confederate soldiers could feel their stomachs pressing against their backbones as the sure knowledge of defeat swept over them. Soldiers blue and gray had fallen by the thousands in the horrific carnages of Spotsylvania, Petersburg, and Cold Harbor as the South tried to hold to its own, but its doom had been sealed a year before with the fall of Vicksburg. Now the only futile hope was that Lincoln would go down in flames, either by electoral defeat or assassination, and that his successor would broker a peace that would preserve the Confederacy. In Halifax, smug Haligonian capitalists were still busy profiting from Southern desperation, trading guns and shoes for tobacco and cotton. But no one needed a crystal ball to see that this profit was finite, that eventually the flow of Southern gold would dry up and leave the town to its old sleepy ways. That cold reality did not sit well with Sandy Keith, who had finally risen to spheres of wealth and power, who was a player in the secret operations of nations, who was important enough to be shadowed by Federal detectives, and who would never quietly return to life as his uncle's humble clerk. He now looked beyond the war, readying himself for an exit from the little town that could not contain his ambitions.

It began with the arrival in Halifax of Luther Rice Smoot, Quartermaster General of Virginia. The son of a brickmaker from Washington,

D.C., Smoot had overblown political ambitions and was generally full
of his own self-importance. He had once run for Washington City
Council on the immigrant-hating "Know-Nothing" ticket and obtained
a job as a clerk in the finance division of the Indian Bureau of the U.S.
Department of the Interior, where he worked in a variety of capacities.
In 1856, using his new connections, he left for Leavenworth, Kansas,
and went into the banking business with William Russell, a wealthy military contractor who was also running the overland mail service, the
Pony Express. Falling into deep financial trouble because Mormons
had attacked his wagon trains, Russell was implicated in a scam to steal
$870,000 worth of bonds belonging to Indian tribes from a trunk lying
carelessly around the Department of the Interior's offices. To his personal and financial embarrassment, Smoot was implicated in the embez-
zlement, and was called to Washington to testify at a Congressional
hearing that revealed a complex business network of government officials, frontier investors, and eastern bankers, including Gazaway Bugg
Lamar. There was a shocking level of insider trading and corruption: a
culture of swindlers who certainly thought nothing of cheating Indians
and bamboozling the public, all behind the smokescreen of a government office. The great orator and abolitionist Henry Ward Beecher
thundered from his pulpit against the short-sighted greed of politics and
commerce, demanding a renewed national morality and declaring,
"Money is insane." War was looming, and the investigation was interrupted by the first shots at Fort Sumter just in time to save the suspects,
including the incompetent Secretary of War, John Floyd, from further
scandal. No stranger to wheeling and dealing, Smoot went on to volunteer his particular skills to the Confederates as an army supplier, always
with his own profit in mind.

Comfortable in a world of name-dropping, group loyalties, and secret handshakes, Luther Smoot was well connected for shady dealings
in Canada where he came to know Sandy Keith. When he was not
busily dispensing tents, flies, axes, picks, tents, saddles, jackets, socks,
and pack mules to the beleaguered troops on the Virginia state line,
Smoot was cooking up some personal business for his own profit.
Blockade running, as he knew, was infinitely more lucrative than
working as a supply officer. Thus, Smoot inevitably ended up smoking
cigars with Sandy Keith at the Halifax Hotel. Also present was Sandy's
old comrade, Dr. William Almon, of *Chesapeake* fame. Smoot had an

elaborate scheme in mind, one which only made sense in the frenzied atmosphere of the time. Smoot wanted Keith to go down to Philadelphia and buy him two steam locomotives for moving cotton along the Southern railroads that suffered from a lack of equipment. Smoot could then get his cotton from the interior of Virginia to the sea on his own engines, "the most profitable business he could engage in" as he said, and definitely more exciting and less frustrating than being a quartermaster who had recently been accused by a field commander of gross incompetence.

Money, technology, and power: These motivations appealed deeply to Sandy Keith, who agreed to help Smoot with the plan. The trick was to get the locomotive engines past the customs officials in Philadelphia. There could be no hint that Smoot was the buyer of the engines or that they were destined for the South. Therefore, Smoot, Keith, and Almon enlisted George Lang, a tall, bearded, muscular builder from Scotland who was the co-owner of a slate quarry in Nova Scotia. Lang fit right in with the plotters, for he too had delusions of grandeur and liked to pretend he was more than a humble stonecutter, falsely boasting to have supervised construction of Edinburgh's 200-foot-high Sir Walter Scott monument. Through his building trade, he was well connected with the Keiths. Lang built Keith Hall, helped probate John Keith's estate, and was a member of the North American British Society, whose members included Sandy Keith's brother, Donald, owner of a thriving furniture factory. More brawn than brains, Lang agreed to serve as the nominal buyer for Smoot's engines. Keith was to ostensibly act as Lang's agent, buy the engines in Philadelphia, and transport them to Halifax where Lang would receive them. Keith would then run them through the blockade to Wilmington. There, Smoot would be eagerly waiting to become a big railroad man. All the while, Keith was scheming to manipulate the situation to his own best advantage. He secretly cared nothing for Smoot or the Southern cause, and envisioned himself as more than a conduit for trade. Underestimating his victim, he believed that Smoot, in all of his self-importance, was going to be a very easy dupe. He did not realize he had met his nemesis.

In mid-July, disguised as his favorite alter ego, "A. K. Thompson," Keith slipped into the City of Brotherly Love. With about $85,000 of Confederate investors' money at his disposal, Keith checked in to the swanky Continental Hotel, a six-story palace known for its lavish table, fine accommodations, and "vertical railways," elevators that whisked guests to their elegant rooms. Followed by adoring fans, jolly Prince Bertie had slept at the hotel on his rounds of North America, and here the famous detective Allan Pinkerton had earnestly warned the newly elected President Lincoln, stretched calmly in an easy chair, of the first known plot against his life. While Godfrey Hyams sneaked into Philadelphia to arrange delivery of Luke Blackburn's bioterrorist weapons, Keith left the Continental and went up Bush Hill to the huge Norris Locomotive Works.

The Norris Works were an exciting place to visit for a technological enthusiast like Keith. The Norris brothers were famous for producing the first locomotive engine, the *George Washington,* which could climb a steep incline under its own steam power. Before the war, they did a brisk international trade, leading one observer to exclaim with patriotic pride, "American locomotives in England, in Russia, in Austria, and soon, probably, in Rome, whizzing up to the Vatican!" With the prosperous bustle of a hefty wartime business, the Norris Works, covering the area of one hundred city lots, poured with black smoke from the forges and rang with the metallic sounds of state-of-the-art lathes, drill presses, shearing machines, and bolt cutters. From the first forging of the boilerplate to the final painting of the nameplate, U.S. government agents watched carefully over the manufacture of the engines, guarding against sabotage, profiteering, and smuggling.

Despite this vigilant official presence, on July 11, Keith boldly entered the Norrises' counting house and ordered two locomotive engines, discussing boiler specifications, wheel gauges, axle diameters, and cylinder strokes. The Norrises expected payment in advance, and Keith promptly settled his account. His order was sent on to the trestle boards of the civil engineers to begin the thirty-day project of building a first-class locomotive engine. Although all appeared to be moving ahead, the situation would have appeared odd to an outside observer. Smoot had given Keith $25,000 for the engines, which cost, at most, $12,000 apiece. So far so good. But Keith had in his possession at least $60,000 more with which he was living a prince's life in the Continental Hotel. The extra money had come from two more gullible investors whom Keith had managed to bamboozle into investing in locomotive engines: $20,000 had come from the Petersburg Steamship Company, whose agents thought that Keith was dealing with the Rodgers Company in New Jersey, and $40,000 had come from George Lang's quarrying business partner, a corrupt Haligonian banker and former railroad engineer, James Foreman. These were immense sums, and a sign of the trust Keith had earned. He was holding well over a million dollars by today's standards, and he did not plan to part with much of it.

By mid-August, as General William Tecumseh Sherman began his successful assault on Atlanta, the new locomotives, with their shiny black steam funnels, were ready for transport to Halifax. They were hefted by crane out of the last workhouse onto a railcar, taken to the dock, and put aboard a ship, all under the watchful eyes of a Federal official. Now Keith made his move. Either he or a hired informant, perhaps Hyams, contacted officials in the War Department and advised them of the engines' true destination in the South. On August 16, government agents inspected the engines and found that they were of the wrong wheel gauge for the Canadian rails. They seized the engines as property of the enemy. Playing the innocent victim, Keith told his three investors of this sad, unavoidable, and unexpected turn of events, claiming that the locomotives had been seized because of his notoriety as a Confederate secret agent. Knowing nothing of the other dupes, each investor believed that his money had been spent and lost on the engines. Keith had played one against the other and now returned to Halifax with at least a $60,000 profit. The investors realized too late that they'd been swindled. The Petersburg Steamship Company gave up without a fight. Nearly ruined, James Foreman started a huge legal fight with George Lang and began a deep descent into swindling and embezzling that would eventually cost him his palatial home and send him into exile from Halifax. And, at the sobering realization that he'd been sorely cheated, his ambitious fantasies crushed, Luther Smoot began a dogged ten-year quest to get his money back. Obsessed with the engines locked in the warehouse, he would eventually exact his revenge from Sandy Keith, setting events into motion that would lead finally to the terrible catastrophe at Bremerhaven.

Keith now established a modus operandi of apparently losing goods in transport and making an immense profit from the loss. Though he was still juggling the locomotive swindle, he tried the scam again on Major Norman Walker, the Confederate disbursing agent in St. George's, Bermuda, a sociable fellow who organized blockade-running operations and was known for his genteel, hospitable welcome to all Southern investors. At their cozy little cottage in Bermuda, Walker, his wife Georgiana, and their four "little Confederates," entertained visitors like Luke Blackburn and the glamorous Confederate lady spy, Rose O'Neal Greenhow, with extravagant dinners of smuggled delicacies, accompanied by amusing tableaux vivant of Biblical scenes such as the ermine-bedecked Queen Esther kneeling before the Sultan Ahasueras. A Virginia socialite who hated the war mostly because it curtailed her shopping, Georgiana Walker suffered from eye ailments that did not prevent her from making contemptuous observations about the "African aristocracy" of the island who were "incapable of self government, born to be slaves & yet forced to be free." The Walkers had reconstructed their narrow little civilization of kid gloves, Confederate flags, and white supremacy in Bermuda so that well-heeled Southerners felt right at home. But when yellow fever began to kill their friends, Norman Walker decided to move his operations to Halifax.

In August 1864, Walker made a visit to the northern port to check out operations, and assigned Keith as his agent to buy $40,000 worth of pork from a dealer in New York. Walker was shocked when Keith produced only a meager sixty pounds, hardly enough for Walker's own soirées. It must have been a golden pig indeed at almost seven hundred dollars a pound. Keith explained that on its way north, the pork had been confiscated and hauled off to a warehouse by government agents in Boston. At the same time, Keith made a great show of petitioning Nova Scotia's Provincial government for the return of the pork, for which he said he paid $23,806. Keith complained of his own "great pecuniary loss" and argued that "the pork in question was purchased by him on his own account and in the ordinary course of his business." He could think of no justification, he said, for its confiscation. The idea that the provincial government would somehow champion Keith's case against U.S. customs authorities was patently absurd. Anyone who knew Halifax and Sandy Keith could tell that it was all a blatant lie and that the pork was destined for starving troops in the South. But it gave Keith an excuse for holding onto the rest of Walker's money, claiming tangled legalities, while Walker and his family entertained themselves on a trip to Paris.

Still oblivious to the increasing futility of their political cause, the Walkers returned from Paris and moved in early October to Halifax, where Benjamin Weir greeted them and told them of the shocking death of Rose O'Neal Greenhow who, fleeing on a blockade-runner chased by the Union squadron, had drowned near Wilmington, her pockets hastily and foolishly stuffed with heavy gold coins that took her right to the bottom when the boat capsized. The insanity of money seemed the order of the day. The Walkers settled into a small house and were frequently entertained at evening soirées at Dr. William Almon's where they were received "with much kindness & attention, & found the society intensely Southern." Yet Georgina observed that in mid-November her husband became graver and looked older than he had before, and though she guessed that Norman was suddenly suffering from the horrors of the distant war, his mood coincided with his realization that he had lost his $40,000 investment in pork. Even as he was cheating them, Keith must have greatly admired the Walkers, for later he would claim to be from their hometown, Petersburg, Virginia, and the plausibility of his lie would depend on the stories they told him.

Now that Norman Walker was his near neighbor, Sandy Keith was under pressure to make good on the pork, but he managed to stave off all of his increasingly impatient investors while he was carrying out his final scam on his Montreal business partner, Patrick Martin. By the fall of 1864, Montreal had become a magnet for arrogant, desperately deluded Confederates, worn down by the war and shadowed by a throng of Federal detectives. Lame, ill, physically and psychologically wounded, they stumped around the elegant rooms of the infamous St. Lawrence Hall, planning grand speculative adventures that would win them the war, restore their pride, alter the world economy, and make them all filthy rich. Their leader was Jacob Thompson, the former Secretary of the Interior, now chief Confederate agent in Canada, charged by Jefferson Davis to commit depredations across the border and fire up the Northern copperheads to revolt against Lincoln. Among the plotters was Luke Blackburn, and a peculiar concentration of Baltimoreans in the city would eventually raise suspicions that the Lincoln assassination was first conceived there, especially since one of the visitors was a black-haired dandy, the Shakespearean actor John Wilkes Booth.

Of all the many would-be outlaw cavaliers on the nomadic, dreamlike fringe of the war, John Wilkes Booth would rise to the greatest infamy. Like Keith, Booth bore a heavy patriarchal burden, for he had been raised in his tragedian father's unfinished manse, Tudor Hall, as damaging in its intimidating legacy as Keith Hall. Also like Keith, Booth was an aggressive finagler and a speculator, with his own investments in blockade-runners and oil wells, the type of man who would end up not on the gory battlefield but negotiating deals in elegant hotels. Yet he was sincere and passionate in his ugly motivations, zealous in his support of slavery, and full of vengeance. In Montreal, to the usual acclaim, Booth performed one-man shows of *The Merchant of Venice, Julius Caesar,* and *Hamlet,* peppered with readings of *The Charge of the Light Brigade.* But all the while he was busy networking with the cigar gladiators in Canada who offered at least moral support for his violent plans. Grown weary of acting, he was beginning to envision his greatest performance ever; he had hatched out a bizarre conspiracy that he presented to anyone who would listen, finally taking him to the doorstep of Patrick Martin.

During his ten-day stay in Montreal in October 1864, wearing his velvet coat and yellow fox hat, Booth visited Martin at his house. Martin's wife and daughter were greatly taken by his dark-eyed charm, his oiled black poodle curls, and his drooping moustache. Booth presented Martin with his plan. He intended to kidnap Lincoln in his theater box. After he'd doused the gas lights, he would sneak up to the box, tie up the President, lower his huge, heavy body down over the balustrade and take him by boat to Virginia. Either that, or Booth would simply intercept the President on his way back to the White House after a theatrical performance and spirit him off. One of the conspirators, Samuel Bland Arnold, a farm laborer who was completely awed by the charismatic Booth, referred to this daffy plot as "purely humane and patriotic in its principles." Booth needed the help of Patrick Martin's old connections in Maryland to transport the purloined president from house to house, muscling him to Virginia. There, they would hold Lincoln hostage in exchange for Confederate prisoners of war. Always up for any scheme that smacked of the daring rebel, Martin was impressed and agreed to provide Booth with money and letters of introduction to friends in Baltimore. In a slightly croaking voice, for he suffered from frequent laryngitis, Booth also asked Martin to see that his entire theatrical wardrobe be shipped south onboard one of Martin's two blockade-runners. Valued at $25,000, Booth's wardrobe was a very substantial investment with which to entrust with Martin, who agreed to watch over it.

Enter Sandy Keith. As unobtrusively as ever, always on the look-out for deluded men, Keith inserted himself into these doings. He and Martin still had a business partnership and a shared interest in the schooners, one of which had been acquired through the Lamars. Martin believed that this was to be their last run, the last hurrah of a failed conflict, and he planned to make a tidy nest egg before the war's end, which he saw looming on the horizon whether Booth succeeded or not. Making arrangements in Halifax, Martin allowed Keith to acquire a very hefty insurance policy on the ships and their cargoes in Martin's name, and he entrusted Keith with his papers and gave him power of attorney in the event of his death. But Keith was holding a deadly secret: He had already figured out that he could make much more money from the loss of the ships than from the sale of their cargo.

Keith had learned some months ago that marine insurance was an excellent game when he lost the *Caledonia*. The Lamars helped Keith acquire the ship, a lead-colored paddlewheel boat, fitted out in Liverpool. Keith was its owner in name only. This was standard practice, for the Lamars were in the business of buying large steamers, seemingly for ordinary trade but really destined for blockade running. They had to make sure that their ships' titles were held in neutral countries so they could not be captured and held by Federal agents. The ships had to be technically owned by persons outside the South, and this role usually fell to a British citizen like Keith. The *Caledonia* actually belonged to H. W. Kinsman, a dry goods merchant in Charleston, South Carolina, who insured his investment for $32,000, leaving the papers in Keith's seemingly capable hands. Its movements carefully observed by Consul Jackson, the *Caledonia* made one brief voyage from Montreal in April 1864, depositing the reluctant raider Francis X. Jones in Halifax where, meeting Keith, he imagined himself at the center of vast and labyrinthine plots. The ship then sailed for Nassau, but sank before it left sight of Nova Scotia. Sandy Keith sashayed down to the insurance office and collected the settlement for himself. Furious at the loss, Kinsman could collect no insurance because he was unable to establish his ownership of the vessel. He was now stewing in Charleston, readying himself to hunt down Keith and claim his debt. The list of Keith's enemies was rapidly growing.

Keith had similar aspirations for his latest blockade-running enterprise with Patrick Martin. Without arousing suspicion, Keith exploited

Martin's relish for adventure, urging him to sail on one of his rickety schooners as supercargo. Martin could have entrusted the goods with hired hands, and his wife, daughter, and other friends considered the whole plan extremely risky and begged him to stay behind or take passage on a sturdier, safer ship. Any seasoned mariner knew that the sudden, treacherous gales of November brought freezing hurricane-force winds and blinding whiteouts that drove ships crashing ashore, for there was nowhere to run on the seaway during such a storm. But Keith was persuasive, and the foolhardy Martin was up for it. The night of the voyage, in the crowded, narrow alleys of old Montreal, Martin laughed and drank with some British garrison officers he knew, and they watched him blithely and confidently board one of the ships. When they arose the next morning, both schooners were gone.

The *Marie Victoria* was the first to perish. Sailing up the St. Lawrence River in calm waters, she was mysteriously wrecked near the piloting station of Bic, carrying Booth's three trunks, full of velvet doublets, gold-trimmed togas, Indian shawls, and tin swords and crowns. All of the crew managed to swim to shore but the ship and its cargo were lost. As his wardrobe disappeared beneath the waves, unknown to him, Booth was on another leg of his odyssey, using Martin's letter to introduce himself to two country doctors in Maryland, including Samuel Mudd, whom he hoped would aid him in his obsession with kidnapping the president. He then went on to New York to rehearse for his role as Marc Anthony in *Julius Caesar*, for which he was forced to perform in a borrowed toga and lace-up sandals. One of his friends, the actor Samuel Knapp Chester, asked what had happened to his costumes. Booth replied that they were still in Canada, in the care of Patrick Martin. As the *Marie Victoria* sank near Bic, Martin was sailing away on his other schooner, never to be seen again.

Meanwhile, in Halifax, Sandy Keith was hosting another Confederate operative, the exceedingly rash Lieutenant Bennett Young, a self-proclaimed "wizard of the saddle," who had just eluded a posse after leading the infamous raid on St. Albans, Vermont, on October 19. With twenty-six other men, he had reconnoitered the town disguised as a hotel guest, and then had suddenly appeared in Confederate uniform, demanding the townspeople to surrender and robbing the banks of $200,000. Popping off their Colt revolvers, the raiders attempted to burn down the buildings using Greek fire, a favorite incendiary chemical of Confederate operatives that was supposed to combust on contact with air, but that never seemed to actually work, probably because of the ineptitude of its users. Galloping away, Bennett fled to Canada and to that most welcoming of men, Sandy Keith, who offered his characteristic hospitality while awaiting news of his latest investment. Keith was a very busy man these days, keeping up a number of swindles while greasing the engine of Confederate trust by taking in men like Bennett.

When he heard of the loss of Martin's ships, Keith prepared to strike it rich. Whether through accident or design, his manipulation of Patrick Martin had paid off. He asked Martin's buddies, the British garrison soldiers, to appear in Halifax and testify at the insurance company that they had seen Martin board one of the lost ships. This proved to the satisfaction of the insurance agents that Martin had not absconded, but was in fact dead. Keith collected Martin's claim, as much as $100,000, refusing to give any of it over to Martin's wife and daughter who had no legal recourse and were left destitute. Despite his amiable façade, Sandy Keith was a cold man, possessed by his secret ambition and immune to the pleas of women.

Years later, after the Bremerhaven explosion and the revelation that Sandy Keith was the "Dynamite Fiend," some of Martin's old crowd immediately speculated that Keith must have blown up Martin and his ships with hidden devices. Captain James Wright, who had once run the blockade with the "genial, whole-souled, and brave Martin" on the *Marie Victoria,* believed that the unbelievable coincidence of the loss of both schooners provided "conclusive evidence of design by the consummate villain, Alexander Keith." Wright theorized that an accomplice onboard the *Marie Victoria* had somehow tampered with the hull, while on the other schooner Keith had probably placed a time bomb like the one he would later use on the *Mosel.* Thus, he ensured the loss not only of the ship's cargo, but of Martin's life. Similarly, Martin's old companion in various plots and schemes, George Kane, told the eminent Civil War journalist George Alfred Townsend that he had met Keith in Halifax and directly observed these events. Keith was a "bad fellow" and smarter than Martin, Kane said, and had probably sunk both ships with explosives.

Based on what Kane had told him, Townsend theorized that Keith had been immersed in a Southern "conspiracy junto" to develop explosives and explosive weapons for acts of terrorism, and would have known about the "horological torpedo" invented by Confederate secret agent John Maxwell and used for an infamous attack against Grant's army. As Maxwell told his superiors, his device was "an ordinary candle box containing twelve pounds of gunpowder, procured at a country store. In the box was packed a small machine . . . which was arranged by means of a lever to explode a cap at a time indicated by a dial." Carrying his concealed time bomb and blessed with dumb luck, Maxwell sneaked behind enemy lines on August 9, 1864, and made his way toward the busy Union depot at City Point, Virginia, where Grant was headquartered. Maxwell approached an ammunition barge and began speaking to a German who could not understand him and motioned him aboard. Maxwell handed another sailor the box and told him to stow it below by order of the captain. The sailor obeyed, and Maxwell moved off to a safe distance to wait for the fulfillment of his diabolical plan.

After an hour, the bomb went off with a tremendous blast, blowing up the ammunition that was on the ship, creating a chain reaction to other weapons stores. The head of the ordnance department at City Point, Morris Schaff, witnessed the destruction: "From the top of the bluff there lay before me a staggering scene, a mass of overthrown buildings, their timbers tangled into almost impenetrable heaps." Some two hundred people died and many more were terribly maimed; Schaff could never forget the sight of a man standing calmly with his scalp torn away, the convoluted tissue of his brain starkly exposed. Confronting the argument that his methods were beneath a true soldier and a gentleman, Maxwell regretted only that he had killed "a party of ladies," chalking it up to "the Providence of God." Townsend speculated that, given the bloody success of the machine, the Confederacy had made further investments in it, and that Keith had probably seen a model and made one of his own to blow up Martin's ships.

Maxwell had chosen the City Point depot in revenge for an attack on Petersburg, Virginia, Norman and Georgiana Walker's hometown. Because of his friendship with the Walkers, it is likely that Keith had at least heard of Maxwell's bomb. But there were other connections between Keith and Confederate bomb makers. About two months before the *Maria Victoria* sank, Thomas Courtenay, a Confederate secret service agent, sailed into Halifax aboard the Lamar's ship, the *Old Dominion*, whose purchasing and supply agent was Sandy Keith. Courtenay was distantly related to George Kane. He was passing through Halifax with a shipment of cotton to trade in England for army supplies. An Irish immigrant with high aspirations, Courtenay sold marine and fire insurance and ran a successful shipping company in St. Louis before the war, transporting cotton from the plantations. Early in the conflict, the Confederate government chose Courtenay to head of a band of "destructionists," whose mission was to develop terrorist technologies and sabotage boats on the Mississippi River, a main supply artery for the Union.

Courtenay's most infamous contribution to these acts of terrorism was the coal torpedo, a bomb disguised as a large lump of coal, about the size of a man's head. Packed tightly with gunpowder, it was surreptitiously placed in a ship's fuel supply until some hapless stoker shoveled it into the boiler. It was not exactly a new idea: Insurance swindlers had typically used disguised fuel logs packed with gunpowder to sink their own ships. But Courtenay's innovation was to adapt this idea to the coal-stoked steam boiler. Using his coal bombs and other flammable agents, saboteurs operating out of Toronto may have been responsible for the burning of as many as sixty steamboats on the Mississippi. Lacking any of the usual moral standards against using hidden devices that might injure unwitting civilians, the destructionists were motivated as much by profit as by bitter hatred. The Confederacy encouraged gifted, patriotic engineers to invent terrorist weapons and offered very substantial rewards for destruction of enemy property. Courtenay was very proud of his invention, and during and after the war attempted to hawk it, unsuccessfully, to foreign governments. Courtenay stayed for a month in Halifax on his mysterious business, perhaps supplying his expertise to other agents, before sailing for England with his wife and children. That was surely long enough for Keith to learn all about the coal torpedo.

Furthermore, Keith was connected to the would-be bioterrorist and disgruntled snitch, Godfrey Hyams, who would later lead police officers to a house in Toronto and pull twenty-five homemade grenades out of the water standing in a moldy basement. Hyams knew all about bomb-making operations that supplied weapons for terrorist raids across the border. These were the kinds of men Keith met on the fringes of the war, and if they did not precisely make up an organized conspiracy junto, they surely shared an interest in inventive terrorist weapons and unorthodox methods of war. Keith was always thinking beyond the war, to how he might put his new knowledge to work.

Any evidence that Keith had used a coal bomb, a clockwork bomb, or some other device to sink Martin's ships is vague and entirely circumstantial. But what is certain is that an idea had been planted in Keith's head, a lucrative idea that involved covert bombs and shipwrecks, and one that he secretly nurtured and refined for a decade. The most exciting times of Keith's life were his days as a blockade-runner and a secret agent, for later in life he would become nostalgic at any opportunity to speak of these golden days, becoming a legend in his own mind. But he would always keep the murderous side of his activities deeply hidden. In this greedy, ruthless little world of terrorists and spies, there was no honor, only self-aggrandizing fictions and amorality that allowed casual slaughters of civilians, even of parties of ladies. Allowing the perpetrator to escape unscathed, the new terrorist weapons could kill at a distance and make such casual slaughters ever more palatable. Keith was certainly not the first or last man to apply technologies to devious peacetimes uses. War disrupts the fiber of everyday life, not only through shell shock and trauma, but also by uprooting conventional ethical moorings. Though his rage would lie dormant for a time, Keith's already weak moral center seemed completely annihilated by the war.

In the meantime, Keith had to extricate himself from the entanglements of his various swindles. Though he had held his victims off for an astonishingly long time, they would soon figure him out and demand satisfaction. Those who had imagined Keith as their faithful, loyal, obsequious servant were in for a rude surprise. Keith put all of his cards in place. As a final gesture of defiant greed, he forged a number of false bills of exchange, relying on his good name at the Halifax banks. He would cheat the town networks too, swindling his old friends right until the very end. He then convinced the starry-eyed Mary that she should go with him on the greatest adventure of her love-struck life. He held out to her the greatest promise: Neither of them would ever have to bow and scrape again.

FIVE

MAN ON THE RUN

In Horatio Alger's classic tale of a poor boy's rise to riches, Ragged Dick takes his country friend on a tour around New York, showing him all the most magnificent buildings of Manhattan. "That's Taylor's Saloon," says Dick. "When I come into a fortun' I shall take my meals there reg'lar." Taylor's Saloon on Broadway: an elegant dining palace with two grand entrances opening into a sea of marble, with fountains and faux Greek statues brilliantly lit by a hundred gas jets. Next to ten-foot-long windows with fabulous views of the city, diners feasted on roast beef and drank sherry cobbler, a sugary alcoholic punch made with pineapples and oranges. There, late at night, young women were rumored to meet their ruin, either because their wooers made them insincere offers or because the vanilla ice cream gave them such ecstatic pleasure. It was an epicurean feast for wealthy whites; the restaurant refused to serve blacks. Within its warm dining hall, on bitter January evenings, sat the brewer's son, Sandy Keith, and the hotel maid, Mary Clifton, wealthy beyond their wildest dreams.

Keith had slipped out of Halifax alone at the end of December 1864. Boldly presenting himself in person at the provincial office, he first made a passport request that was instantly mired in diplomatic red tape. Passports were a new attempt to prevent terrorist raids across the border, though no one was entirely sure how to identify raiders or prevent their crossings without holding up legitimate trade.

Keith, however, was very well known to one of the gatekeepers, Consul Mortimer Jackson, who not only refused to countersign the passport document, but instantly alerted the War Department. Under the scrutiny of his old suspicious neighbor, Keith revised his plan. He decided to slink across the border as "A. K. Thompson," an identity he would take permanently. "Thompson" and its variation, "Thomas," were two of the most common names in the United States. They provided a very effective alias, like the names Smith and Jones, and lots of sneaks, including several Confederate secret service agents, used them to confuse the law. There were many real Thompsons in Keith's life, from a temperance leader in Halifax to Jacob Thompson, head of Confederate operations in Canada. In his eternal quest for an identity that was so much larger than his own, Keith often took aliases of powerful men he both hated and admired.

Still owing the Confederate purchasing agent, Norman Walker, a large quantity of confiscated pork stored in Boston, Keith made a great show of telling his family and good friends in Halifax that he was leaving for the United States to reclaim it. He freely discussed the dangers of the trip, reassuring them that he would soon achieve his goal and make good with Walker. In buoyant holiday spirits, they cheerfully wished him well on his adventure. Keith was so smooth, so confident, that they suspected nothing. He traveled overland to St. John and sailed through the treacherous winter winds on the Bay of Fundy. Despite the panicky vigilance on the border, he sneaked past the militia patrols and through the pine forests of the Maine coast. With him were a weekend bag and two leather valises stuffed full of bonds and cash, all the luggage he needed. In a few days, he wired to his friends that he was on his way home, mission accomplished. "Drink a glass of wine with me at 12 o'clock," he said. At the news, all the jolly fellows toasted Sandy's success, expecting him back by midnight to buy them all champagne and entertain them with his latest fanciful exploits. But to their great surprise, Keith never arrived.

Instead, he stayed in Boston waiting for the loyal Mary, who slipped out of Halifax and traveled down to meet him, a frightening journey for a young woman traveling alone through raider-infested waters. But she was driven by that love and hope that can strip away all caution; and besides, Keith now had a spectacular amount of money that could help him charm a much more skeptical customer than a dreamy-eyed chamber maid. In Boston, Keith had one more last minute bit of business. As an agent of the Confederate government, he had arranged to ship thirty bales of cotton through Boston for sale to the textile mills in lowland Scotland. But instead, taking advantage of the soaring price of cotton, Keith forged a bill of lading, received the cotton, and sold it, keeping the profit of about $5,000 for himself. He would have two weeks before this swindle was discovered when the vessel arrived at its destination in Glasgow without the expected cargo. This was enough time for him and Mary to slip out of Boston and fade into the noisy anonymous streets of New York.

As days went by and Keith did not return to Halifax, it began to dawn on his fellows that they'd been cheated badly, that this trustworthy, discreet, and respected figure, known for his sociability and enterprise, had run off with a small fortune. While Keith slept on feather beds and indulged his mighty appetite at the finest restaurants in New York, the news spread rapidly as his victims tallied up their losses, with estimates ranging from $150,000 to $300,000 dollars. With these proceeds, Keith and Mary lived in high style in a city where wealthy businessmen lined their pockets with wartime investments, fingers deep in the prosperity of the Northern economy. In the predictive mood of the New Year, the news trumpeted the coming victory of the North and the grand future of its manufactures and its railroads, soon to reach from New York to San Francisco. With all the crass ambitions of newly found wealth, the Swells were rapidly overtaking the old-moneyed Brahmins. Appropriately opening at Wallack's Theater on Broadway was Edward Bulwer-Lytton's play, *Money*. In it, the social pretender Sir John Vesey, once played by John Wilkes Booth, explains his rules in life: "First, Men are valued not for what they *are*, but what they *seem* to be. Secondly, If you have no merit or money of your own, you must trade on the merits and money of other people." Vesey's humble secretary, his cousin Albert, suddenly inherits a fortune, apparently gambles it away, and then wins it again, declaring in the end that while love and truth are essential, one should never be without "plenty of Money!" It was a play that resonated with these times of great fortunes lost and gained in which Keith was a rather minor, but particularly cold and deceptive player, gambling with the merit and money of others. How was he different from any of the great capitalists who took ruthless advantage of others? Keith, a lowly clerk, had gambled on the fortunes of his own friends and family relations, stolen them blind, and come away with plenty.

Despite his extremely successful embezzlements and astonishing rise to wealth, Keith was not immediately happy in New York. Sherman was burning and pillaging his way toward the sea in a fever of violence, the Southern economy was crumbling, and Keith was losing money, hand over fist, in bad investments. He always claimed to his postwar friends that he lost $100,000 gambling on Wall Street, an immense sum gone in only a few weeks time on the queasy roller coaster ride of wartime speculation. Though his losses were a swift blow, Keith managed to hang onto much of his ill-gained fortune. He had a permanent case of bad nerves, obsessively worrying that the secret emissaries of the vast and powerful network so feared by Francis X. Jones might be right behind him. In an ironic echo of his bioterrorist plotting, he was not only weakened by stress but grew feverish with some ailment that prostrated him. Mary tended him, fed him broth, wiped his brow, and cleaned up after his mess. Their situation rapidly disintegrated.

Though not in any conceivable way a vast cabal, a few furious men were actively chasing Sandy Keith now that his true nature had been revealed. For them, he became a symbol of their defeat and loss. One of these pursuers was H. W. Kinsman, whom Keith had cheated out of the insurance money on the *Caledonia*. Another was Robert Grissom, pilot of the Lamars' ship, *Little Hattie*, who had given Keith $4,000 in gold that had disappeared. Grissom was also acting for Norman Walker, who had lost $40,000 on the dubious pork shipments. And a third was Luther Rice Smoot, who had never received his locomotive engines. Keith had reason to fear other tough guys such as the cagey pilot Mike Usina, who had also lost $40,000 in dirty dealings. None of his pursuers were the Haligonian bankers he had swindled with false bills of exchange. Though they bore deep grudges, they all accepted the loss as the price of profiteering and would not shame the powerful Keiths. But the Southerners were not so forgiving or obsequious.

Grissom was the first to come close. He figured out that Keith's destination was New York, and gave Keith's photograph to a private detective who tracked his man as far as the elegant surroundings of Taylor's Saloon. Before he could be collared, Keith got wind of the detective and prepared to run. His worse fears had come true, the bloodhounds were almost at his door, and he was gripped with the chilling anxiety that he would be killed for his crimes. He couldn't stay in New York for the Confederate blockade-runners and agents were a tight-knit group, and news of his whereabouts would travel fast from New York to Halifax to Wilmington, putting into motion the rest of the men he had cheated. He decided to leave poor Mary alone in a strange, new city, assuring her he would send for her as soon as he could. He gave her not a penny for her survival. Though he'd privately corresponded with his family members, and even received a visit in New York from his brother, he now left them behind forever.

Keith fled Manhattan onboard a train clattering toward St. Louis, as far west as he could imagine, almost to the edge of the frontier. The journey took two days, over the Appalachians, across the fields and lonely prairies of the Great Plains. In winter, everyone complained about a rail journey, a long agitated dance that made the body tired and sore. The cars were crowded and hellishly overheated by immense iron stoves. Men secretly smoked strong tobacco near window cracks and a few boisterous young rowdies were always present, drinking too much whiskey and vociferously arguing politics late into the night. News-boys passed through the cars selling trashy illustrated news, and servers offered apples, gumdrops, and yet more tobacco. At night, the shared sleeping cars were stifling and smelly with body odors. Most people had to suppress their visions of the frequent train crashes and derailments that filled the nineteenth-century newspapers, which never held back from unmitigated gore. As the train passed through army outposts and barracks, passengers had new fears of Confederate saboteurs haunting railroad bridges.

A first-class car—for Keith planned never, from now on, to travel less than first class—was an oasis of serenity where a gentleman did not need to mingle with the odiferous riff-raff. He did not have to wait for the bathroom, for each room had a water tank and a basin. He could smoke his cigars without angry looks from finicky matrons. The beds folded up, leaving plenty of room for him to sprawl in an over-stuffed armchair, looking across the Appalachians, along the Ohio River, through elegant Cincinnati, across the bleak winter farm fields of Indiana and Illinois. Aside from the comfort and good cuisine, wealth also provided Keith with the privacy he needed, for he feared the eyes of his victims more than any broken rail.

The train arrived near St. Louis on the east side of the Mississippi River. Passengers took a ferry, for there were not yet any bridges over the turbid water. In deep winter, it was possible to cross over the ice on foot, and it had been an unusually frigid season. A sudden concentration of warehouses, mills, factories, and houses both humble and grand, St. Louis spread from the Mississippi, edging against vast swamps and lonely, wild prairie. It was a staid place, founded by French trappers and traders, and as one visitor put it, "Chicago amuses, amazes, bewilders, and exhausts the traveller; St. Louis rests and restores him." Still, overly refined folks from the east were sometimes appalled at the rough manners of the townspeople, who openly loved their liquor and smoked in the streets. Of the slouching, old, high-gabled homes remaining in the French Quarter, the visiting Charles Dickens wrote that they seemed to be "grimacing in astonishment at the American improvements." Though the city had experienced tremendous growth, was the new center of an expanding railroad, and would soon embark on grandiose plans to become nothing less than the greatest city on Earth, no great crowds yet gathered in its newly paved thoroughfares. The greatest physical energy of the city was at the docks, where dozens, sometimes hundreds, of steamboats moored.

By the time Keith arrived in January 1865, the Civil War had drained the population, devastated businesses, and created violent, bitter divisions among Missouri's citizens. A slave state, Missouri had voted to stay in the Union, but its Governor, Claiborne Jackson, was an avid secessionist and formed a government in exile. Though the Union army maintained a firm control over St. Louis, vitally important for its river supply, the city harbored Confederate couriers, spies, and the infamous boat burners who frequently set Union transports aflame. Just a few weeks before Keith arrived in the city, the steamer *Maria*, loaded with Federal troops, wagons, and mules, had been sabotaged while lying at anchor, killing twenty-five soldiers and severely burning many more. The burning *Maria* had been cast off in a high wind so that when the ammunition supply exploded it wouldn't destroy the docks. The *Maria*'s engineers believed that "some fiend [had] placed a shell, or other explosive missile, among the coal used for fuel, which was thrown into the furnace and produced the disaster." The *Maria* was not the only ship to perish in such a way, and among the boat burners had been a team organized by Jacob Thompson in Toronto to reconnoiter and attack the St. Louis levee. The plot failed because the destructionists were armed with the overrated chemical agent, Greek fire.

As one of the leading centers of Confederate covert operations, St. Louis was well known to Keith through stories that he had heard from his many Southern guests. He had a good friend in St. Louis, a Frenchman who worked as a steward in the Southern Hotel, and who welcomed Keith and helped him settle in. To explain the arrival of his mysterious friend to his curious co-workers, this Frenchman claimed that he had once operated a hotel in the blockade-running port of Nassau, and that he and Keith had both lived there. In a world ripe with Thompsons, the Frenchman too called himself Thompson, and it was a great joke between the two men to pretend that they were cousins. The Frenchman's friends often teased him about this because Keith appeared English or Scottish, not French. Everyone thought the cousin story was fishy, but it was cheerfully tolerated.

Keith enjoyed living in fine hotels, which suited his fleeting, vicarious existence, and the Southern Hotel was one of the best, newly constructed of elegant, warm yellow limestone. It was a vast, gas-lit place, consisting of 361 guest rooms and large public rooms with richly upholstered divans looking out on the thoroughfares at Fourth and Fifth Streets. Later, Theodore Dreiser, who worked as a news reporter in St. Louis, wrote that the Southern was "my favorite cure for all despondent gray days—where all was warm, brisk, colorful, gay, in fact. Here was no least sign of poverty or want, but only of comfort or luxury. Here everyone was at least apparently prosperous—busy about one money-making scheme or another—or enjoying the peace of this atmosphere." Its splendid dining hall offered the regional specialties: venison and wild turkey caught on the prairie. Here, Keith could more successfully imagine himself a fine gentleman among the traveling merchants and politicians. He had so much money about his person that the hotel refused to keep it in its safe, unwilling to take responsibility for such a vast sum.

Back in Manhattan, no longer able to afford the decadent luxuries of Taylor's Saloon, Mary had been forced back into her old life, working as a maid at French's Hotel. She labored there, wondering desperately when Keith would finally send for her. It was a strange place for the mistress of a major Confederate operative to find herself. Only two

months before, French's Hotel had been one of the targets of a team of
rebel agents organized in Toronto. On the night of November 24, 1864,
they had doused the rooms of several fine New York hotels, including
French's, with Greek fire, hoping that over a dozen conflagrations
would spread and burn down the city. By one of those many strange
coincidences, John Wilkes Booth and his brothers were performing
Julius Caesar at the Winter Garden Theater next to one of the hotels.
When the audience panicked, the performers stopped and Edwin
Booth spoke calming words from the stage. The terrorists once again
failed to employ the Greek fire effectively, and the conflagrations did
little damage. The owners of French's, who were furious at the rebel
attack, would have been quite surprised indeed if they knew that the
sad woman scrubbing floors and carrying towels was a mistress to a
foremost Confederate operative.

Mary was not to stay in the employ of French's for long, for she
soon felt a blow worse than abandonment: she was pregnant. As the
days wore on, it was becoming more and more obvious that her lover
had abandoned her, after all she had done for him. Growing heavy
with twins, she worked for enough money to pay her passage and
sailed forlornly back to Halifax.

As Keith rested and restored himself in the Southern Hotel, hiding
from all his victims, including Mary, the momentous events of these
months—the passage of the Thirteenth Amendment abolishing slavery,
the fall of Richmond, Lee's surrender at Appomattox, the assassination
of Lincoln—hardly touched him. John Wilkes Booth's life ended on
April 26, 1865, when he was shot through the neck in a burning barn,
twelve days after he had become so enraged at abolition and ashamed
of his own cowardice that he put a bullet through the President's head
on that fatal night in Ford's Theater. The loss of his expensive theatrical wardrobe with no insurance compensation could not have helped
Booth's state of mind. He played only three major theatrical roles in the
months after leaving Montreal, and immersing himself in violent, obsessive plotting for what he called "the sharpest play . . . ever done in
America."

After Booth's death, in late May, the U.S. Consul in Quebec,
William Gurley, was informed that the *Marie Victoria* had been sal-
vaged. At his own expense, for he felt an urgent duty to recover any
evidence of Booth's guilt, Gurley rushed 157 miles to claim the actor's

trunks containing his sodden costumes and a few photographs and letters. Because of the fevered excitement of finding the trunks, holding
possible evidence of conspiracy in the Lincoln assassination, no one
was much interested in why the *Marie Victoria* sank. But the trunks
turned out to be of little investigative value, and were eventually auctioned off for a mere $500 and then acquired by Booth's brother,
Edwin, who burned them in a strange midnight ceremony. It would
take ten more years for anyone to link Sandy Keith with John Wilkes
Booth and the ill-fated *Marie Victoria.*

But even as the attention of the nation turned to the drama of the
assassination trial and the necessities of Reconstruction, a few of
Keith's victims had not forgotten him. Their detectives were flashing
around his *carte de visite.* These were popular, mass-produced cardboard
photographs that the vain could have taken on any busy thoroughfare,
and blockade runners took pride in having theirs fall into the hands of
the Feds, whom they always bragged of outwitting. Sandy's images
were floating around from Halifax to Virginia. His hands and face
looked plump and babyish, his eyes small, his jacket, with immense
pockets, too big on his large body, a watch fob arcing neatly over his
chest. A great liability of the photograph, which one tended to give all
one's friends, was that it might end up in the wrong hands. And so it
happened that an enterprising detective arrived at the Southern Hotel.
There, he confronted Keith, who had believed himself to be safe out in
the hinterlands. Keith knew that money could get him out of just about
any scrape, and he bribed the detective with $5,000, a very effective
sum. But others were coming and he knew he had to run again. His
friend, the Frenchman Thompson, knew the perfect sanctuary: out on
the desolate Looking Glass Prairie.

SIX

MAN ABOUT TOWN

One spring day in 1865, carrying only two valises, Keith bumped along in a drafty coach, scaring the prairie hens on the muddy road to Highland, a remote town in the Illinois countryside, thirty-five miles east of St. Louis. He had one eye nervously over his shoulder, looking for a posse of his angry victims. With him was his alleged cousin, the Frenchman, who had family in Highland. Keith agreed to their final destination because it was far away from any railway line. He needed safe asylum, deep in the soft wide sea of the Looking Glass Prairie.

Keith later told a story suggesting he had been in that far country of Illinois before. As a secret agent, he claimed, he had been sent with money to help the rebels at Camp Jackson, just north of St. Louis, site of one of the more infamous events of the war and still a sentimental favorite in the mythic lore of Southern resentment. In April 1861, Missouri secessionists began to gather arms at the camp, planning to attack the St. Louis arsenal. When the arsenal's commander, Captain Nathaniel Lyon, heard of this, he marched his soldiers through the city toward the camp, as the excited residents—men, women, and children—poured out of their houses and followed along. Although the soldiers at Camp Jackson gave up peacefully when Lyon arrived, the crowd grew increasingly angry and menacing. Pistols were waved, rocks were thrown, and Lyon's soldiers randomly opened fire. In the end some one hundred civilians lay wounded and twenty-eight more

dead, one an infant in its mother's arms. At this point, Keith said, he
was on his way to Camp Jackson, but had only gotten as far as Trenton, a whistle stop ten miles south of Highland. Hearing the news of
the massacre, and still with a great deal of money in his possession, he
stayed for a while with a family in Trenton. Then he returned home, as
he blatantly lied, to the South. Keith probably got this story from Confederate agent Francis X. Jones, who had actually participated in the
Camp Jackson affair. There are no other existing records to show that
Keith was involved. But whatever real and imaginary excitements
Keith had experienced in his former life, he had chosen the Illinois
prairie as his escape from them.

He would ingratiate himself with the burghers of Highland, who
had emigrated from Switzerland in the 1830s to found their odd little
enclave in a prairie grove. Poetic, musical, dreamy types, these emigrants called their settlement Highland because a government sur-
veyor told them that the countryside resembled his native Scotland.
The gentle rises hardly earned the designation "hills," but the settlers
named them after Swiss mountains and fancied that each of their
gently-rounded tops looked like watch crystals. Most pioneers considered the prairie a hostile, pestilential wasteland. They hated hacking at
the muddy matted roots to create farmland; feared the prairie fires,
blizzards, and tornadoes that swept across the vulnerable plains; and
were maddened by biting insects and relentlessly chirping frogs. It
would be many years before the prairie became a romantic site, before
Carl Sandburg could write so ardently: "I have loved the prairie as a
man with a heart shot full of pain over love." But for the Swiss, weary
of upheaval in their homeland, the prairie was love at first sight, a wel-
coming and bounteous place, a pleasant little Switzerland without
strife. Their visions and desires flowed into the landscape and imbued
it with grandeur. To attract town-builders who could also contribute to
the extremely limited gene pool, the founders of Highland wrote home
of the vast luxurious prairie, stretching as far as they could see. They
imagined thousands of their cattle roaming across the expanse.

The town burghers settled into peaceful lives with their families
and servants, ruled with moderation over their Shangri-la, and timed
their days with the Swiss pocket watches that their rough American
neighbors found strange and wonderful. The burghers had plenty of
time for leisure, quaffing earthy beer from the local brewery. Gifted

with wealth and fine European educations, they developed a lively cultural atmosphere for a small town, with an orchestra, a literary society, a special club for singing, and one for their favorite sport, competitive sharp shooting. Many of the men had learned to shoot during their required military service in the Swiss army and developed a recreational taste for it. Highland hosted sharp shooting fêtes, with prizes and plenty of drinking. The prairie was an excellent place for the shooting sportsman, as Prince Bertie and his friends found on their visit to the Looking Glass Prairie: "Notwithstanding that the birds were very wild, tolerable success attended their shots." The somber climate of war had suspended many of these happy activities, though the town still found time for patriotic amusements, like public performances of regimental bands.

Like many Maple Street towns, Highland was inbred and suspicious of uninvited outsiders. The aristocratic, well-educated Swiss found their American-born neighbors rather dull, with "no aesthetic appreciation, as is shown by their monotonous, crude music and singing and by their preference for everything loud, bright, and unusual." The only two blacks who tried to settle there were a barber and a hosteler, who became so lonely and forlorn that they quickly left. Social problems, such as drunkenness, youthful rowdiness, and vagrancy, were blamed on outside agitators. Like the uncorruptable and upright town of Hadleyburg in a Mark Twain short story, Highland was "sufficient onto itself, and cared not a rap for strangers or their opinions." And as Twain understood, such a town's moral pride cried out for a passing stranger to come along and corrupt it. From the first, Highland's clannishness was reinforced by its languages. During the Civil War, many started learning English to get the war news, but the town's 1,400 citizens still mostly wrote and spoke in their native languages, German and French. The town's two newspapers were in German, and were filled with political and cultural news from home. It was difficult to fit in socially or transact business without fluency in German and at least some knowledge of French.

Highland proved a perfect place for Keith to hide. Who would ever suspect him of secreting himself in a tight-knit, pro-Union, German-speaking enclave in the backcountry of Illinois? It would be difficult for his pursuers to even inquire about him. And it would not be hard for Keith to charm Highland's provincial gentlemen with his wealth

and apparent friendliness. It was the kind of crowd he had played before. It was a strange coincidence that Keith should end up in Highland, for he had been born in a place called the Highlands thirty-eight
years before, in a similar agrarian landscape of low rolling hills. After
the excitement of his wild urban existences, this quiet, rural place must
have felt something like his childhood home.

Arriving in town, the Frenchman took Keith to the small, modest
cottage of his wife's sister, Susan, and her husband, Fred Pagan, who
helped run a family business, a hydraulic wine and cider press. Keith
was hoping to board in the Pagans' house, but though the couple was
sympathetic to his plight, they had no room for him. Keith was very
nervous, fussing over one of his valises and expressing reluctance to
take it to a hotel. Fred and Susan agreed to hold it for him until he got
settled. Later, they couldn't help peeking into the curious bag. It was
stuffed full of money.

After being turned away by the Pagans, Keith and the Frenchman
proceeded to the Highland House, a three-story hotel run by Jacob
Weber, a prosperous businessman, ardent defender of the Union, and
one-time president of the Maennerchor Harmonie, the local choir. The
Highland House was a comfortable place, with sixteen guest rooms,
two big parlors, a great dining room, ten horse stalls, and two beer cel-
lars. The hotel was lively, noisy, and full of women and children, mostly
Weber's own brood, as well as the usual boarding house crowd of
single men. The townspeople gathered often in Weber's popular beer
garden, singing old songs, bragging about successes or crying about
failures in the shooting competitions, and arguing politics. Lincoln
slept at the inn, as he presumably did everywhere in Illinois, and the
bootjack he allegedly used to wedge his great feet out of his great boots
is carefully preserved to this day in the town's library.

Though Jacob Weber wondered why Keith had only one small
valise with a few clothes, he saw that the stranger was planning to settle in at Highland House for a long rest. To the Highlanders, Keith
seemed to have dropped from the clouds. When asked, he mumbled an
explanation about moving to the countryside to recover from rheumatism, not an especially convincing story. The boggy prairie was not
generally known for its medicinal benefits, and a nineteenth-century
sufferer would likely take the waters at a hot springs rather than move
out to the bug-ridden muck. And the townsfolk had the strong impres-

sion that Keith seemed in perfect health. Furthermore, he could not even speak the town's languages. Yet the lack of communication was to Keith's great advantage, for he could disguise his rough edges, speaking instead in the impressive language of money. Once he had settled in, he began flashing his money around, and the hotel servants gossiped about the bonds, gold coins, and wads of cash left lying on his bed. Jacob Weber advised Keith to better conceal his money, but he replied, "Oh that is all right. Everybody is honest here." Keith had Weber order crates of the best French champagne exclusively for his use. Then, every so often, he would treat everyone, rich and poor alike, to a glass of it. These magnanimous displays deeply impressed the whole town. Within a few months, as the war wound down to its end, Keith became a beloved figure welcomed in Highland's best society, among its wealthiest merchants, bankers, and politicians.

His new best friend was John Suppiger, a member of one of the town's founding families, having emigrated from Switzerland with his parents. His cousin, Joseph, who ran a steam-driven flour and saw mill, was the town patriarch. With few choices available, John married his cousin, Louise, after living for a time in a room at the Highland House. When Louise died, he married Catherina Meyer, daughter of a Swiss artist, Wendelinus Meyer, and his aristocratic, but solid and plain-speaking wife Margaretha. John and Catherina ran a successful general store at the corner of Walnut and Main. John was a sociable fellow, active both in the orchestra, where he played the flute, and in the sharpshooters' club, which kept up weekly practice during the Civil War.

When Keith met him, in the last days of the war, John Suppiger had become enormously popular because of his leadership during the draft crisis, when the town had to meet a steep quota of forty-five men for the Union Army. Suppiger and his brother-in-law, Charles Seybt, had raised money to pay several volunteers, thus fulfilling the town's patriotic duty while protecting its wealthier sons from military service. The burghers may have loved sharpshooting, but had no desire to see their sons practice this skill amidst the horrific carnage of the battlefield. Many did not consider this conflict as involving them. Suppiger and Seybt, while politically involved men of action, were concerned with town building: wheeling and dealing, joining professional societies and social organizations, acting as philanthropists, running their own businesses, diversifying their interests, and speculating on property and the new railroads.

Keith gravitated toward men like these. He wanted to be like them, popular and respected, the persona he'd won and lost in Halifax. And in Highland he saw his opportunity, for it was easy to impress a society that saw great mountains in small elevations. Just a few jokes, a hint of mystery, a flash of money, and a case of champagne got him farther than he could have imagined. And he never had to stray far from Weber's beer garden.

Keith began to learn German, though he was not a very quick student. He took lessons from the aging Julius Hammer, widely known as a miser, but still a very popular teacher, a member of the singing society, and the town's best storyteller. In Keith, he met an equally impressive spinner of tales. During their sessions in the one-room schoolhouse, Keith told Hammer elaborate fictions of his past, presenting himself as a wealthy speculator. He said that he had lived in New York and had been given a place there in his uncle's business, where he had quickly risen to chief officer. His uncle, however, had pressured him to marry his cousin. He was so averse to this arrangement that he ran away to Canada. There, he went into the fish business, successfully trading with Southern ports. Somewhere along the way, he began speculating on Wall Street, and made a great deal of money, but had lost $100,000 of it. He left Canada, he said, because the dreary climate made him ill, and he had come to Highland to get well. Rolling up his sleeve, he flexed his arm at Hammer, showing his indeterminate tattoo: an elaborate "A" or "K." Keith may have had a new identity, but, as Charles Dickens might have said, he was "the son of his old self," with indelible marks of Sandy Keith in the new, fanciful mix of truths and lies that made up "Alexander King Thompson."

Julius Hammer was with Keith in Weber's beer garden during one of Keith's champagne parties, when he waved a letter from a New York attorney and told the crowd he'd received an unexpected windfall of $15,000. On that night, Keith was introduced by mutual friends to Cecelia Paris, a charming French milliner who arrived from St. Louis to stay at Highland House that summer. Mary was instantly forgotten, and Keith fell madly in love with this twenty-year-old dark-eyed young woman, half his age, in whom he could see so much of his own nature. Cecelia was a troubled girl, with a rash, devil-may-care attitude about life. Like many a rebellious teenager, she'd had a falling out with her mother, Louise. The trouble seems to have been caused by Cecelia's romance with a poor clerk in a St. Louis bank. Louise had reason to fear the poverty, ruination, and despair that might befall a young woman if she made a bad match or slipped from modesty and propriety. Louise had once faced the threat herself, back in France, when she was alone and pregnant with Cecelia. But Louise had saved herself from ruin by marrying John Paris, one of the sons of a large family in Alsace-Lorraine, whose patriarch was a lawyer.

John and his bride, along with Cecelia and her stepbrothers, immigrated to St. Louis to run millinery and dry goods businesses, and as she was growing up, Cecelia had learned the art of bonnet making. Louise became the imperious proprietor of her own shop on St. Louis's downtown North Fourth Street, and was well known for actually being French. Nearly all milliners in the country pretended they had fashionable Parisian origins, taking on the fine airs of Madame. But Louise was a real bona fide Madame Paris (or at least close enough), a role she played to the fullest. The milliner's trade, in which Cecelia grew up, encouraged such pretensions in fashion-conscious milliners. Milliners and their wealthy clients were slanted mirrors of each other, the one always aspiring to be like the other. But both knew very well who had the real power, the power of money. The clients often exercised their power over shopkeepers by complaining and refusing to pay. And over the clients were their husbands, who controlled the purse and frequently complained about their wives' spending habits. Even in the shops themselves, milliners practiced a strict social hierarchy, with the apprentice at the bottom of the table, passing materials along, and the trimmer at the top, adding the fancy lace, feathers, and bric-a-brac. In the middle was the fitter, who worked with the framework for the hat. As benevolent queen or tyrant, Madame ruled over all. Everyone knew her place in a millinery shop, and everyone wanted to rise above it.

Cecelia was no exception. She was a refined young lady, educated in France, able to speak several languages, and she chafed against her role in rough wartime St. Louis. She had been packed off to Highland, to the world of what she called the "pleasure seekers," to help a family friend: the recently widowed Margaretha Meyer, mother of John Suppiger's second bride, Catherina. Two of the Meyers' grown daughters,

Francesca and Margaretha, were still at home and ran a millinery shop, and had taken an apprentice, Catherine Carmel, from down the street. They were successful entrepreneurs, catering to their aristocratic clients, faithfully making charitable donations to the town's many wartime fund-raising activities. Cecelia came to this independent, creative female household to provide another skillful hand. But she often expressed dissatisfaction with her own life and imagined herself as "sequestered . . . shut off from the world by great tracts of woodland and ranges of hills." Like many a teenage neurasthenic, she claimed she was dying of consumption, that romantic disease of European poets, musicians, and women in unrequited love. She would marry a rich man, she confided to her friends, and live a "short and merry life."

At Highland House, her dream seemed to have come true in the person of an "English-looking gentleman," who was "tall, broad shouldered, with a ruddy complexion and a profusion of light brown hair." He impressed her by flashing $75,000 worth of bonds, and she forever remembered the precise amount. It is easy to see what the two saw in each other. Both from humble origins, refugees in a small town, they aspired to the high life, free from labor and care. They imagined themselves as finer beings, worthy of the best society, fully deserving of the good life and elegant, expensive things at whatever cost. In Keith, Cecelia found her path to wealth and an easy life, and in Cecelia, Keith found the style and refinement he needed to cement his new identity as a rich gentleman, an identity acquired at great risk. A young, beautiful, fashionable woman on his arm fortified his image of himself. She taught him to be more refined, scolding him for his vulgarity, especially his ravenous bad manners at the table. Their relationship had clear lines of power. Despite Cecelia's formidable social talents, Keith called her "little hennie" and "little pettie," and she mockingly referred to herself as "your most obedient sarvant, sir!" To everyone in Highland, they appeared a deeply happy, loving couple. After a whirlwind courtship, as the summer came to an end, they married. Their wedding took place in the home of the Meyers, with the local justice of the peace, John Menz, presiding. John and Catherina Suppiger stood as their witnesses. To further impress his bride, Keith bestowed $15,000 upon his new father-in-law, John Paris.

Keith and Cecelia settled into domestic bliss, dividing their time among the Highland House, the Southern Hotel in St. Louis, and a house a few miles north of Edwardsville. Keith felt confident enough to occasionally make himself visible in St. Louis, where he sometimes introduced himself as "King," reflecting his regal aspiration and self-delusion. He even considered buying a house in St. Louis near his in-laws. But the man who would be King was having a bit of difficulty with his money. In Highland, he had to entrust John Suppiger with $70,000 because the local bank could not handle such a large sum in savings. (This bank would later swindle its clients in dirty land deals.) He frequently went off to Trenton, the whistle stop south of Highland, to engage in some mail transactions with a New York banking firm, August Belmont & Co. A robber baron who infamously appeared at a Waldorf-Astoria party in $10,000 gold-inlayed armor, August Belmont was the U.S. representative of the British House of Rothschild. The Rothschilds had invested and lost heavily in Confederate cotton bonds, a likely reason for Keith's connection to the bank. Some of Keith's secret doings required the services of John Eagan, a St. Louis policeman who had a side business as a private detective. Cecelia never asked about Keith's business, his little trips, and strange acquaintances, contented to let him lavish money on her.

Cecelia did notice that Keith was given to frequent nightmares about assassins holding knives to his throat. He finally began to divulge enough about his past to make himself believable without giving away his crimes. Before long, he could not stop talking about his recent blockade-running days. He poured out stories that mixed fact and fantasy that put him in the best possible light: adventurous, romantic stories a young woman would want to believe, about the sea and military life. He admitted that he was concealing his real identity. Lying that he was born in Brooklyn, he spoke with great reverence of his Scottish mother, but distanced himself from his father, whom he said was English. He claimed he had moved with his family to settle in Petersburg, Virginia, an echo of stories he had picked up from his old Southern friends. Keith's victims, the Walkers, had lived in Petersburg, where Georgiana's well-heeled family was admired for its "refined and recherché" entertainments, displaying the "grace and chivalry of Virginia in her palmiest days." That was the ideal life Keith imagined for himself and Cecelia.

But Petersburg was also a foreboding choice for a lie. As Keith would have known, in July 1864 the Union Army had set an underground mine, full of four tons of black powder, to blast through the

Confederate defenses near Petersburg, leaving a crater 170 feet across and 34 feet deep. Confederate General Bushrod Johnson described the "astonishing effect of the explosion, bursting like a volcano at the feet of the men," producing "an immense column of more than 100,000 cubic feet of earth to fall around in heavy masses, wounding, crushing, or burying everything within its reach." The ensuing melee, which finally ended in a Confederate victory, was forever known as the "Battle of the Crater," a story Keith surely knew from the Walkers and other Southern refugees. Keith's lie carried a hint of his obsessions with murder, mayhem, and great explosions. Though she was skeptical about some of Keith's stories, Cecelia missed this clue, and would not realize her husband's darkest tendencies until some years later.

Though the couple seemed very happy when they were together, their Edwardsville neighbors would later recall that they had sometimes caught Cecelia crying alone and speculated that she was mourning the loss of a first child. In the gossipy climate of a small town, even the most personal crisis could not go unnoticed. Nor did the neighbors fail to observe the unusual behavior of Madame Paris when she first came down from St. Louis to visit her daughter. Then, they heard loud arguments, Madame's angry shrieks rattling the window panes and driving the cat from the house. The dog, they remembered, escaped with half a tail, never to return. When Madame came back a second time, she was given a ride by a local farmer, who did not know who she was. The farmer amiably began to gossip about a former visitor to the Thompsons, a "restless old snoozer" with a voice so loud it could shatter the ears of a mule. Her manner was so imperious, he went on, that if she gestured to the cows they would voluntarily offer their hides to her. Madame recognized herself in this description, and laid into the farmer, grabbing his beard and yanking out his whiskers. Calling him a "hairless old pumpkin head" and the "muddle-brained grandson of a lunatic," she threatened to reach down his throat, jerk out his intestines, and throw them over the Blue Ridge. Ten years after the Thompsons' brief sojourn in Edwardsville, Madame Louise Paris was still the stuff of local mother-in-law folklore.

Still, for a few precious months, life was relatively pleasant for Keith and his bride. The war was over, times were good, and there was little reason for Cecelia to suspect that the increasing happiness she saw in her husband was partly relief in a very narrow escape. Then the icy north winds of December blasted across the prairie, and as she huddled under the quilts in the Highland House, Cecelia's new husband suddenly disappeared.

SEVEN

THE FOX AND THE HOUND

In a parlor in the now considerably quieter town of Halifax, Mary Clifton met with a prying visitor, an acquaintance from warmer and happier times. She wondered if he might help find her lover, the father of her twins, who had abandoned her a year ago on another winter's day. Pale and wan, she had grown so desperately sad that had she recently tried to poison herself. In her head, she sometimes heard the cautionary words of the popular ballad: "Oh, they'll buy you fine trinkets, fine garments and flowers,/ And they'll call in at tea-time to pay their devours,/ They'll swear that they love you by the light of the mune,/ And propose (marriage) — no, sherry cobbulars at Taylor's saloon." Her false-hearted lover, Sandy Keith, had never returned. Now she considered whether she should tell what she knew to another of his victims: the hard and relentless Major Luther Rice Smoot.

Smoot could not forget the wrong Sandy Keith had done him. His fight for the justice he believed he deserved sustained him through the disorientation of defeat. The former Chief of Confederate Ordnance, Josiah Gorgas, echoed the feelings of many Southerners when he wrote in his diary on May 4, 1865, "The calamity which has fallen upon us in the total destruction of our government is of a character so overwhelming that I am as yet unable to comprehend it. I am as one walking in a dream, & expecting to awake. I cannot see its consequences, nor shape my own course, but am just moving along until I can see my way at some future day." But the practical, materialistic Smoot had never been the dreamy type and he stared at defeat with a singular purpose. Though he returned with his wife and son to Baltimore and began working his investments and planning a cigar factory, he was obsessed with regaining the $25,000 (half a million in today's terms) he had expended on two brand new Norris locomotive engines still locked in the customs warehouse in Philadelphia. On October 26, he received a full pardon and amnesty from President Andrew Johnson. Though Smoot's part in the rebellion made him liable for substantial penalties, executive clemency was granted as long as he took an oath of loyalty, paid all legal costs of his pardon, never owned slaves, and never claimed any confiscated property. He duly accepted the pardon, but he stubbornly refused to acknowledge the final point and began petitioning the government for return of the locomotives, claiming that they had been wrongfully confiscated and were never intended for purposes of war. He knew the petition had a very small chance of success, so he pursued another course: relentlessly hunting down Sandy Keith.

Motivated by some combination of revenge, unrequited love, and a desperate need for financial support, Mary Clifton revealed her secret. In her condition, it had hardly been possible for her to hunt down Keith herself. Now she betrayed him: She knew Sandy Keith was somewhere in St. Louis. It was all the information Smoot needed. Arriving back in Baltimore, he immediately dashed off a letter to his cousin, Thomas Ratcliffe, who worked as a merchant in St. Louis, enclosing Keith's *carte de visite* and offering a $1,000 reward for information. Ratcliffe took the letter down to the St. Louis police station and asked the detectives sitting at their desks to see the chief, who was out to supper. "Is it an emergency?" they asked. Ratcliffe replied, "No." He then explained his mission and passed around Keith's photograph. Recognizing the smooth-faced, puffy-cheeked man with "little eyes like a pig's," Detective John Eagan offered to lead Smoot to him. Feeling no loyalty towards his former employer who had once used him for his own mysterious purposes, Eagan jumped at the promise of reward. After Ratcliffe wired his cousin the next day with the good news of Eagan's cooperation, Smoot took the first train from Baltimore. Not to be deterred, he traveled two days into heavy weather, for snow was falling densely on the plains. Twenty trains had ended up snowbound, and near St. Louis cattle were dying of hypothermia and starvation. As Smoot traveled into Illinois, Lincoln's body was disinterred so that it could be ceremoniously reburied with his two children in a temporary vault in Springfield. Smoot was on his way to confront a man who once had a shadowy connection to the assassin of the Great Emancipator.

When Smoot arrived in St. Louis, he met with Detective John Eagan. Smoot gave Eagan a portion of the promised reward money, and told Smoot that he had discovered that Keith and his new bride were spending the Christmas holidays in Highland, staying at their beloved Weber House. Smoot next consulted with lawyers before he traveled to Springfield, Illinois to obtain a warrant for Keith's arrest from U.S. Marshal David Phillips. Phillips agreed to join Smoot on his way to Highland and make the capture. Eagan was asked to come along, too. They were odd traveling companions indeed. Phillips was known for breaking up an Illinois gang of the Knights of the Golden Circle, or Copperheads, the secret secessionists in the North. He was also a personal correspondent with Lincoln, advising him of various plots, including the kidnapping of free blacks who were transported through the president's home state of Illinois for sale in Kentucky. In writing Lincoln, Phillips called the scheme an "outrage on humanity." Yet here he was in an overheated regular-class passenger car with Smoot: a supporter of slavery, a "Know-Nothing" Democrat, a traitor who supplied the rebel army, a conspirator with the very people that Phillips fought so hard to defeat. But with the war over, conciliation was the word of the day, and Phillips, a firm believer in justice, could not deny that Smoot had been wronged.

The men detrained at Trenton, and then froze in a bumping coach, arriving in Highland at dusk. Stamping their feet in the snow and blowing on their hands, they hung around the Weber House until they saw Keith and his wife coming toward them. Full of Christmas cheer, the couple had just been at a party with their friends, and obliviously passed by their pursuers and entered the hotel. The men too went in and took a room right above that of their target. In the early hours of the morning, they went down the stairs and Eagan pounded on Keith's door while Smoot hid behind in the dark. Keith jumped out of bed and went out, still in his nightclothes. In the flickering light of a candle, Keith recognized Eagan, who politely apologized for his intrusion and introduced Marshal Phillips. Then Smoot emerged from the shadows.

Keith reared back in horror, breaking out in a terrible sweat, surely envisioning an impending demise right in the hallway of this remote country hotel. Smoot angrily demanded his money. Ever the manipulative operator even in his fear, Keith began to argue that he was too poor to pay it; he had no money. But it became obvious to him that Smoot and his companions were dead serious and would not desist. They demanded that he come with them, and Phillips delivered the arrest warrant. Keith went back into his room, hurriedly dressed, stuck his revolver in his pocket, and went out. He did not say a word to Cecelia.

Although it was intensely cold in the deep winter, Keith sweated profusely in his dark sack coat as the men made their way to St. Louis, arriving at dawn. The river below St. Louis was choked with a gorge of ice, the ferry marooned on the Illinois side. The men intrepidly walked across the ice, past steamers awaiting their destruction in a sudden thaw that would send them crashing down the river. Despite the frigid cold, Keith was still drenched with sweat, a sheen of perspiration showing across his broad face. As they walked through the streets of St. Louis, Keith fingered the cold revolver in his pocket, and said dramatically to his captors, "My God, I've a great mind to blow my brains out now!" They confiscated the gun. In custody at the St. Louis police station, Keith kept trying to negotiate with Smoot, first saying he had no money and then that he had some, finally driving Smoot to such distraction that he stomped off to ask an old friend to help him deal with Keith. Weirdly, this friend was none other than the equally hated and celebrated conqueror of Atlanta, Savannah, and Richmond: General William Tecumseh Sherman.

Now holding command of the Military Division of the Mississippi whose main duty was to protect the expanding Pacific Railroad, Sherman was living in St. Louis in a spacious mansion provided by the townspeople so that he could recover from his war efforts. His headquarters, where he could almost always be found, lay in a three-story brick house on Walnut Street, just a few doors from the Southern Hotel. He was known to be easily accessible, and he allowed Smoot an audience, listening to his woeful tale of swindling and cheating and deals gone sour. Smoot wanted Sherman to provide him with soldiers to intimidate Keith into giving up the money. In his blunt, taciturn way, Sherman told Smoot that though he'd like to oblige him, Federal soldiers were no longer available for such work. The war, he told Smoot, was over. But Smoot, ever stubborn, did not exactly agree.

For several days, Smoot went back to the police station and tried again to get his money. Tired of his imprisonment, Keith was getting worn down, and he finally offered Smoot $5,000. When that offer was refused, he said he'd borrow some money from his old friend, his alleged cousin, the Frenchman. That offer too was refused. Finally, he said that $19,500 was all he had in the world, and agreed to give Smoot $10,000 in bonds, which he said were half his worldly savings. Smoot was becoming exhausted too. He accepted the compromise, and Keith was released on New Year's Day, 1866.

Smoot and Keith checked into the elegant, ornately decorated Liddell Hotel, uneasily sharing a room, for Smoot was not planning to lose sight of his hard-won catch. He'd spent his holidays at this arduous effort, nearly two weeks away from his child and delicate wife, and now he wanted to go home. Though the bank was closed on New Year's Day, he and Keith went around the streets of St. Louis trying to find the bank officers at their residences, but looked into only darkened windows. They finally managed to hunt down a cashier, but he said another bank teller was required to open the vault. The bank teller, however, was off on holiday visits in the remote town of Belleville, Missouri. Desperately wishing to be free of each other, Smoot and Keith grew increasingly irritated and impatient. Finally, when the teller returned that evening, he agreed to open the vault. In the bank, Keith signed for the bonds and delivered them over to Smoot, having gotten away with paying less than half the debt. But Smoot did not let him get away without a stern lecture, advising him to pay up the rest of his accounts and settle with all his creditors, lest more trouble come his way. Smoot asked Keith if he had encountered another of his victims, H. W. Kinsman, owner of the ill-fated *Caledonia,* who was also trying to hunt him down. Keith answered, "No," and abjectly begged Smoot to keep his whereabouts secret. But Smoot was in no mood for forgiveness, and told Keith he was making no promises.

Not entirely satisfied but satisfied enough, Smoot paid Eagan the rest of his reward plus extra for expenses, and went back to Baltimore. In the summer of the next year, 1867, the U.S. Treasury Department sold off the Norris locomotive engines for a meager $11,087, provoking Smoot into a furious battle, claiming he had suffered "ruinous loss" and that his "civil and political rights" had been violated. Nearly ten years later, well after the Bremerhaven disaster, Smoot was still submitting claims petitions demanding compensation from the government. He named Keith, the "English agent who had "formed the design of defrauding him," and included testimony from Keith's old friend Dr. William Almon, who, like many folks back in Halifax, also held a lasting grudge. In the end, Smoot lost: the Senate Claims Committee declined to act on his petitions. And for all of his efforts, Smoot's fame would finally rest on forcing Keith out of hiding and propelling him across the sea to the scene of his greatest crime. If Smoot had dropped the matter of the locomotives, if he had never gone to Highland, if he had left his nemesis alone in that dreamy town, perhaps Keith's crimes would have only been petty swindles, tall tales, and bad speculations, and he would have existed only as a trace in a few diplomatic records buried in the National Archives. But it was not to be. In his infamy, Keith would come back to haunt Luther Smoot, long after Smoot had consigned him to memory.

After Smoot left St. Louis, Keith was overcome by a state of extreme anxiety. He moved from the Liddell to his comfortable old haunts at the Southern Hotel where he hid, shaking with fear, just down the street from General Sherman. Strangely, he called for Detective John Eagan to come and meet him in his room. Thinking that the whole ordeal had been a simple, personal matter of bad debts, Eagan was surprised to find Keith in a mysterious, unmanly state of dread, nearly prostrate with nervousness. Keith began by explaining that though he knew Eagan had led to his downfall, he forgave him. After all, he told the detective, he understood that the betrayal was solely a matter of business. In Keith's deformed moral universe, lust for money justified any means, including betrayal, deception, and, eventually, even mass murder. Their relationship reestablished to his mind, Keith asked Eagan to cash a $500 bond for him and express the money to Highland. Without explanation, he then begged Eagan not to leave him that night. The detective agreed, saw Keith off at 5 o'clock the next morning, and went down to the Adam's Express Company to send the money, just as he had promised. For many years, he kept Keith's carte de visite, marveling at the strangeness of the man.

Now that he had once again been hunted down, even out on the far reaches of the prairie, Keith knew that many others would follow ceaselessly, more violent and angry men, his old network of friends-turned-enemies, even more hardened by war and defeat. His relentless ghosts would not give up, and he feared that eventually one of them, far worse than Luther Smoot, would find him and kill him in revenge. He needed to go farther, much farther, to such a remote place that it would not be worth the effort of his pursuers even if they did discover his location. In the few hours it took him to reach Highland, he had cemented his plan. He would sail away to one of the farthest points on the transatlantic route. It was a fateful choice.

For ten days, Cecelia waited at the Highland House, wondering what had happened to her apparently adoring husband. She had begun to lose hope, forlornly guessing that he must have abandoned her for no reason, right in the midst of their seemingly cheerful holiday celebrations. Then he suddenly materialized again in an extremely agitated state. Bad men were chasing him, he told his new wife, and she must pack up, for they were to leave at once. She never revealed to anyone how much he now told her of his real past, but it was enough for her to agree to his frantic plan. In a panic, they hastily made final arrangements, took the stage coach, yet again, to Trenton, boarded that now familiar train on the Ohio and Mississippi Railroad, and in furious, stormy, freezing weather, made for New York. By the time they reached a hotel, Cecelia was cold to the bone and prostrate with nervous exhaustion, and had to be given "restoratives" immediately. For ladies, the cure for such a state was often the addictive opiate laudanum, which would knock them unconscious. A few days later, on January 13, 1866, the Thompsons boarded the steamer *Hermann*, sailing through heavy gales to Germany. After a twelve-day voyage, they landed in the port of Bremerhaven, retrieved their luggage, and prepared to board the train. A few oblivious stevedores and dockworkers were unaware that they had just received a glimpse of their horrific destiny.

EIGHT

THE EXILE

Arriving at their final destination in Dresden, the Thompsons took apartments in a fine hotel and began to recover from their recent ordeal with the help of their illicit fortune. They had escaped with at least $45,000 (about one million dollars in today's terms) after the payment to Smoot, and Keith was probably juggling other Wall Street investments. In this new land where they were completely anonymous, the Thompsons left behind all the trials of their old lives. Cecelia marveled at the ease that came over her husband, and she saw a new person emerge from the quivering coward she had witnessed just a few weeks before. Keith now abandoned the name "Alexander" altogether and became the bluff and jolly William King Thompson, wearing a full beard and gold spectacles. Revealing a surprising interest in culture, this rough provincial seemed already to know much about Dresden, knowledge he demonstrated on the couple's early sightseeing tours to the splendid Japanese garden overlooking the royal castle, to the Frauenkirche renowned for organ and choral music in its acoustic dome, to the excellent museums of history, ethnography, mineralogy, art, and antiques. This refinement of taste helped the Thompsons to establish their plausible disguises as a wealthy Southern gentleman married to a genteel, educated lady from New Orleans. In the first year, like many fabulously wealthy Americans, they took a grand tour through Europe—through Switzerland, Italy, and France—before returning to

Dresden to stay. There, they transformed themselves into an impressively rich and well-disposed couple that everyone wanted to know.

As the well-traveled abolitionist Jane Swisshelm later explained, the Thompsons' role-playing instantly opened doors for them in their astonishing rise to high society. Aristocratic Europeans admired Southerners, she said, because of "the aroma of huge estates and great expectations, as well as of past magnificence, attached to them." Keith had learned well from elegant figures like Norman Walker and Luke Blackburn to act the role of gentleman with real panache, and Cecelia's beauty and French accoutrements made their disguise even more plausible. It was an age of poseurs, impersonators, and imposters, fake dukes and dauphins, false claimants, and bogus heirs. As long as their stories were plausible enough, no one was likely to question them, happy to go along with the gilded lies rather than the brutal truth.

With their substantial wealth, the Thompsons were rapidly welcomed into the best society of Dresden, finding their niche especially in the large American colony. There were about 700 Americans living there, attracted by the city's beauty, its culture, and its extremely modest cost of living. Dresden was known, especially in the late 1860s, as a great European center of art and music that was surprisingly affordable, a comfortable family place requiring less than two-thirds of what it cost to live in New York, and best of all, shopkeepers catered to their clientele by speaking English. With the exception of a few New York bluebloods like George and Lydia Griswold, the wealthiest of the American expatriates in Dresden did not come from old money, but were self-made men and their sons and daughters who made up a new fashionable society of globetrotters. In Dresden, they could be merely rich, rather than filthy rich, and still live like dukes and duchesses on the interest from their modest fortunes. In these postwar days of a nakedly avaricious capitalism, an aspirant to the *beau monde* no longer required an aristocratic inheritance. Money provided the short cut. To be a poseur in high society was simply to be one among many, and the brewer's son and the milliner's daughter, with their chameleon-like natures, were embraced without hesitation.

The American expatriates were a clannish group, all living in the same part of town. As one visitor put it, "once one commences to move around in the circle, one soon meets all who compose it." They did not have to speak German, and were mostly isolated and detached from the great events affecting Saxony, their host state. When the Thompsons arrived in 1866, Prussian Chancellor Otto von Bismarck was carrying out his violent promise to unify the German states by "blood and iron." He was fresh from his success in the 1864 war with Denmark, which had ceded two of its territories. Now he was preparing to goad Austria, which also sought supremacy among the German states, into a war he believed he could win because of Prussia's superior military technology. The American expatriate community was far more concerned with opera and card playing than the political turbulence of these events, but Keith quietly watched them with growing excitement.

He grew in status as he was welcomed into the center of the colony, the fashionable American Club, whose members included diplomats and wealthy businessmen. To gain entry into this social circle, visiting Americans would inevitably come there, hoping to take a comfortable leather seat among exchanges of brandy, cigars, gossip, and favors. Keith seemed to have a sixth sense for finding such centers of wealth, and he immediately understood that the American Club was where he would find his best opportunities. For a time, the Thompsons lived in rooms right above the club where they could lavishly entertain the members who came up for a visit. Just as Keith managed to worm his way into the good graces of powerful Confederate operatives, he sought out influential friends, and soon became so popular that he was elected the club's vice president. Still, he kept his identity a bit slippery, sometimes spelling his name "Thompson" and sometimes "Thomas," as it suited him.

The Thompsons' circle was a lively mix of the arty, the unusual, and the adventurous who migrated according to the social seasons. There were giants: Julius Ludovici and Clarence Gray Dinsmore, both members of the New York Titan Club that admitted no one under six feet, two inches, and held classical banquets at Delmonico's dedicated to "Mother Earth, Protectress of the Order." Recovering from a recent bankruptcy, Ludovici was a famous miniaturist, specializing in portraits, who also dabbled in writing, including a trashy historical romance, *Knight Conrad of Rheinstein*, featuring heroic feats of arms, tournaments, and minstrelsy. Dinsmore was the idle son of an enterprising saddler who changed course and worked his way up to become president of the Adam's Express Company. The Dinsmore family was rich enough to own another home in Paris. There was a large contingent of Brooklyn millionaires in Dresden who became intimate with the Thompsons, including Seymour Van Nostrand, a Columbia man, member of the Philolexian Literary and Debating Club, who sported a skull and crossbones tiepin. Keith gravitated toward interesting, well-traveled young men like these, and he was drawn especially to Scots like the young James Alexander Hunt, member of the Seventy-Ninth Regiment of the Queen's Own Cameron Highlanders, who had close family connections with the aristocratic Maitlands of Clifton Hall in Edinburgh. Hunt liked to flirt with Cecelia, whom he admired for her tiny waist, so attractive to grasp on the ballroom floor. Many of the wealthy transients coming through Dresden were hopeful young men and women like Hunt, cruising for even wealthier mates at balls and soirees on the transcontinental circuit.

Never far from his war memories, Keith also made fast friends with several U.S. Navy commanders enjoying a respite after the war, like Lieut. Frederic Stanhope Hill, an inveterate sailor who had served under Admiral David Glasgow Farragut. Hill commanded the U.S.S. *Tennessee*, which cruised for blockade-runners in the Gulf of Mexico, and he had intimate knowledge of ironclads and Confederate torpedoes. Now retired from the navy, Hill was working as a newspaper editor and writing a memoir of his days in the merchant marine. Another good friend was the California pioneer and shipping merchant, Selim Woodworth, who had briefly commanded the U.S.S. *Narragansett*. Woodworth was more famous for having tried to rescue the Donner Party, stranded on a mountain trail in California, but had arrived too late to save them from cannibalizing their dead. Once imprisoned for attempted murder, Woodworth was described by an admirer: "He was small in stature, but had the bravery and spirit of a giant, never to be intimidated either by threats or force of arms." Keith also knew Commodore John Worden, recovering from eye injuries, who had commanded the ironclad U.S.S. *Monitor* in its famous encounter with the C.S.S. *Virginia*.

To the delight of men and the boredom of women, including his wife, Keith relished sharing his own adventures, talking incessantly about his old blockade-running days, deftly inventing stories and leaving cautious silences when it came to the darker truth. His ability to shift loyalties to befriend the former enemy reveals how little passion he had for any political cause, how motivated he was by opportunism, and an abiding fascination with warfare, maritime trade, and technology. Typical of his stories was one he told a visitor from Providence who met him at the club. Keith said he was born in North Carolina and was recruited into the army during the Civil War as an ordinary private. He was wounded in the arm during the battle of Malvern Hills when a shell went off as he was sitting around camp with his mates. Declared unfit for active duty, he took up blockade running, making a fortune running cotton from Wilmington, money he invested in bonds, buying low and selling high. He had tripled his investment and come away with $200,000. He then had married a Southern lady and moved to Dresden. With this kind of story, emphasizing business acumen and military experience with the spice of daring, Keith was able to cement many new profitable relationships. He was a skilled and inveterate liar, choosing his details carefully to resonate with the experience of his listeners.

Cecelia, on the other hand, gave and received fashion advice with her new friends, discussed the progress of their children, listened to their tales of travel, consoled them in their illnesses, and received consolation herself. Selim Woodworth's wife, Lisetta, shared Cecelia's interest in religion and art, and her wax flower bouquets had once attracted Mark Twain who, in a moment of uncharacteristic seriousness, called them "exquisite." Another intimate was the strikingly beautiful Florence "Florie" De Meli, who sang in the choir at the American Chapel, but liked to smoke using a meerschaum cigarette holder. She was a restless woman, married to the much older Henry De Meli, balding and with a full black beard, whom she called "old Boodle." De Meli's maternal grandfather had made his fortune in New York real estate. On his paternal side, the Mellys, originally from Leipzig, had had their name improved to De Meli, claiming a noble Italian ancestry. Real New York bluebloods, like George and Lydia Griswold and their daughter Mariana Griswold Van Rensselaer, a well-known art critic, also frequently came to call. Cecelia's closest friends were the American consul at Leipzig John Steuart and his wife, from Baltimore, who had embraced a permanent exile from the United States and whose granddaughter would eventually marry into European royalty. The Steuarts were avid collectors of curios and antiques, with an excellent knowledge of clocks. On the A-list for dinners, they spent many warm hours at the Thompsons chatting about their hobbies and their children, and Keith once again found himself in the company of diplomats, whom he so admired and wished to be.

Cecelia helped make this possible. Fulfilling the traditional milliner's fantasy of becoming a great lady, Cecelia was a queen of this new society, fluent in English, French, and German. It was considered a privilege to be her friend, for she was greatly admired for her refinement and intelligence. Those she excluded from her circle suffered, and sometimes begged abjectly for her attention. Despite this impressive new social world, Cecelia also kept in touch with a few carefully chosen friends and loved ones back home, and her correspondents chatted about farm life, regaling her with how much milk their new cow produced that year. She remained close to her sister, Fannie, a shop girl in St. Louis, who sent news of Cecelia's old beau, a poor bank clerk who was slowly making his own rise to legitimate wealth. But Cecelia never breathed a word of what she now knew of her strange husband. She had transcended her humble origins and had arrived in a dream.

With plenty of leisure time on their hands, the Thompsons played euchre with their interesting friends, hosted fancy teas and extravagant feasts for the most important people in Dresden, went to balls, concerts, and the opera, and shopped in all the best stores with a passion. It was said that at their house champagne flowed like water. Friends sent them more friends, carrying letters of introduction and calling cards, hoping to gain, as one visitor to Dresden put it, *"entrée* into delightful circles—such circles as one would expect to meet at home." The Thompsons traveled about Germany, as far as the island of Helgoland in the North Sea, and took long walks in the forest, delighting in the peasant women who sold them fresh milk. They began a family, with Blanche born in 1868, William in 1869, and Klina in 1871, and Keith was admired by all for his tender care of his children. Even though the Thompsons had a nanny, Keith fed his children, changed their diapers, and tucked them in with kisses. He was equally solicitous of his wife, bringing her tea and her shawl when she felt the least chill. It was enviously said in the Dresden circle that Keith allowed no whim of Cecelia's to go ungratified. For the Thompsons, it seemed an idyllic, satisfying life, one that Keith would do anything to keep.

The polished veneer of this ideal society was not without its cracks. There were others, like Keith, who disguised wildness, impulsiveness, and cruelty behind their charm and cultivation, and the community, which attracted escapists, had a proportionally high degree of public scandal. In a sensational divorce trial in 1883, the hidden lives of the De Melis were revealed. As her female admirers sat in court passing around a blue smelling bottle, Florie told a sordid story of "old Boodle," explaining that after he had failed as a mining engineer in Colorado and a diamond hunter in South Africa, they had gone to Dresden, where he revealed his cruel side and refused to let her see her parents. When he drank, he was extremely abusive to their young son, kicking and beating him, and striking him with a tome on the history of France. Henry De Meli depended on an allowance from his imperious mother, Antoinette, who hated Florie because she had been a penniless bride. Mother and son plotted to have Florie committed to an insane asylum, but she sold her jewels and escaped to New York, where she struggled without means of support. To the scorn of the ladies in the court, Henry De Meli counterattacked by accusing Florie of flirting with a young German landscape painter—on one occasion playfully dropping confetti in his hair while he knelt before her—and of improprieties with Baron Heino von Geyso, an Austrian army officer.

Old friends from Dresden were deposed as character witnesses, including the well-respected Griswolds and Frederic Stanhope Hill, who declared Florie beyond reproach. Other German witnesses stated that Henry De Meli was not well liked and had been involved in some unforgivable disturbance at the American Club for which he had been cast out. Though lips were closed as to the exact nature of this disturbance, which occurred in 1873, Keith, as vice president, had been summoned to a meeting about it, and afterwards held great enmity towards some of the club's members. It is not clear if he had championed De Meli or not, though Florie and Cecelia remained good friends. The secretary of the American Club, Stephen Austin, testified on Henry De Meli's behalf at the divorce trial, declaring that he never seen De Meli have more than five or six large drinks while many men at the club stopped at no less than twenty. In the end, despite intense public sympathy for a wronged wife, the judge refused to grant Florence De Meli a divorce or custody of her children because, though her husband was guilty of "petty tyranny," he did not directly threaten her life. The community at Dresden always knew of Henry De Meli's drinking and cruelty, and the Thompsons had been closely involved, entertaining Florie's parents when Henry had forbidden her from seeing them.

While the De Melis' problems took a long time to publicly erupt, a scandal that really shook the community involved Cecelia's close friend, Lisetta Woodworth. When Selim Woodworth died in 1871, Lisetta and her five children went back to San Francisco, where she immediately married the son of a former Ohio governor, naval lieutenant Erasmus Dennison, but the union quickly degenerated. When Lisetta sent Dennison a note demanding a divorce, he went over to a friend's house, walked into a bedroom, and put a bullet through his head, leaving a suicide note that read: "My own darling—for you are too noble to have deceived me. Love me as you used to love me. I have killed myself in order that our little ones shall not suffer. Lisetta, my last words to you are, I have been true to you in action and I love you as much as any man can love another: your enemies and mine have done this thing. Beware of them in the future." Cecelia preserved the newspaper article that detailed these sad events. She could certainly sympathize with her friends Florie and Lisetta, for she was no longer naïve to the paranoia, self-destructive violence, and high-strung emotion that a husband might shockingly reveal.

Cecelia's worries about her own mate had not entirely abated. For one thing, there was his obsession with the Seven Weeks' War in the summer of 1866, a few months after they had arrived in Germany. This war, in which Prussia fought Austria to gain hegemony among the German states, took place all around Dresden, the capital of Saxony, allied with Austria. Early in the troop maneuvering in June, the Prussians had marched through the town, pushing south along the Elbe, greatly exciting Keith, who was once more in the thick of military display and conflict. The Keith Highland clan had once fought as mercenaries for the Prussians. Standing in Berlin was a statue of Field Marshal James Francis Edward Keith, a brother of the Eighth Earl Marischal, who fought in Saxony for Frederick the Great. Shaped by the violent legacy of his forebears, Keith felt intimately connected to these events. Day by day, he poured over the newspaper, closely following the battles, many of which were taking place within 150 miles to the southeast. According to Cecelia, who would later remember Keith's morbid interest in the carnage as a warning sign, he became so single-mindedly absorbed in war coverage that he "would lose control of himself and rave about scenes of bloodshed described in it as though he were mad." His imaginary projection of himself into the Seven

Weeks' War was so complete that immediately after it was over, he insisted that Cecelia go with him on a tour of battlefields, although she was weak and grieving from a miscarriage. Stopping little to eat or drink, they traveled across the mountains, through Bohemia's ravaged fields and villages, tracing the paths of the armies. Keith "seemed to gloat over the awful sites and to be oblivious to anything but them." The Thompsons stopped at hospitals, where Keith befriended and cheered the wounded and often wept over them, and when he witnessed a funeral, the coffin borne by the comrades of the dead, he tearfully expostulated, "Poor fellows, I pity them." When the Thompsons returned to Dresden, Cecelia's doctor told Keith he was crazy for subjecting his wife to such a trip in her postmiscarriage state. This admonishment quieted him for a while.

Another troubling sign was his increasingly frequent disappearances. Traveling as William King Thompson, Keith made mysterious voyages to New York, ostensibly on business. On one of these occasions on the steamship *Thuringia* in 1870, he ran into his old Highland friend, Charles Seybt, who was traveling home from Hamburg. Obviously nervous, Keith pretended not to know Seybt, but when Seybt pressed him, Keith finally admitted that he was indeed the same Thompson who had once lived so happily in Highland. Seybt wanted to know why "Thompson" had changed his first name from Alexander to William, and Keith prevaricated. He told Seybt that he was going to buy some land in California and was afraid of being caught by authorities because of his former life as a Confederate secret agent. Seybt found the conversation very odd, and became suspicious of his old friend, who began to regale him with unlikely stories of his war days.

Also onboard ship was George Lentz, who wrote for the *New York Journal of Commerce,* an obvious magnet for Keith who liked to boast of being a big player on Wall Street. The two formed an acquaintanceship. Meeting Lentz three weeks later in New York, Keith said that he was about to return to Germany, smuggling oil paintings in the bottom of his trunks. Keith's behavior certainly indicated that he must have been engaged in some sort of chicanery. From what he told Lentz, lucrative swindles involving fine goods, disguised cargo, and ships were still very much part of his fantasy life. Yet the degree to which elements of this fantasy life were real is not entirely clear.

When Keith's movements during these years were later investigated, it was found that this voyage to New York eerily coincided with the mysterious disappearance of the *City of Boston*. The Inman Line steamer left the port of New York on January 25, 1870, and stopped in Halifax to pick up passengers, including several prominent merchants and army officers from the garrison. Loaded with flour, cotton, beef, bacon, copper, tallow, and wheat, and enough provisions for fifty-eight days, she sailed for Liverpool, never to be seen again. It was widely believed that the *City of Boston* had either encountered a gale or was overloaded with cargo and riding too low. William Inman vociferously denied that his ship was unseaworthy, and sued one of his accusers for libel. Keith was in New York when the insurance claims on the *City of Boston* were paid out, and though no direct paper trail exists, Keith did send Cecelia two banker's drafts at that time, one for £500 and another for £475. This would later raise serious suspicions that Keith had sunk the *City of Boston,* which is still rumored among North Atlantic sailors to be a ghost ship drifting among the icebergs.

The sudden windfall may have come from a much more minor crime, since Keith was running a small smuggling business. He would collect goods like wine, fruit, lace, and silk from Leipzig shopkeepers who wished to export them to the United States but wanted to avoid high duty taxes on them. Then Keith would hide the goods in his luggage to get them past the customs officers in New York. Once in the city, he would station himself in his hotel and dispense these goods to the shopkeepers' friends and relatives. Keith was not quite the art smuggler he claimed to be, but he was engaged in petty crime.

Not long after the trip to New York, the Thompsons began to experience the decline of fortunes that would finally send Keith over the edge. The Thompsons had started their life in Germany with at least $45,000 in ready cash, and probably much more invested. Even with only $45,000, they had enough to live a modest independent existence on the interest, without spending the capital. But they had thrown themselves with such enthusiasm into their new identities as wealthy denizens of the *beau monde* that even in modest Dresden they had to spend the capital to keep up appearances. They burned through the money at a fantastic rate, on entertainment, fashion, and travel. Cecelia adored shopping, she was happily welcomed at all the best shops, and she would later be harshly blamed for her extravagant spending on fine linens, silks, sealskins, furs, and diamond jewelry. In hindsight, the gossips thought her desire to be a grand lady and mother of adorably dressed children finally sent her husband, unable to keep up with her appetite, over the edge into madness. She existed in a dream that her husband's resources were inexhaustible, but it was a dream in which he had heavily invested, too.

It took some time for him to break the enchantment. Like many husbands of the era, he never revealed his financial dealings to Cecelia and she never bothered to ask, not even to inquire about his mysterious business trips to America. Despite his façade, Keith was not very knowledgeable of legitimate international business and recently had found few opportunities to play his old games of cheating and swindling. He invested heavily in the French Atlantic Telegraph Company, which was laying a cable from Brest to St. Pierre in Canada, but he made little profit and began selling off his shares. He kept most of his money in a savings account at Baring Brothers, in London, and watched his fortune disintegrate with every bank statement.

During their best years, the couple had lived for at time at the Hotel Golden Lion near the Castle Pillnitz on the Elbe, once the summer residence of the Saxon kings. But in late 1871, after his fortune had dwindled to less than $5,000, Keith decided to cut expenses by moving to a hotel in dour Leipzig. Here, the Thompsons became embroiled in a fight with a former resident, Warren Gould, who had agreed to lease them his furniture and other household goods. Gould was incensed when Keith reneged on their deal, claiming that the property was overvalued and that not all the promised silverware had been included. From Paris, Gould wrote to Keith, demanding that he honor his agreement "as a man and a Mason," but Keith was coming to the realization that he had been living far beyond his means. His bank account at the end of 1872 stood at around $2,500, a meager fraction of his old wealth. The couple returned to Dresden in the summer of 1873 and rented a home they called the "Villa Thomas" in the suburb of Strehlen. For Cecelia, the "Villa" left much to be desired. It was far from the center of society and fashion, and its kitchen was located in the dank, dark basement where servants were supposed to work and sleep. For this reason, the Thompsons had difficulties keeping domestic help.

Though he maintained his own fondness for first-class travel tickets and fine hotel rooms, Keith attempted to control Cecelia's spending, but she ignored his scolding and ran up huge debts at the shops, which freely extended credit to such a fine lady customer. To one shop alone, the Petit Bazaar, Cecelia owed $1,429, almost $30,000 today. Cecelia laughed with her friends about Keith's stinginess, since a husband's alarm about his wife's milliner's bills was a conventional joke. A husband ruined by hats, especially those of a beautiful young wife, was a laughable figure, and a wife, especially a lady, was supposed to be oblivious of her husband's finances. The *Saturday Evening Post* lampooned the "Political Economy for Ladies" thus:

> Ladies, what is capital? Having more money than you know what to do with.
>
> What is labor? Endeavoring to make your husband understand that you ought to have a new dress every week . . .
>
> What is supply? Your husband's giving you a check to cover your expenses.
>
> What are profits? The mean of enabling you to keep up appearances . . .
>
> What is credit? Running up a bill at your dressmaker's . . .
>
> What is a check? That which every man ought to give his wife when she wants it.
>
> What is a panic? When a wife finds that her husband has not sufficient [*sic*] to pay her milliner's bill.

When Keith complained about the milliner's bill and even tried to cut off his wife's credit at the shops, he was acting out a role that no one, especially a former milliner like Cecelia, took very seriously. However, his situation was rapidly deteriorating. By the end of 1873, his bank account was down to $1,600. It would not last many more years at the Thompsons' current level of spending, and their society friends were beginning to whisper about their decline.

Shortly after the move to Strehlen, Keith announced that he was going to America on some business, and giving many hugs and kisses to his three children and bidding a fond farewell to his wife, he sailed off. Cecelia received a few letters from him, and then he was suddenly silent. Thinking he might be dead, she was in such a panic that she called her mother, Madame Louise, who immediately boarded a steamship for Germany with her other daughters, Fannie and Blanche.

Louise must have felt justified in her bitter, old hatred of Keith, who had turned out to be such a callous husband. A sharp businesswoman, Louise was anything but gullible, and Keith had not been able to purchase her love. She had seen through him despite his generous wedding gift to Cecelia's stepfather, John. When Cecelia received word from Keith that he was on his way home, Louise did not share in her daughter's relief at this news. Louise packed her bags but went only as far as her childhood home in Alsace-Lorraine, then a German territory, where she could be more available if Cecelia should need her.

After many weeks, Keith finally arrived. He was in a dark and furious mood, pounding on the door and cursing, rushing in, according to Cecelia, with a "strange, wild look in his face." After that, without a word of explanation, he sank into a state of deep gloom, cut off his friends, and asked his wife and children to leave him alone. If he had had business investments in the United States, he may very well have lost them in the Panic of 1873, a major depression that began with the failure of a banking firm, Jay Cooke. The company had handled Civil War bonds, and, taking advantage of the massive unregulated growth of the postwar years, had invested in excessive railroad expansion. When Jay Cooke failed, the subsequent crash froze the New York Stock Exchange. Banks foreclosed on their loans and shut their doors, and railroads ground to a halt. On his return from this dire scene, Keith complained about dizziness, and fell into a malaise. He would sometimes rant against his former friends "with a passionate earnestness indicative of actual hatred." Vacationing in Dresden, the Highland miller, Charles Seybt, and his family, occasionally saw Keith coming down the street, but he pretended not to know them and hurried away.

Much of Keith's ire was reserved for Cecelia. According to the nanny, Keith grew so furious at an especially large milliner's bill, that he beat Cecelia in a violent rage. When the nurse rushed in and distracted him, Cecelia jumped out of the window to escape him, and shivered outside, clinging to the trellis and fearing for her children. Finally, after raging around and roaring curses, he gave up searching for her, and the nanny helped her back in. She took to her bed, refusing to speak to him and planned to leave him. But she knew she had nowhere to go, and eventually forgave him. Always imagining herself frail and now under great stress, Cecelia began to suffer from the hereditary rheumatoid arthritis that also afflicted Louise, and she was sometimes unable to get out of bed. As the reality of their situation began to dawn on her, Cecelia realized that she might have to take outside work for the sake of their children. She at least had a marketable skill.

Keith himself would not consider an ordinary working life. To be a member of high society was, by definition, to enjoy an endless leisure, traveling, and collecting. After all of his struggle, Keith would not give up this pleasurable new identity for a return to the messy and dangerous labors of the brewery. But despite his refusal to do any legitimate work, Keith was not a lazy or stupid man. He had all the right qualities of a successful businessman: initiative, enterprise, managerial ability, and impressive social finesse. Having turned over an elaborate plan for years, now driven to its fulfillment by financial distress, he put all his abilities to work for his final and most stupendous crime. His old terrorist impulses, sleeping underneath the cover of his comfortable life, would now rise up in a cold rage. Beginning in early 1873, even before his situation was truly desperate, Keith put his plot into motion. Giving him a sense of purpose throughout his depression, the scheme took two years of planning, the efforts of an unwitting team of technicians, and a heavy investment of his dwindling funds. Using his considerable knowledge of secret weapons collected during his old days as a terrorist operative, Keith diligently applied himself to perfecting his instrument, a bomb so unusual, so technically perfect, and so powerful that it would carry his rage to its sublime finale. If our favorite machines always reflect our own natures, Keith's was the clock, with its secret inner movements and sudden loud strike of the hour. With a clock carefully attached to an immense concentration of dynamite, Keith planned to strike as suddenly, forcing his victims to live or die at a moment set by his own whim. But as he would find out, no machine is entirely predictable, and his clock could force even its maker to step to its own time.

NINE

THE BOMB MAKER

In early spring 1873, a Leipzig clockmaker, Otto Martin, received a visit from his excellent client, the American consul John Steuart, who had an enthusiasm for antique timepieces. With Steuart was a plump, pleasant, red-faced man who seemed to Martin to speak English with an American politeness and "with the clear color of the Yankee dialect." The man presented his calling card: Mr. William K. Thomas. "Thomas" eagerly asked Martin to introduce him to a clockmaker who could produce a very special spring-loaded mechanism that would run for a certain number of days before releasing a lever, starting another machine. Always friendly but extremely mysterious, Keith refused to clearly specify what this other machine was, claiming that it was a trade secret. Martin did not grasp the ultimate purpose of the device, but he became completely wrapped up in the challenge, just like the others Keith would enlist. Keith carefully selected and organized a team of the finest technicians who unwittingly would build his elaborate and deadly creation.

Keith was always in tune with his time, and now he plummeted into the frenetically expanding industrial world full of ambitious people who dreamed of making it rich with extraordinary, novel ideas. This was the age of independent invention that introduced sewing machines, cameras, telephones, typewriters, phonographs, cash registers, and internal combustion engines. It was also the age that introduced landmines, naval torpedoes, Congreve rockets, Gatling guns, and high explosives: weapons as yet unparalleled in their power of death and destruction. Exiled to a raft on the Baltic Sea so that he would not blow up his native city of Stockholm, Alfred Nobel had ingeniously stabilized nitroglycerine with diatomaceous earth, thus inventing dynamite. This terrible new potential for explosive force inspired Keith's evil genius, and like any successful inventor, he adapted and refined ideas that were already floating around.

His idea originated with the primitive candle he used to blow up the Halifax powder magazine. The same basic concept evolved into an immensely complicated time bomb. The surreptitiousness of the Civil War's terrorist weapons inspired him with the means and the modus operandi. The gentlemanly Luke Blackburn, now governor of Kentucky, had disguised what he had imagined to be malevolent bioterrorist weapons in innocuous shipping trunks. Maxwell's clockwork bomb and Courtenay's coal torpedo had revealed to him just how vulnerable ships could be, and now he planned to target transatlantic passenger ships using his own invention. Best of all, these bombs could be left at the scene while the bomber sneaked away to safety, never witnessing the bloody consequences of his deed. The explosion would destroy any evidence, any remaining trace of the perpetrator, and he could return to the bright façade of his respectable life, where none could see the shadow self within him. Slowly and deliberately, Keith located talented craftsmen who would realize his ambitions as an inventor without recognizing his murderous motivations. Always able to exploit the human frailty of pride, he preyed on their obsessive fascinations with machines.

The enthusiastic and unsuspecting Martin suggested that Keith would need the very best engineer for the job: a "talented imagination who could really think themselves into his ideas." That man was the famous clockmaker, J. J. Fuchs of Bernburg, who was known throughout Germany for his innovative long-running mechanisms for grandfather clocks and church bells. Since Keith's German was atrocious and Fuchs could speak no English, Martin volunteered to bring the two together and act as interpreter when Fuchs arrived for the renowned Easter trade fair in Leipzig. Keith was so excited that he visited Martin several times before the fair, anxious for his meeting with Fuchs.

When the clockmaker came, Martin took him to the Villa Thomas but no one was home. Fuchs went again by himself, but, as Martin predicted, found Keith's German too choppy for explaining his complicated plans. Gleaning enough to understand that for some reason Keith needed a silent, ten-day clock, Fuchs promised he would try, but without knowing Keith's ultimate purpose, he dismissed the project as unimportant. He dawdled with it for a few months until an exasperated Keith gave up on him. Having taken a great interest in the project, Martin expressed regret at the collapse of such a good business opportunity for Fuchs, and felt that Keith had not trusted the clockmaker enough to give a full explanation of the mechanism. Martin tried to persuade Keith that only Fuchs, with his extraordinary mechanical talent, had the skill to carry out such a task. Then Keith moved to Dresden and the whole affair was, for the time, forgotten.

A year later, in the spring of 1874, Keith traveled to Vienna, now feeling the crunch of his diminishing finances and desperate to act. In order to facilitate his explanation of the desired mechanism, he took another false identity: Teadro Wiskoff, a bogus Russian businessman who owned a silk factory and needed a machine to cut thousands of strands of thread at once. In his disguises, Keith always liked to toy with obscure symbols and words meaningful only to him. Perhaps he intended to evoke the spider, spinning a web of deception to lure victims to their death, and amused himself with his choice of name, which sounded like Wise Kopf, Wise Head. For this performance, the inveterate role-player inflected his crude German with a heavy Slavic accent. His inquiries around the city took him to Ignas Rhind, a well-known, innovative watchmaker who had invented and exhibited an eight-day clock. Keith seemed to Rhind a genial, warm-hearted man, laughing and joking as he made his order. He presented the clockmaker with an irresistible challenge: to design a completely noiseless twelve-day clock that would release a powerful spring lever. Picking up a hammer, he dealt a loud blow to Rhind's bench to demonstrate the necessary force. "Wiskoff" seemed very determined and knew exactly what he wanted. Rhind agreed to do the work for 200 florins, equal to about $100. Keith gave Rhind half the sum when he produced the blueprint a few days later. The blueprint was then passed on to another technician, Carl Glückshall, who was to construct a working model, and took an irritatingly long five months to complete the work.

When Keith impatiently returned to the shop in September, his amiable manner had changed, and he angrily berated Herr Rhind when he tried the mechanism. He pounded on the table. Hadn't he told Rhind he needed a strong spring that would act with great force? Rhind's weak spring would never work. Keith refused to pay for the clock and demanded improvements to the spring lever. A conscientious mechanic, stung by the questioning of his skill, Rhind agreed to keep trying. It took three more months of experimenting with different springs for Rhind and Glückshall to produce a model with sufficient power. For them, it was simply an interesting technical problem, while for Keith, it was the only conceivable way to save himself.

While Rhind and Glückshall worked on the clockworks, Keith began acquiring another vital component of his bomb: dynamite. This new explosive, patented by Nobel in 1867, introduced a compact energy that transformed the modern world. Amazingly light and portable, its power was exhilarating. Huge crowds turned out for blasting demonstrations, where they experienced the truly sublime, the disintegration of old buildings and ships, the clearing of harbors and fields, the destruction of entire mountains. Dynamite struck awe and terror into those who witnessed its capabilities. And yet in 1874, hardly anyone really understood its potential as a weapon because of its stability. Despite enthusiastic efforts, military developers had found it useless for landmines, cannons, and torpedoes. But because of his background, Keith had realized that an ingenious union could be made between dynamite and the older concept of the time bomb. Dynamite's safety and portability made it ideal for covert bombs once Nobel had solved the problem of detonation. It needed a primary detonator, like a blasting cap, to set it off. Its stability meant that a bomber would not put himself at risk when carrying or transporting the substance. Furthermore, while a bomber would need a massive amount of gunpowder to blow up a huge ship, a relatively small amount of easily transportable dynamite would do the same trick. A mind like Keith's was quick to see dynamite's nefarious potential.

Even though the sale of dynamite did not yet have much official oversight, Keith was cautious in his purchase. For this negotiation, Keith took another disguise: W. J. Garcie of Jamaica. Keith was no doubt remembering his youthful visits to the Bahamas. There was also a dark-haired, devilishly handsome, completely innocent young dandy named Garcie who circulated among the Thompsons' friends in Dresden. Just before Christmas in 1874, disguised as "Garcie," Keith ordered a small quantity of lithofracteur, a variant of dynamite, from the Brothers Krebs explosives factory at Kalk, saying that he needed it for his business in Kingston. He had very carefully chosen his explosive brand, for Krebs advertised lithofracteur as producing less fumes than Nobel's dynamite. This quality made lithofracteur especially valuable to a secretive bomber who wanted to make sure customs officials could not detect the telltale scent.

When Keith returned to Rhind's shop in late December under the guise of "Wiskoff," Rhind demonstrated that the lever now fell with enough force to crack the table. Keith paid the other half of the agreed price and was pleased enough to offer the clockmakers forty dollars extra for their work. Keith told Rhind that he was returning to St. Petersburg in Russia, and asked him to mail the device to him in Bodenbach, a growing industrial town in Bohemia, on the border of Austria and Germany, about thirty miles down the River Elbe from Dresden. He would arrange for it to be sent to Russia from there, and then pay Rhind the remainder of his bill. Busy attending to domestic life as Cecelia was pregnant with May, their youngest child, Keith did not go to Bodenbach to pick up his model until February of 1875, two months after it had been completed. It was only then that Rhind received the rest of his fee.

Keith now had a working prototype with which to experiment. He kept his dynamite and his model secreted in a storage building in back of the Hotel de Pologne in Leipzig, where he had a cordial relationship with the owner, Frau Noack. Here he did his crafting and assembling. Like any mad bomber, he also had to have known of a remote location for actually testing explosions of dynamite and blasting caps, for he had to know the exact force he needed for detonation. Despite her husband's deep involvement in these secretive activities and his troubled emotional state, Cecelia appears to have had no knowledge of her husband's insidious project. She was still in Strehlen, pregnant again, tending to three young children, supervising unhappy servants, and dealing with creditors and landlords. Within several days of tinkering, Keith had determined that even with its force, the Rhind mechanism was too weak to detonate several hundred pounds of dynamite.

In March 1875, Keith went to Fuchs's shop in Bernburg, accompanied by a porter who was carrying the thirty-pound Rhind prototype. After so many months, Fuchs was amazed to see Keith again, especially after Keith had treated this man so dismissively. With much more polished German than Fuchs remembered, Keith again spun out his story of needing a machine for a new invention in silk production. The clockwork had to run for twelve days, be completely silent, and maintain its even motion in any position. And it had to be larger and operate with greater force than the flimsy model Keith was providing. If Fuchs succeeded, Keith said, he would order twenty more of the devices. He obviously had a very large operation in mind. Though the story may now appear farfetched, Fuchs accepted it without too many questions. He had previously built a clockwork mechanism that brought together threads from twelve sewing machines and kept count of how much silk had been sewn on each machine. Keith's persona as a wealthy businessman was so carefully crafted that Fuchs had no suspicions and agreed to the work. He charged Keith 375 marks, or about $100.

At that time, with the materials and standard designs at hand, it was impossible to make a truly silent clock. The swinging regulator of the pendulum had two end rods that slipped in and out of the first gear, starting and stopping the wheel, creating the loud tick-tock that kept insomniacs up at night and made time bombs easy to detect. But as Martin had promised, Fuchs was no normal watchmaker. He turned out to be a brilliant technician, making an almost silent mechanism using an airbrake instead of one of the rods. All other clockmakers who saw his work were stunned with admiration, even after the Bremerhaven disaster, when they realized that Fuchs had been duped into aiding and abetting a fiend. Completely oblivious to his customer's obsession and greed, Fuchs advised Keith to secure this clock securely to a board to make it even quieter. Keith was enormously pleased and tipped the clockmaker an extra $25. But despite these many months of careful effort, Fuchs's mechanism would be Keith's downfall. Later, Fuchs said, startlingly, that if he had known the true purpose for the device, he would have made it sturdier and less prone to jarring, as if his technical skill would absolve him of the guilt of his involvement.

Now that he knew the clock was ready, Keith acquired enough dynamite to make an extremely powerful weapon that could blow a hole in a 3,000-ton ship. Disguised again as "Garcie," he went back to

Krebs in March and ordered 700 pounds more of lithofracteur, keeping an eye on it as he traveled aboard a train from Cologne. Arriving in Leipzig, he had the unmarked explosives, kept in three boxes, stored in the station's luggage room. He eagerly waited for Fuchs to arrive, bearing the perfected timepiece. In April, Fuchs met Keith at the Leipzig train station. Still playing his gratifying role as an enterprising businessman, Keith took Fuchs into the storage room, where he showed him the boxes, saying they were full of factory parts destined for Russia. All he needed, he told Fuchs with satisfaction, was the clock. They called for two railroad workers to lug Fuchs's mechanism and the parcels to a storage shed in the yard of the Hotel de Pologne. Within weeks, other strange articles filled the shed, including four attached zinc boxes with an iron ring at the top, and a specially built, double-compartmented barrel marked as containing ironware and branded with the letters "G.S.T. 10." Keith carefully kept the shed locked, and strictly forbade the hotel concierge, who knew about the boxes and other mysterious deliveries, from saying anything to Cecelia. Now Keith prepared for his trial run. He packed the explosives into the zinc boxes, putting iron bars into empty spaces to act as shrapnel and increase the effect of the explosion. He put two of these boxes into the bottom of the barrel, for which he had made a canvas lining. He attached the clockwork to five layers of boards screwed together, and carefully poised the spring lever to fall on a blasting cap, fitting the whole machine into the middle of the barrel. He then placed four more dynamite-packed zinc boxes over the clockworks, ready to go. He planned to strike in June, at the height of transatlantic travel.

In the midst of Keith's surreptitious machinations out in the shed, his old Highland friend, John Suppiger, along with Suppiger's wife, Catherina, and two of their children, John, six years old, and Adelina, twenty, traveled east from Highland to New York and then boarded the S.S. *Schiller*. Departing on April 27, in the earliest days of the tourist season, the *Schiller* was bound from New York to Hamburg with stops in Plymouth and Cherbourg. John had not wanted to go on this trip, but Catherina, just recovering from a serious illness, talked him into returning to their Swiss homeland, perhaps for the last time. There was a big Highland contingent onboard, including a retired farmer, Christian Hirni. The Suppigers were traveling with their twenty-year-old nephew, Louis, going to Europe for advanced medical

training. Also with them was Sigmond Stern, originally from Wurten-
burg, Germany, who was planning to ask for Adelina's hand in marriage. Stern was a prosperous owner of a clothing store in Greenville,
some miles up the road from Highland. In all, there were 254 passengers on board, with an unusually high number of women and children
who hung over the bulwarks waving as the ship left port. There was
also $300,000 worth of gold coins, packed in six wooden barrels in the
hold. Many of the first-class passengers were wealthy ladies and gentlemen carrying substantial sums of gold and jewelry.

Built only two years before for the German Transatlantic Steam
Navigation Company of Hamburg, the *Schiller* was a fine ship, one of
the grandest of its day, and it made good time across the Atlantic,
avoiding the perils of shoals and icebergs. Children ran about on decks
while their seasick mothers warned them to take care. As the ship approached Plymouth and the treacherous Isles of Scilly at a brisk speed,
it encountered a thick, enduring fog. Three days later at about
9 o'clock at night, half a mile from shore under heavy seas, it went
headlong into the reef, was flung back, and crashed again broadside.

As the ship listed heavily in the dense fog, the passengers scrambled on the slippery decks. Brandishing knives, men, including some
sailors, muscled their way into the lifeboats. The ship's officers fired
their pistols at them but were unable to get them out. These lifeboats
were swamped and all in them were drowned. Then the great funnel
came down and smashed two other lifeboats to pieces. As great waves
crashed across the decks, one after the next of the remaining passengers and crew were swept away. Clinging to each other, women and
children huddled together in the deckhouse. But this too was swept
away as their anguished husbands outside watched in horror. Crying
for help from the lighthouse, forty people lashed themselves to the
masts, but these eventually split and fell into the sea, drowning all who
clung to them. Only forty-four people were saved from the wreck, and
were found drifting with the tide in their life jackets. Of the one hundred women on board, only one survived. Not a single child was saved.
The Suppigers and their friends all perished that night.

Because Cecelia kept in touch with her stepfather and sister, she
would surely have heard the tragic news of her old friends and passed
it along to her husband. Hearing about the very human impact of this
maritime disaster apparently had no effect on Keith. In fact, he most

likely viewed accidental shipwrecks as good news to him, for they would make the one he would cause look less suspicious. Nor did summer travelers put off their plans despite knowing how dangerous sea travel could be. Well over 10,000 ships sank every year, mostly small boats with inexperienced crews. Lloyd's of London listed every manner of disaster: ships driven to shore by weather, colliding with icebergs and whales, struck by waterspouts, set aflame by spontaneous combustion, plundered by pirates, taken possession by convicts, and blown apart by coal dust, steam, or gunpowder. Then there were dozens of ships that sailed off, never to be seen again. The Lloyd's list contained such poignant entries as: "The *Honest Endeavor* sailed from Hull, Nova Scotia bound, and had not been heard of for three years." Between 1851 and 1873, seven iron steamships simply disappeared, which was the worst fate for surviving families since they could never be entirely sure of what happened to their loved ones.

While most passengers felt safe on large steamships, two spectacular wrecks in 1873 had deeply shaken public confidence in sea travel. In January, a steamer crashed into the immigrant ship *Northfleet* anchored off Dungeness, Scotland, taking 300 lives. In April, the White Star liner *Atlantic* was driven to shore by the wind at Mars Head, near Halifax, taking 547 lives. This wreck was so horrific that it filled the news for weeks as mangled bodies, mostly of women and children, washed up in the surf. Readers devoured tragic stories of such disasters, and the painter Winslow Homer was inspired to create a romantic illustration of the wreck for *Harper's Weekly*, showing a beautiful young woman, dressed in a spotless white gown, stretched out on the beach as if she were sleeping. But the wholesale alarm the *Atlantic* wreck caused among travelers preparing to make their summer voyages provoked the *New York Times* to reassure its readers: "The loss of the steam-ship *Atlantic* naturally tends to produce a feeling of distrust on the parts of those whose business takes them down to the sea in ships. A moment's reflection, however, suffices to show that ocean steam-ship travel is as nearly a perfect immunity from disaster or accidents, accompanied with loss of life, that occur from various causes on land." As with airplane disasters today, shipwrecks could be dismissed as anomalies. Newspapers promulgated various psychological strategies to prevent anxiety about traveling on ships. For example, as the *New York Times* pointed out, there were plenty of comparative risks in everyday life. In the week after the *Schiller* sank, which killed the Suppigers, thousands of excursionists sailed from New York, and tens of thousands more would make the exodus to Europe during the rest of the year. Despite ocean disasters, travelers in large numbers still swayed seasick on the decks, suppressing fears of the unpredictable forces of technology and nature. But they had not yet learned to fear a savage mind, ruthless in its designs, plotting their random destruction.

In a sudden and surprisingly cheerful mood at the beginning of June, Keith announced to Cecelia that he was once again leaving for America. He first had the barrel, which weighed hundreds of pounds, sent by rail to the depot in Bremerhaven where he went to receive it. He then armed the bomb by setting the clock for ten days, and set it above a compartment packed with iron filings and dynamite. Harkening back to his old Civil War tricks, he filled the top and sides of the barrel with a layer of a powdery white substance to disguise its contents. He then arranged to have it shipped onboard the North German Lloyd steamer, the *Rhein*, sailing for New York with its usual contingent of emigrants. He wrote to his bank, Baring Brothers: "You will please effect insurance on the steamship *Rhein*, Captain Brickenstein, which sails for New York tomorrow, via Southampton. Insure for property onboard shipped by me, value, say nine thousand pounds (£9,000)." Baring Brothers agreed to insure the barrel at a hefty premium of a little over £46, adding, "We shall be glad to know the nature of the said property and how it is packed. Possibly the rate would have been less if you had furnished us with these particulars." The bank never received an answer to its query. Keith did not dare draw any special attention to his deadly barrel. He paid the highest premium without argument.

With the barrel destined for passage on the *Rhein*, Keith sailed ahead on the *Republic*. He told his cabin roommate, Fred Boultbee, that he was traveling to Virginia to visit his property, which had been damaged during the war, and to see his dying mother. Soon after, he changed to a private room, claiming that the first was too small. The trip was uneventful. On June 21 Keith arrived in New York and checked in at the Hoffman House on Broadway. Using his real brother's first name, he was disguised as "George S. Thomas" of St. George's, Bermuda, one of his old blockade-running haunts. He kept a low profile, and though the hotel clerks noticed that he received mail from Bremen and Leipzig, they rarely saw him. They remembered him as a stout man with a florid face, his gray hair combed forward at the sides. His dark gray eyes behind his golden spectacles were always keen and restless. Carrying himself with a very erect posture, he wore a black cravat and dark, almost clerical clothes. His only embellishment was a fancy watch of unusual workmanship. The clerks remembered that he "was always very neat about his linen." Sometimes, he "was very jolly and made everybody about him enjoy the best of humor, while at other times he would be very sedate and remain alone for a long time." Living off the proceeds from a forged bank check for $750, Keith had enough money to go out shopping for presents for his little ones. He eagerly waited to hear the newsboys cry that the *Rhein* had mysteriously disappeared at sea, like the *City of Boston* a few years before. That would mean a substantial gain to him of $45,000 insurance money, restoring his affluence and his pride. That news never came. The *Rhein* sailed blithely into the harbor intact, the malfunctioning bomb still hidden in a barrel in the hold. The experiment had failed, but Keith was not too discouraged. An inventor and an entrepreneur had to weather his failures. He could try again.

Still disguised as George, Keith took a carriage down to meet the *Rhein* as it sailed into New York harbor and picked up his barrel, now purporting to the customs officials that it contained small goods valued at $148. The barrel was marked with his supposed initials, "G.S.T." He must have had some nervous moments transporting an armed bomb away from the dock. In his room, he carefully unpacked the barrel, laid the parts of his bomb on the floor, and investigated them. Fortunately for the passengers, something had gone wrong with the detonating system, always the most complex part of any bomb. Keith kept the clock for the trip back to Germany, but was reluctant to risk transporting the barrel. It still contained a large quantity of dynamite, and he decided to leave it for a few months in New York and covered the whole thing over once again with plaster. In order to avoid paying duty on the barrel, he worked through a broker, Edward Skidmore, who would arrange to have it appraised and shipped back to Germany on Keith's order. Keith told Skidmore that the barrel contained polishing paste. Fortunately for Keith, the appraiser, L. B. Foster, was widely known among his colleagues for his incredible stupidity. Foster drilled a hole in the barrel, gave the powdery contents a cursory examination, and declared it worth $600. With the barrel still in storage but with the precious clock in hand, Keith sailed back to Germany on the *Republic*. When Keith boarded holding very little luggage, the captain expressed great surprise at seeing him again, especially since his name was not on the passenger list. Keith mysteriously explained that he was "anxious that some parties should not know of his return."

In September, Keith drew the last of his money from the bank and bounced a check for £110. Baring Brothers wrote a dreaded "returned check" letter to him on September 27: "We beg you to take note that as your account already shewes a balance of £80 at your debit, we have been unable to accept your draft of 21st instant for £100 on your account; and we have therefore informed Messrs. Robert Thode & Co [Keith's Dresden bank] that the draft has been accepted for their honor." Robert Thode, who was eventually swindled out of £1,100 by his client, later remembered his long association with Keith, whose face he always thought "betokened natural sense, energy, and good natured qualities."

Keith talked another bank into giving him a large line of credit to get him through these rough times before he could make good on his technology investments. Not long after, he was ready to try his scheme again. He returned to Brothers Krebs for three rolls of detonating cord, thirty-two blasting caps, four watertight bags, and one hundred more pounds of lithofracteur. In addition, he commissioned his locksmith in Dresden to construct two more special metal boxes with finger-sized holes in the top. He rapidly constructed a second bomb, this time concealing it in a portmanteau. Although he usually avoided danger, he had considered the risk of traveling with the bomb against another possible failure if he did not personally oversee the portmanteau's handling and placement. This time, his desperation and greed outweighed any fear of his own destruction. Again onboard some steamer, he planned to insure that his device was working properly, taking a high-risk venture whose consequences he could not foresee.

TEN

THE JOLLY GOOD FELLOW

Two months after his failed attempt on the *Rhein*, Keith announced that he was going on another business trip and once again gave his family a loving farewell with many fond hugs and kisses. He loaded his cumbersome boxes and luggage into a carriage, promising to be home soon. Cecelia missed him greatly, and wrote to him complaining of the dreary wet autumn weather and her inflamed joints that hurt so bad that she could barely write. Shut up indoors and driving their mother to distraction, the children were very restless, screaming and running about. Eagerly awaiting promised gifts from abroad, they sent letters with "oceans of kisses to their papa," drawing them as circles and squiggles, a special one for each child, a code of kisses. With these signs from an oblivious world of domestic affection, Keith went about his perverse idea of breadwinning.

He first traveled to London for a few days and then to Liverpool on October 7, checking into the swanky Northwestern Hotel at the terminus of the London and Northwestern railway line. There he stayed a week, at a cost of eight shillings a night, twice that of most other hotels in the city. One of Liverpool's two leading hotels, the Northwestern was huge and very modern, hosting passing dignitaries like Seyed Burgash-bin-Saîd, the Sultan of Zanzibar. Just outside in the square was a stone stage specially built for the violent marital quarrels of Punch and Judy. Keith often left his room and went out to

indulge his appetites, visiting the small famous chophouses that filled
the streets with the smell of sizzling mutton and beef. Relentlessly
gloomy and dingy from coal smoke, Liverpool was a bustling place,
annually receiving over 20,000 ships from all parts of the world,
loaded with a great variety of colorful passengers along with bacon
and ham, rum and brandy, rice, sugar, cheese, wool, and a large
amount of cotton destined for the busy English textile mills. Many
bobbies patrolled the town, nabbing pickpockets and prostitutes who
lacked enough pence for a bribe. Wearing peaked caps with a red
band and white moleskin uniforms, porters heaved boxes and bags up
and down the hill to and from the docks. The city was packed with
business traders and travelers, many wearing glossy top hats, ele-
gantly fitted trousers, and long Albert coats with red roses in the but-
tonholes of their silk lapels.

Liverpool had been a center for blockade-running transactions
during the Civil War and had intimate associations for Keith, who had
acquired the ill-fated *Caledonia* there, perhaps the first ship he had
scuttled. The town's business leaders had historically enjoyed immense profits from their transport and sale of human beings. The
renowned Shakespearean actor George Frederick Cooke once admonished a Liverpool audience, "There is not a brick in your town
that is not cemented with the blood of a suffering African." Though
Britain's slave trade ended in 1807 and many of Liverpool's citizens
were staunch abolitionists, others had no compunction about maintaining social and economic relationships with the slave-holding
American South. During the Civil War, the city grew fat with trade in
Southern cotton and the fitting out of ships for the Confederacy. As a
broker and agent for the Lamars, Keith was involved in these transactions and undoubtedly maintained business connections in the city.
After the war, England provided a safe haven for Confederate agents
fleeing prosecution. Later, detectives would wonder whether Keith
had accomplices in Liverpool, for few could believe that he had de-
vised his plot by himself.

In his hotel room, Keith went about his business, tending his dynamite, tinkering with his temperamental device, planning his investment
strategies, doing a cost-benefit analysis, and dreaming of making it rich
again. Calling herself his "own darling comforter" and sending him a
thousand kisses, Cecelia wrote to him on October 11, chatting about

the stern new nanny, the childrens' progress in their studies, and how laughing baby May was holding her head up all by herself.

I trust you have been well both in body as well as in mind since you left—do not worry yourself about your *chickees* at home we will be so contented & happy when you come back again—I'll go out walking with you every day I do long so to have a good long walk again. The children send their papa lots of kisses and are so anxious to see the pretty books you bought for them—your little maie sleeps between willie & blanche since the new bonne has arrived before she would not be put into any other bed but yours as she thought you would come sometime in the night and then you would find your bed all nice & warm & your little pet in it waiting for you—just now she is sitting by me telling me to speak very kindly to you & not as cold in my letter on account of you not coming back as soon as we expected. . . .

Keith had indicated to Cecelia that he would return in a few days, and did not tell her he was sailing for America. Despite tender letters from home, he suddenly stopped replying and would not answer Cecelia's frantic telegrams. Once again, she had no idea what had happened to him and "fears of some dreadful accident" filled her mind. She was quickly running out of money to pay the servants and feed and clothe the children.

As ships went in and out of the harbor, Keith took a long week to put his plan into motion. For two nights, he did not stay in his room, and the gossipy hotel porters believed that he had gone to a bordello. Although he was always up for a party, Keith had to accomplish some very risky parts of his plan while in the city. He had to wind the twelve-day clock in his hotel room and then get the armed bomb onboard without suspicion or accident. The bomb had to go off within a ten-day window of opportunity, between the ship's landing at Queenstown, where Keith intended to get off, and its arrival in New York. If he started the clock in Liverpool, and then was interrupted by some unforeseen circumstance, he could dismantle the bomb, but would have to wait days while the clock ran down. There was no way of stopping and resetting it. Each day of delay meant more visits from harsh creditors, more risk of arrest and social embarrassment. Therefore, the timing was crucial. He also had to scam insurance agents into believing that he was a wealthy businessman traveling with expensive goods. The whole scheme was senseless if he failed to get the insurance, since then there would be nothing to collect after the shipwreck.

When Keith was ready to go, he went the mile and a half down to the dock, passing the many policemen who kept the city under tight surveillance. He was looking for the ship he would condemn to a terrible fate. He approached the S.S. *Republic,* a ship with which he was well familiar, and talked to his friend, the steward, whom he'd met earlier in the year. The steward referred him to Stern & Sons, a travel agency in town. To throw off any possible suspicion of his movements, Keith lied to the agents that he had never been in Liverpool, though he had sailed from there on the *Republic* just a few months before. He then chose his victim. Claiming to be interested in the size of the berths, he inspected the *Celtic,* the largest of the plush new White Star steamships that made a fast crossing between Liverpool and New York, via Queenstown, Ireland. Afterwards, he was seen talking intently to a man on the dock who would never be identified. Satisfied that the ship felt right for his malevolent purposes, Keith booked a first-class cabin on the *Celtic,* costing eighteen guineas. It was a cheap time to travel, since immigration had fallen off, and the steamship lines were deep in a price war. Keith was betting on making a modest investment in return for huge gains.

Now Keith faced the greatest challenge of his acting ability. He had to convince his travel agent at Stern & Sons that two ordinary-looking boxes, covered in worn black oilcloth, were actually full of twenty dollar gold pieces worth £12,000. Suspicious, the agent asked why he was traveling with such a huge amount of cash rather than bank drafts. Keith played one of his favorite roles: the Southern gentleman. He replied that he needed cash as soon as he reached New York to pay claims on land in Virginia, owned by his father before the Civil War. This was so urgent that he could not wait for his identity to be verified and the drafts validated. The travel agent bought the story and attempted to get the boxes insured. But when Keith returned, the agent said Keith would have to present the boxes for inspection, counting out the money in front of a more hard-nosed insurance representative. Keith quickly withdrew, suddenly claiming that the insurance premium was too high. He then resorted to the White Star offices. Its agents told Keith not to worry, that the boxes would be stowed safely in a special room onboard the *Celtic*. But when Keith insisted on insurance, the White Star agents asked that the boxes be opened and the money counted. Keith again declined. Now the whole plan had collapsed, but Keith was on a run-away course, driven by his own obsessions with appearance and time. The clock had been set. He had made the decision to travel with his bomb, and was committed to going through with his plan even though there was no apparent gain. That he was willing to pursue this evil course suggests that he was motivated not only by money, but also by technological curiosity and pure malevolence toward his fellow human beings. He had to experiment to see if his new device would actually work.

On the chilly, rainy morning of October 15, Keith took a steam-tender out to the *Celtic*, anchored in the Mersey River, and boarded her. He was a nervous and disappointed man. He seemed very troubled about his heavy treasure boxes, but the purser assured him that they would be safely stowed with the ship's valuables. Keith continued to fake concern about them in a last-ditch attempt to get a receipt for them, but finally gave up. Not so visible was his real inner anxiety about one of his bags, his unusually heavy, firmly corded portmanteau. This was taken aboard by two very muscular porters and placed in his room. Keith surely heard the bomb imperceptibly ticking, like Poe's tell-tale heart.

On the trip from Liverpool to the first scheduled stop at Queenstown, Keith faced yet another fearful disappointment. He found that he would have to share a room with another traveler, Colonel Donn Piatt, a tough customer for a con job. A former Union officer, Piatt was a well-known Washington journalist. In 1871, with George Alfred Townsend, he started the *Washington Capitol*, and covering national politics found "the House a Cave of the Wind and the senate a preposterous fog bank." He had an unswerving irreverent insight into personality and celebrity, and was famous for his caustic satire of political figures. He delighted in exposing the flaws of politicians, dubbing Ulysses S. Grant "His Inebriated Excellency." So biting was his ridicule that Piatt even called himself "the Ink Fiend" and considered his pen to be loaded with dynamite. Despite his sarcastic edge, women admired Piatt for his soft, pale hands. He loved the pampered life of a gentleman—he was once ambassador to France and built a Flemish castle in Mac-o-chee, Ohio. Therefore he was very unpleasantly surprised and disgruntled at having to share a stateroom with Keith when there were several empty rooms available. When he demanded another room, the ship's officer assured Piatt that his roommate Keith would be disembarking shortly at Queenstown, a one-night journey. Piatt was immensely relieved that he'd soon have a room to himself for the rest of the crossing. Entering the cabin, Piatt was annoyed to find it filled with large, strange-looking boxes that could not be stowed under the berths.

His irritation was immediately relieved when he met Keith, who masterfully performed the wealthy businessman. Despite Piatt's reputation as a sharp-eyed observer who was never fooled by pretension, he was Keith's kind of audience, a man who disparaged idols because he envied the trappings of wealth and power. In fact, the Ink Fiend found the Dynamite Fiend "a very agreeable man" with "as pleasant a countenance as one cared to meet." Pleasingly well dressed, hair smoothly brushed, and beard neatly trimmed, Keith greeted Piatt cordially, offering him an entire box of the finest Havana cigars, not to be found in all of England. Impressed with Keith's aura of respectability and generosity, Piatt refused the cigars, explaining that the smoke would make him seasick. Most steamship passengers feared the demon of the ocean, the dreadful nausea that would overtake them on the first days of the voyage. The rolling, pitching, and bucking of the ship sent them into glassy-eyed paralysis and even gave them woozy hallucinations as they huddled under their woolen blankets. The smell and sound of passengers puking into the metal pans attached to their berths was one of the worst experiences of a sea voyage, and the Atlantic passage was known for being especially turbulent. The addition of the cloyingly rich smell of a cigar could easily send a strong-stomached man heaving.

The traveler had reason enough to fear seasickness, as well as the powerful currents, tremendous gales, squalls, dense fogs, and icebergs of a transatlantic crossing. Equipped with luxuries and the latest appliances, such as fresh running water and electric call bells for the stewards, the cabins were situated over immense furnaces and potentially explosive steam boilers. Making a transatlantic crossing, Charles Dickens had nervously described the steam boiler as a "fire in hiding, ready to burst through any outlet, wild with its resistless power of ruin and

1. Alexander Keith
Source: Nova Scotia Archives and Records Management (NSARM)

2. Code-breaker David Homer Bates
Source: Picture History

3. Luke Pryor Blackburn
Source: Kentucky Historical Society

4. John Wilkes Booth (left) performing in *Julius Caesar*, 1864
Library of Congress

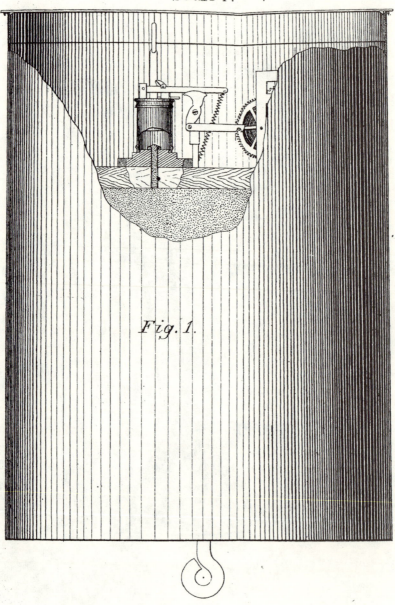

Scale ¼.

Fig. 1.

5. Civil War clockwork bomb
Source: W. R. King, *Torpedoes*, 1866

6. Mechanism of John Maxwell's bomb
Source: W. R. King, *Torpedoes*, 1866

7. The Highland Sharpshooters
Source: Louis Latzer Memorial Public Library

8. *(opposite)* Cecelia Thompson, c. 1865
Source: Staatsarchiv Bremen

9. *(above)* Cecelia Thompson, c. 1875
Source: Staatsarchiv Bremen

10. *(right)* Alexander Keith, Jr., c. 1860
Source: Staatsarchiv Bremen

11. *(opposite)* Alexander Keith, Jr., c.
1865
Source: Staatsarchiv Bremen

12. Alexander Keith, Jr., c. 1875
Source: Staatsarchiv Bremen

13. *(above)* William Thompson
Source: Staatsarchiv Bremen

14. *(right)* Blanche Thompson
Source: Staatsarchiv Bremen

15. *(left)* Klina Thompson
Source: Staatsarchiv Bremen

16. *(below)* Mechanism of Keith's
bomb
Source: *Deutscher Hausschatz,* 1876

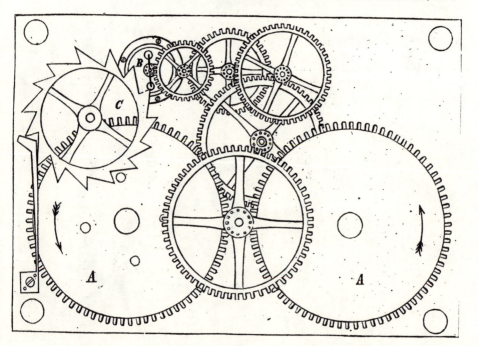

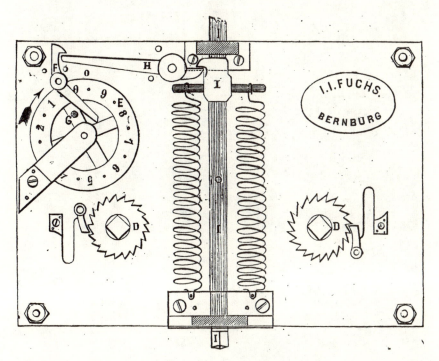

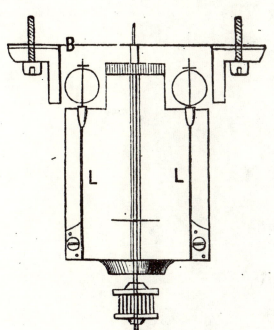

17. *(above)* Mechanism of Keith's bomb
Source: *Deutscher Hauss-chatz*, 1876

18. *(left)* Mechanism of Keith's bomb
Source: *Deutscher Hauss-chatz*, 1876

Mosel und Simson kurz vor der Katastrophe.
Originalzeichnung von Marinemaler Fedeler in Bremerhaven.

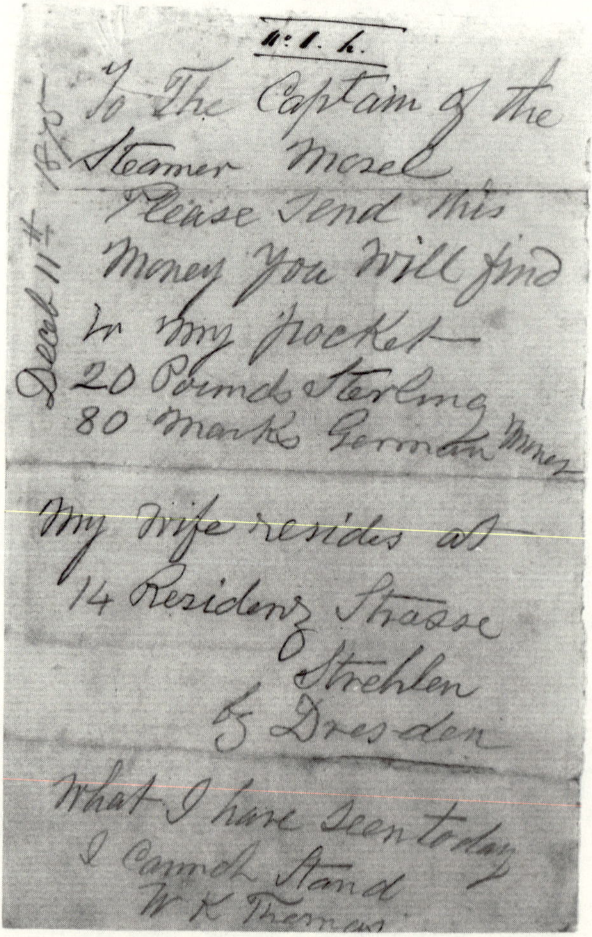

19. *(above)* The *Mosel* in harbor, just before the explosion.
Source: *Die Gartenlaube,* 1876

20. *(left)* Keith's suicide note
Staatsarchiv Bremen

21. *(opposite)* Keith's death's head
Staatsarchiv Bremen

(handwritten note, image 20:)

n. 1. h.

Dec. 11th 1875

To The Captain of the Steamer Mosel

Please Send this Money You will find in my pocket
20 Pounds Sterling
80 Marks German Money

My Wife resides at
14 Residenz Strasse
Strehlen
by Dresden

What I have seen today I cannot Stand
W K Thomas

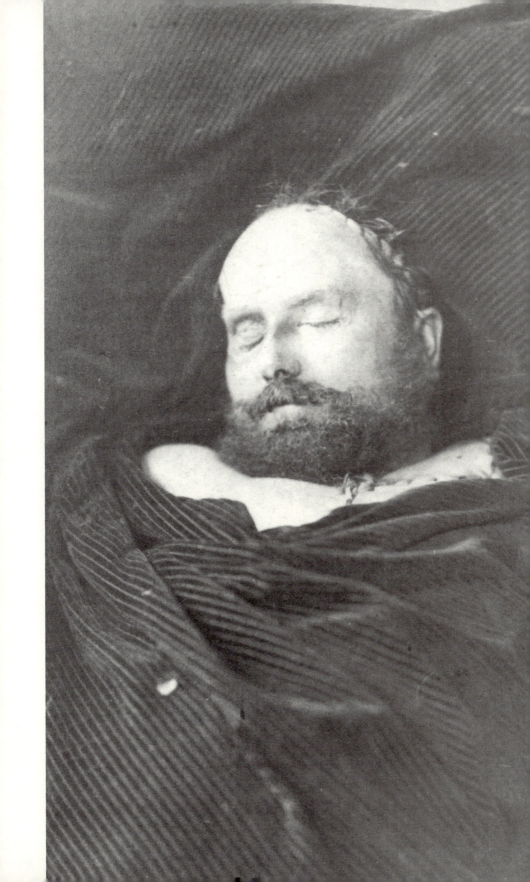

"Dynamit-Explosion," Bremerhafen, den 11. December 1875.
THOMAS, der MÖRDER.

22. Postcard, 1876
Source: Picture History

death." Such a description might have applied to the murderous Keith, who disguised his violence in the cool planning of technological projects and lulled everyone he met with his sanguine exterior. He was hoping to mimic a boiler explosion.

Having made some forty transatlantic crossings, Keith appeared complacent, explaining to Piatt that he was not bothered at all by sea travel. His sea legs were as good as his land legs—he couldn't tell the difference. "It must be very rough," Keith joked, "when I cannot shave myself every morning." Obsessively compelled to talk safety with nervous passengers, Keith presented himself as a model of serenity. He went to bed early that first night, and seemed to fall deep into quiet slumbers. The first-class cabins were located amidships, so that passengers were furthest from the cranking noise of the ship's iron screw and the queasiness of the roiling sea. Reassured, Piatt also slept peacefully that night, unaware that in Keith's portmanteau a set of wheels was turning, teeth ratcheting the seconds to destruction.

Keith, however, was in for a shock when it was announced that the ship would not make its scheduled stop at Queenstown. The ship's personnel observed that Keith seemed highly agitated, and for good reason. He had put into motion a plan that had already failed, and things were growing steadily worse. He had not been able to insure the box, and now he was caught in his own noose with the bomb's twelve-day clock inexorably ticking away. Now he had to disarm the bomb, a complicated, delicate operation, for he well knew that too much jarring, a simple miscalculation, might jig the mechanism into a premature detonation. This would take privacy, time, and enough room to move around. But he was ensnared with Piatt, lying next to enough dynamite to atomize them both and blow the whole ship and all its passengers into flotsam and jetsam. When the ship sailed past Queenstown, Keith was still trapped on board, even though Cecelia and the children expected him home at once. He went to the purser and demanded a private berth. Fortunately for all the passengers on the *Celtic*, Piatt was moved to his own room the next day. Keith then locked his door and would let no one enter.

Despite Keith's friendly façade, strange and surreptitious doings went on in his room, late at night. There were strict ship's rules on the use of oil lamps and candles, and the ones provided were placed out of reach of passengers. But Keith had managed to get a candle so that he could work in secret on something in the portmanteau. During his strenuous labors, he splattered chemicals and candle wax all over the walls and floors, staining the carpet. When he later disembarked, the porters would discover that the portmanteau had grown surprisingly light. Afraid that he'd be caught going through customs, Keith had surreptitiously tossed the dynamite overboard.

Throughout all this, with amazing self-possession, Keith maintained his gregarious persona, though for a time he was literally sleeping with dynamite. He only broke once, when the bilious, fastidious Captain Kiddle reprimanded him for spitting tobacco on the deck: "What do you do that for, sir, when the ocean makes the largest sort of spittoon all around you? Ladies walk this deck, sir." Lingering from his old days as a rough Scottish brewer's son from the remote Highlands and the wild Canadian provinces, Keith's crassness stained his careful image for a fleeting moment. The reprimand from an officer of such military bearing stung hard. Keith grew enraged and told Piatt he would have his revenge on the captain when the ship reached New York. He quickly regained his composure, and made amends with Kiddle, engaging him in close conversation, walking with him on the promenade deck.

All through the voyage, Keith courted his once-intended victims. On the surface, he seemed to all he met on the *Celtic* as a genial man, a gourmand who loved rich living. As always, he was memorably funny and charming. His room was near the saloon, which ran the breadth of the ship and was full of mirrors, infinitely reflecting the self. It was often full of wealthier passengers looking out at the stars and the ocean, writing diaries and letters, drinking champagne, reading romances, or trying to recover from seasickness with broth, hard biscuits, and hot brandy. There, Keith befriended the bartender, who admired his prodigious eating and drinking. Keith also made the acquaintance of the ship's doctor, who was taken by his amiable manner and often strolled the decks with him. Keith could not help meeting many of 296 passengers, most of them under the age of twenty-five, children like his own that he had intended to kill. The promenade deck resembled a city street, with children frisking and playing games, young parents scolding, romantic newlyweds strolling hand in hand, older couples beginning or ending their grand tour, and the new transatlantic businessmen of the Gilded Age briskly exercising their legs.

Dinners at the long tables were social affairs, lasting hours, and Keith would always order "rations for three on one plate." They typically began with oysters and an elaborate tureen of green turtle soup, flavored with basil and Madeira and decorated with mock turtle eggs made from chicken meat and egg yolks. This extravagant dish was followed by several courses of fish, fowl, and meat, including the usual salmon with lobster and cucumber sauce, broiled ham, boiled mutton with capers, sirloin of beef, lamb and mint sauce, and roast squab. Then came creamy pudding and pastries, fresh fruit and cheeses. The nightly feast was accompanied by long discussions of business, politics, and religion. Keith's gluttony and vulgar manners were always noticeable, but he was such a nice fellow that everyone politely ignored them.

On more turbulent days at sea, only the jolly good fellows came to the table at each of the four meal bells. A familiar group on every passenger steamship, these gregarious merchants laughed and drank together, sharing anecdotes and making fun of the nauseous. After all, real men did not suffer from seasickness. They liked to display their superiority by eating heartily, chumming with the captain and crew, paternally watching over women traveling alone, and organizing philanthropic donations for the steerage passengers. One of their favorite games in the smoking room was to wager twenty or thirty dollars on how many miles the ship had gone in twenty-four hours, according to the ship's log. Keith played the role of the jolly fellow, the international man of business, somewhat mysterious, with an exciting, slightly dangerous past. He was making his own wager on time. As he cupped his claret, warmed to the temperature of blood, he must have secretly burned with envy of his wealthy companions. Despite his humble origins, he had become master of this social game, rising above the boiled-beef crowd down in steerage. But he was in danger of tumbling off the high deck.

Despite luxurious dinners, a transatlantic crossing was a tedious affair, and after a few days passengers began counting the hours and minutes to landing. To ward off the anxiety and boredom of the rich, White Star steamers offered nightly entertainments: poetry readings, inspirational lectures, piano recitals and concerts, tableaux vivant, and dances on the moonlit deck. During after-dinner brandy and cigars in the smoking room, Keith indulged in his favorite game: poker. Once, he participated in a little amateur dramatics: a mock trial in which a

black woman sued a Jew for breach of promise. Keith played the role
of jury foreman, and got a big laugh for his performance in a play that
emphasized the arrogant superiority of wealthy saloon passengers. Yet
Keith always maintained a certain reserve, and his origins were something of a mystery in the bored, gossipy world of the ship. Some
guessed from his slight accent that he was a German of high class; others thought from his pleasant manners that he must be an Englishman
or an American. None knew that they would barely escape a terrible
wager by their pleasant fellow gambler.

One night, on especially rough seas in a driving rain, Piatt was
watching the storm from a shelter above the gangway. Keith, who
often paced the decks alone at night, approached him and asked if he
were seasick. In an uncharacteristically sentimental mood, Piatt answered no, that he was meditating on how tiny they were in such a
vast expanse of water, how insignificant it would be for such a small
ship to sink beneath the heaving ocean. Piatt must have seemed the
great innocent to Keith, whose brain was churning with violence and
desperation. Enamored with his own secret powers, he had coldly
planned the death of this amateur philosopher; he could cause a catastrophe much like any of nature's worst storms. Taken in by the appearance of modest respectability, Piatt still did not recognize the real
dangers of a hidden human violence beneath the surface of this
friendly man. Later he would compare Keith's murders to the casual-
ties of war: "It is when crime gets out of its well-known grooves that
we recognize its magnitude."

As they stood on the deck, damp with cold rain and salty spray,
Keith did not philosophize with his potential victim. Instead, he hauled
out nuggets from the advertising of the White Star Line, explaining
that its ships, constructed as seven watertight compartments, were
much safer than Cunard's more modest ships. A terrible Cunard disaster, he told Piatt, would soon reveal the perils of ocean travel. Keith
was ignoring the Cunard Line's exemplary safety record as well as the
recent wreck of the White Star ship *Atlantic,* and he turned out to be no
prophet, for the most famous shipwreck of all would be a White Star
steamer: the ill-fated *Titanic.* But perhaps having been frustrated by his
White Star attempts, Keith's thoughts had already turned to his next
potential victims as he imagined a Cunard ship, with a great wound in
its side, slipping under the waves, a tragedy wrought by his infernal

machine. In his strange duality, Keith emanated security, safety, and a genial nonchalance that fooled even the best.

When the *Celtic* arrived at New York's Pier 52 after the thirteen days' voyage, Keith disembarked with luggage still containing the clock, which had been slightly damaged in his frantic dismantling of the bomb. Keith also still had one of the mystery treasure boxes that he gave to the ship's purser, telling him to guard it well, because it contained $30,000 in gold coin. He attempted to get a receipt for it, but the purser refused. Still spinning the web of deception, Keith thought he might get the plan to work on a ship traveling back across the Atlantic, but once again he failed. The purser diligently carried the box and placed it on the dock, telling the pier superintendent that it was extremely valuable. The superintendent scoffed that the worn-looking box couldn't possibly be worth that extravagant amount. Keith was quickly discovering that bureaucrats and minor officials were not nearly as easy to fool as the aspiring gentry. He grew nervous about his story, because he then came up to a customs officer and told him that the box was full of rifle cartridges. He was going on a hunting safari out West, he said, a story that emphasized his genteel, manly character. At Keith's request, the box was left for a week on the dock after a customs official gave it a cursory examination. Unclaimed, it was moved into a storage room.

For four days after his arrival in New York on the *Celtic*, Keith hid in his room at the glamorous, luxurious Fifth Avenue Hotel. In an age of anxiety about urban conflagrations, the hotel advertised its safety to its guests: modern elevators and state-of-the-art fireproof construction. Despite his desperation and lack of means, Keith was still living the high life, gravitating always toward the social center of politics and business, where he saw his place. The Fifth Avenue Hotel bustled with the busy lives of ruthless and powerful men; there they held meetings, made transactions, traded ideas in anterooms and dining rooms, greased the political machine, and perfumed their sales with the smell of fine cigars. Keith probably did not think of himself as any worse than these new exploiters who did not usually kill their victims outright, but wore them down with poverty and exhaustion. It was an age of greed.

With this trip, Keith had spent his last resources and wasted precious time. He wired Cecelia on October 26 that he was returning immediately and sailed back on the *Republic*, taking his clock. At the Villa Thomas, Cecelia and the children were eagerly awaiting his return, when he suddenly burst into the parlor, threw himself down beside his wife, and began to cry. He said, "Oh, how I longed for this moment! I was in the house all last night." Cecelia pointed out to him that the house had been locked. He answered, "Well, I was about it. I walked around it again and again." Believing that her husband was suffering from some delusion, Cecelia tried to persuade him that he could not have been at the house. He finally admitted that he could not have been there, but had imagined it so perfectly he thought it real. Now extremely sensitive to her husband's violent mood swings, she was happy that he soon became cheerful, laughing and playing with his children.

But all was not well in Villa Thomas. Whatever few reserves Keith had were gone. He had not made good yet on his debt to the bank, as he had promised. There were other creditors who would soon be on their way. He faced arrest and imprisonment for his debts, the loss of his house, and abject poverty for his wife and children. Preparing for the foul weather outside, he put on his thin coat and scarf. "I do not want to grieve you by telling you," he told Cecelia," but I have to go away for a week or two." She began to cry. As he walked to the door, he turned and said, "I must go now, but this will be the last time."

ELEVEN

THE TRAVELING HUSBAND

Fearful of arousing the suspicions of the insurance underwriters in Liverpool, Keith now changed his base of operations to Bremen, a center of emigration and trade with businessmen crowding its hotels and transatlantic steamships regularly plying its busy nearby harbor. The city was known for the reasonable rates of its marine insurance companies that provided coverage for over $25 million dollars worth of goods every year, a powerful magnet for Keith. With all the transient business in Bremen, Keith hoped it would be easy to secure insurance without too many pesky questions. He checked into the Hotel Stadt Bremen, where, as he wrote to Cecelia, he had "a very comfortable room and a good bed." He then arranged for his dynamite-filled barrel, left in New York since June, to be shipped to him. He planned to strike well before Christmas so that he could get home to his wife, who was growing increasingly impatient and distressed with his odd behavior. She would be greatly appeased if he returned home a wealthy man. Studying the shipping schedules to find his next victim, his eye landed on a North German Lloyd steamer, the *Deutschland*, which was to sail in a few days.

He rented a carriage house on a busy street to serve as a workshop and began to reassemble his bomb. He took breaks from his work for lunch, which included a healthy quaff of beer, in his hotel. Then he went back to his engineering, thinking over what had gone wrong in his previous efforts. Carefully inspecting the clockworks, Keith found that they had been dirtied and damaged in the failed attempt on the *Celtic*. On November 29, he took the machine to the shop of a Bremen watchmaker, Friedrich Bruns, and discussed cleaning and repairs with Brun's assistant, Zimmerman. When Bruns later saw the clock, he was stunned at the skill with which it was made. Technically familiar only with small watches, he was astonished at the nearly silent efficiency of such a huge mechanism. He feared that his own skill would be lacking, but was excited by the challenge of fixing it. The work would mean a delay of some days, and the bomb would not be ready for a passage on the *Deutschland*. Keith now changed his target to the *Mosel*, but this would not save the *Deutschland* and her passengers from another disaster.

On December 4, the *Deutschland* sailed from Bremen for New York, carrying 230 passengers and crew. Three days later, one of her lifeboats came ashore on the coast of England, near Rochester. It held the exhausted quartermaster of the *Deutschland* and two other men who had died during their harrowing thirty-eight hour journey. The quartermaster, August Beck, reported that during a heavy snowstorm the steamship had gotten completely lost and had run aground on one of the treacherous sandbanks of the Kentish Knock, near the Thames Estuary. Captain Edward Brickenstein had ordered the lowering of a few lifeboats. Beck had been manning one when its tether snapped, collapsing the boat and throwing its occupants into the sea. Beck and two other men managed to heave themselves back into the lifeboat, but did not have the strength to row back to the ship against the blinding snow and driving wind. One of these men, a steerage passenger, had smashed his head against a hoist when he leapt frantically into the lifeboat and soon succumbed to his wound. Beck's other companion, a sailor, was lightly clad and had no socks or shoes, and though Beck tried desperately to keep him alive by vigorously rubbing his hands and feet, he too had died. When Beck reached shore, with the corpses at his feet and his hands nearly frozen to the oars, he was blackened with frostbite and near death. With the unexpected strength that comes to some people under extreme conditions, he had managed to row to shore. He remembered ruefully that his wife had had a premonition of an unlucky voyage for him.

As Beck told his story, a rescue ship managed to finally reach the *Deutschland*. The surviving passengers also told a grim tale. Many of them had been awoken by the sound of a loud crack as the ship's propeller broke. Alarmed, they hurriedly dressed and went out onto the freezing deck, where the captain assured them that rescue was nigh. However, no ship could reach them in the gale, and after some twenty hours, the ship began to flounder in the rough seas and high tide. The passengers, most of whom had taken refuge in the saloon, were ordered back onto the deck. Some experienced what disaster psychologists know as freeze panic, and unable to move forward or back they remained below decks. Numbed with shock, others automatically followed the voice of authority and took shelter wherever they could, huddling in the wheelhouse and clinging to the rigging. One by one, they were swept away.

Those who managed to keep their hold experienced the sluggishness, disorientation, and hallucinations of hypothermia. Feeling the uncontrollable desire to rest, a few simply let go and fell into the sea. One woman hung herself in the saloon. A man in the rigging slashed at his wrists with a penknife. Another tried to shoot himself, but was dissuaded by a woman who admonished him not to die the death of a coward. Shortly after, she fell and was drowned. A pair of new friends, Adolph Hermann, a Prussian farmer, and Bertha "Anna" Petzold, a physician's daughter, clung to the ropes together, using the time-honored remedy of whiskey to keep them warm. When the purser above them let go, he nearly took them with him as he tumbled to his death, but they hung tight. Adolph thought Anna was "the bravest girl of the century," and the couple would later announce their engagement, declaring that they had found love amidst their terrible ordeal. A Swedish passenger, Otto Lundgren, was not so lucky. He had managed to survive the *Schiller* disaster that had killed Keith's old friends the Suppigers only a few months before. It was his strange fate to again encounter the hostile sea, but this time, he would be counted with the missing. In all, sixty-four persons died during the long, cold day and night. Many of them were women and children.

When the remaining passengers and crew were near death, roped to whatever anchor they could find, the tug *Liverpool* managed to reach them. Her skipper, John Carrington, an old salty dog, said that it was the most perilous rescue he had ever attempted. On rough seas, 150 passengers and crew were pulled from the wreck and taken to Harwich. Those survivors who still wished to brave the ocean were given some oranges and twenty-seven shillings in charitable donations and put on a train for Southampton where they waited for the next ship. If they felt at all relieved, they would not be for long. The North German Lloyd Company, owners of the *Deutschland*, had offered them passage on Keith's next target, the *Mosel*.

As he came to the end of his machinations in Bremen, Keith heard news of the *Deutschland* wreck and wrote to Cecelia: "The people who were saved were 28 hours in the rigging during that dreadful cold wether drenched with salt water day and night, and got frozen and dropped off the rigging into the sea to be herd of no more. I new the Captain very well, he is the Captain that Mrs. Stewart [the American consul's wife] went over to America with and she liked him so much, he is not lost." What a strange letter this was. If Keith had fulfilled his original plan to bomb the *Deutschland*, no one would have survived, including his alleged friend Captain Brickenstein. A popular and capable officer with sixteen years' experience, Brickenstein had just recently been made captain of the *Deutschland*, and the fatal voyage was his first trip out with her. Prior to this appointment, Brickenstein had captained another Lloyd steamship, the *Rhein*, targeted by Keith in June. Oblivious to his brush with evil, Brickenstein had blithely piloted the *Rhein* with Keith's ticking barrel onboard, but had escaped destruction. Keith had thus twice intended to annihilate Brickenstein, who had never done him any harm and for whom he expressed an interest, for he always liked to befriend captains. To be sure, any acquaintance with Keith was an extremely dangerous business. In Keith's imagination, which romanticized violence, the shipwreck he caused would be just as harrowing and grand and tragic as the newspapers made the *Deutschland*'s.

He wrote Cecelia, his "little hennie" and his "own little darling," every few days from Bremen, complaining of having the sniffles, of the dreary weather. His letters were full of kisses and loving words for Blanche, Willie, Klina, and little baby May.

My darling Pett. This being one of the days that you and I like so much, raw cold and bleake with a little rain. I thought that I could not occupie myself better than to sit down, and write a few lines to those that are so dear to me. . . . I have all of your fotographs and I have them open on the table before me, so that I can have some consolation on this miserable day. I enjoy them as much it brings me as near as I can get to you just now, you sweetes of darlings. Oh if I had lotts of money what a good time we could now have with such pretty dear good children. I hope you are all enjoying as well as possible in my absence there are lotts of Americans going and coming to this place every week one steamer going to America, and one returning full of passengers all complaining of the bad times.

Cecelia was growing more and more worried that her husband had not returned. She rightly suspected that he was lying and about to disappear on one of his trips to America again. At first, she tried to wheedle him, writing that she was so lonesome she was sleeping with their little ones, and that they were all frightened. Their friend, George Griswold, she wrote, had disappeared for a whole night in New York and his friends had reported him missing to the newspapers. When Griswold reappeared he claimed to have fallen and struck his head on a curb. No one in his old American circle in Dresden really believed the story, suspecting instead that Griswold had an extended rendezvous with a mistress. Cecelia called Griswold "a dirty old beast" and admonished her husband, "You better take care they don't say something of that kind about you old fellow!" She wrote that if he did not return soon, "I'll be *jealous* for I begin to have all manner of *thoughts* about you." Although he was busy booking passage on the *Mosel* and getting his bomb ready, Keith replied to her, "You must not be afraid I will run away to America again. I do not intend to go for some time again so you can rest quiet on that subject. I must remain here for a few days longer." With a far worse crime in mind, he assured her that he was not seeing other women: "Keepe your mind at eas as I know you are always having some awful dream or other, that disturbs your equelebrium for a day or two."

On December 9, just two days before the *Mosel* was set to sail, Keith sent his wife 200 marks to buy rubbers for the children and take care of other small expenses. Cecelia was not happy with the money, for, she wrote, "it proves that you are going to be away much longer than I hoped you would be!" Cecelia's letters, usually neat and cheerful, now began to ramble, revealing her sense of entrapment, frantic fear, and anger:

the servants are frightened to death to sleep below in the kitchen, they say they are sure they will be murdered some night and hear all kinds of strange sounds so that I have lost all patience with them & would have pitched them out long ago if I could get decent ones to stay. And another thing, we are fairly snowed upon the snow lies four feet deep all around the house & on the balcony it is almost up to the windows—imagine thaw weather setting in everyone says that it will be impossible to stir out of the house during all the spring . . . you know it was bad enough before you went away and one seldom sees a droshcke pass now so that when one would like to go to town one could not—for instance tomorrow we are all to go to Funkes little baby & all of course I cannot go on account of not being able to take the little baby out, it is too far to carry her or to take her little wagon the snow is too deep & it is too cold anyhow so if we could get a droshcke to take & bring us [we] might possibly go, but no one will undertake the job—after dark you can't hire them to drive out so far & now it is dark at four o'clock. I assure you I have not been out of the house since you left but once to Funkes and another time I got ready to go but it looked so hopelessly cold & the snow was so deep that I've turned back—it makes me quite sick to stay in the house so much, I need *air* and crave it just as much as I crave meat without it I cannot live.

Still afraid that he was seeing another woman, she finally turned to threats:

> *I want to know positively whether you are coming back before Christmas or not!* Tell me the honest truth—I can stand *that* much better than uncertainty—You are very wrong in letting me be in the dark & keeping me in suspence like a little child—I am old enough. . . . *Therefore no secrets any longer towards me;* tell me plainly how long you are going to be away. (I do not wish to know what is keeping you) Christmas is coming along so very fast & if you are not here a few days before, I'll take my children & go away with them. . . .

Keith replied, trying to appease her. Playing the role of a devoted husband who had to carry out his necessary business as the breadwinner, he referred vaguely to the unavoidable delays of his work that would soon bring them relief from their bills. "Now do be patient a few days longer," he wrote, "and you will have your fattie with you all winter." He would be home for Christmas, he told her, "if the devil was to stand between you and I."

Ignoring the pleas of his wife, he had now booked a ticket on the *Mosel* from Bremen to Southampton. Everything was ready, despite some annoying difficulties in the preparation. He had tried a grand scheme to get twenty-seven chests insured with the Bremen financial firm Kafesch and Stossky but could not seal the deal, finally complaining that the premium was too high. He finally managed to get insurance on a barrel of supposed caviar for 3,000 marks, or about £150. It was hardly enough to make up his expenses for the past two years. But he also had another box that he once again represented as being full of greenbacks. As had now become his futile, obsessive habit, he would try to get the box insured onboard ship. And if nothing else, he could see if his bomb really worked.

In Southampton, the passengers from the wrecked *Deutschland* waited for the *Mosel*. They had experienced a reality well outside the nineteenth-century literary imagination of a picturesque shipwreck in which passengers penned last notes to their loved ones and even the most debased harlots and villains repented of their deeds and met death with calm resignation. The survivors knew themselves as human beings who had struggled in the most painfully human ways. Anna Petzold was not an eighteen-year-old girl who'd found her savior, as the newspapers portrayed her, but a mature twenty-five-year-old woman who'd spent a grim seven hours in a life preserver, gripping the ropes, watching her fellow creatures fall to their deaths. Despite the tales of heroism and salvation, the *Deutschland* survivors had been beaten by the waves, blackened by frostbite, and traumatized by their witness of chaos and untold horrors. Subject to flashbacks and recurrent nightmares, they had been forced to question the ordinary meanings of their complacent lives and even their God. Their dead friends and loved ones from the wreck had been stripped of any valuable mementoes by greedy, unscrupulous salvagers. Now Keith was moving toward them, declaring sympathy for their suffering while setting the worth of their collective lives at a mere 3,000 marks.

TWELVE

THE DYNAMITE FIEND

On the morning of December 11, 1875, Sandy Keith rose, had his usual full breakfast in his Bremen hotel, and wrote a letter to his wife, whom he knew was growing more and more frantic about his absence. "I have had a troublesome work on hand that has detained me longer than I expected," he explained, "but I am in hopes all will be right now so that I can remain quietly with those that I love so much, and that likes me so well." The wreck of the *Deutschland* was on his mind as he stepped out into the winter morning with his luggage. He could no longer afford furs, and wearing only a thin cloth coat, he passed through the streets of Bremen, where Christmas vendors filled every niche, displaying their wares of shining toys and trinkets, the scent of *Stollen*, sausage, and roasted almonds reminding Keith of his insatiable hunger and his lack of means to fulfill it.

Envisioning the catastrophe he was about to cause, he hurried to the rented carriage house and arranged for some porters to transport his heavy barrel, telling them to exercise special caution with it. He then took a carriage to the *Bahnhof*, where he would board the train from Bremen to its harbor, Bremerhaven. The station, with its narrow halls, was bustling with people coming and going, but the mood was subdued as travelers read in their newspapers of the *Deutschland* wreck. Working impressively hard at maintaining a calm and genial persona, Keith boarded the train. The carriage was crowded with emigrants, scrubbed clean for the two-week voyage, their hand luggage packed with woolen blankets and picnics of wine, bread, cheese, and sausage. Stowed in a rear luggage car, the bomb was armed and ready, the spring poised to land on the blasting cap and blow all the train's passengers to kingdom come. The passengers felt a need for conversation and began to talk openly about their fears. Keith participated in a lively way, combating the scenarios of shipwrecks with the tone of a much more experienced ocean voyager. Just as he handled his wife Keith handled his fellow travelers, convincing them of his benevolence, his friendliness, and his pleasant character, hiding the truth of his malevolence behind his golden spectacles.

At the harbor, Keith left the barrel behind in Lloyd's luggage hall. The snow was beginning to melt now, and his way down to the ship was wet and slushy. He stood on the dock in the salt air waiting to board the *Mosel*. A mountain of iron, the ship loomed over him, dwarfing its tug, *Simson*. Keith had carefully calculated just how much dynamite it would take to blow up such a giant and where his bomb should be placed for maximum effect, and his planning would soon reach its apotheosis. The *Mosel* would become another romantic ghost story, a sister of the *City of Boston*, haunting the transatlantic routes. By then he would have gotten off in Southampton and traveled home to the Villa Thomas to await his modest success and then, just in time for Christmas, heap the table with bon-bons, fruit, and gifts for his eager children. Before him was a gloriously sunny day, ice breaking up and floating into the harbor from the River Weser. It was auspicious weather for an ocean voyage. He saw dockworkers and sailors bustling about making last preparations, yelling out gruff commands. Many travelers had gone onboard, and felt relieved by the splendid size of the ship, the warm welcome from the ship's staff, and the order and punctuality with which their effects were taken and stowed. A throng of passengers and their loved ones still congregated on the south side of the quay, opposite the lighthouse. Unwilling to say their last goodbyes until the final bell, they huddled in the sun to stay warm, clutching their hand luggage, the women holding their babies closer and pulling their shawls tighter around them. Businessmen hurried about, making last-minute preparations.

Charles Mueller was also standing on the dock. He was a merchant of human hair, one of the major German exports since after the war, when fashionable American women had developed a mania for expensive blonde wigs. Mueller had bought 126 pounds of yellow hair and was now returning home to Milwaukee. He thought he recognized Keith and approached him: "Excuse me, but are you not from Milwaukee?" Keith responded in German that he was indeed an American, but not from that city. Chatting with the stranger, Mueller found Keith a very amiable man, "a scholar and a genial fellow." They switched comfortably to English, talking of their accommodations, and when Mueller said he was traveling only second class, Keith, with his usual sociability, said they would meet onboard anyway. Calm and jovial, with nerves of steel, he gave not the slightest hint of his dark purpose.

The two men made their way up the gangway and parted. Keith went to his first-class cabin, purchased on credit, and arranged his belongings before coming back up onto the deck, his favorite spot for voyaging. He preferred always to be outside, watching his past and future shores. He milled about with the other passengers, looking out at the shining ocean or down at the dock where stevedores were still hauling luggage, businessmen were finishing up with firm handshakes, and small knots of families and friends were wistfully hugging and kissing and bidding their last farewells. Young Fritz Zumann raced ahead to board the ship, while his brother lingered behind with his aunt and uncle on the dock, unwilling to let go so soon. Keith watched all these proceedings with cool detachment. When a policeman from Bremerhaven approached him and demanded his papers, Keith remained calm. "Do I look anything like a criminal?" he asked. But the man insisted they go below and get his passport. They went down the narrow stairs to Keith's cabin, where the policeman confirmed that Keith was not the man for whom he was looking.

The ship's last bell rang out. The lingerers now bade their final farewells and rushed to the gangway. Families and friends waited to see the great ship leave its moorings, sadly watching their loved ones waving from the decks high above them. Workmen were still clattering down the dock, accompanying a horse drawn cart with the last of the baggage. Near the *Mosel*, they began attaching a large, extremely heavy barrel to the winch when it slipped and fell. The mechanism inside lurched, the hammer prematurely snapped down onto the firing cap, and the dockworkers suddenly vanished in a tremendous explosion.

All that was left of the horse was its hooves, lying on the boards like a surreal nightmare.

After leaving his new friend, Charles Mueller had walked to his cabin and was milling about the hall when he was suddenly struck with a great blast of fiery wind, an immense blow that threw him down a set of stairs. Everyone on board the ship had been thrown to the ground and was unable to move for several minutes. When Mueller was finally able to get to his feet, he asked the steward nearby what had happened, and the steward replied that he believed the ship's boiler had exploded. In a state of dreamlike shock, Mueller went out onto the deck and struggled to help the wounded and the dying. In the carefully controlled, matter-of-fact way that people recount their traumas, Mueller said: "I covered up the nakedness of several of the dead, both men and women. I saw a Hebrew on a trunk stripped of his clothing and apparently wounded, his head was falling back and he appeared to be suffocating. I took some bedclothes out of the trunk burst open by the explosion, and made a comfortable seat for him. Five minutes afterward he died." Mueller then "attended a young lady screaming for help, denuded of all her clothing to her waist." His first thought was to cover the humiliation of her nakedness. Though Mueller lost only his cargo of hair and some bolts of silk he intended as a present to his wife, the pain and horror of these moments were forever etched in his mind.

Standing in the cabin below, Keith and the police officer too had been thrown down by the concussion. Keith instantly knew what had happened but said nothing. He quickly gathered some of his possessions into a saddlebag, and the two men ran up the stairs and out onto the deck. Keith's only wish was to escape the carnage on the ship. A rain of iron and wood, blackened bodies and body parts had fallen onto every part of the ship, even flying through gangways. The windows had shattered, and the bow, including two strong iron struts, had caved under the pressure of the concussion. All the passengers above, after recovering from the violent shock, had rushed over the promenade deck to the stern where they stood shivering, bewildered and confused, their ears ringing from the blast. A witness described what they saw below on the quay: "A monstrous field of corpses spread out before us. The misery and the moans of horrifically dismembered reached our ears. Burning scraps of clothing covered their amputated limbs. With tear-filled eyes we turned away. The misery was too great. The knowledge of having been spared such a terrible death increased our feverish agitation. Everyone rushed to the gangway. It had disappeared." Highly agitated, Keith ran up to the captain, struck half deaf by the explosion, who was yelling out commands to his crew. Keith insisted to him that that he must get to Bremen for he had an urgent telegram to send. The captain pointed out the obvious fact that the gangway was gone and there was no getting out. They were all trapped.

Keith went to the rail and looked down on a scene of incomprehensible carnage, the bloodbath he had caused but had never imagined he would have to witness. It was all supposed to take place out on the desolate ocean where the victims would quietly disappear. He believed in the new emerging rule of war, with its remote technologies that could kill at a distance, where the faceless enemy would fall without provoking the guilt of witness. Obsessed with war, he embraced violence only in an impersonal and cerebral way, without risk to his own person. He was a strategist, not a soldier. But now he faced war's chaotic reality, bodies blown to bloody bits, showered across the decks and floating in the harbor. The gaping hole. The shattered glass and twisted iron. The acrid smell of smoke and the terrible sharp smell of blood. The unidentifiable bodies in the water. The low murmur and terrible vulnerability of the stunned, the wounded, and the dying. He tried to kill his thoughts and his senses by drinking deeply from his schnapps flask, but alcohol would not shield him.

He went back down to his cabin and picked up a pencil. In a large, shaking hand, he first addressed a note to Mrs. C. F. Thomas: "God bless you and my darling children, you will never see my [*sic*] to speak to again. William." Then he wrote another:

To The Captain of the
Steamer Mosel
Please Send this
money you will find
in my pocket —
20 pounds sterling
80 marks German money

My wife resides at
14 Residenze Strasse

Strehlen
by Dresden

What I have seen today
I cannot stand
W K Thomas

He took off his jacket, sat down on his couch, and fired two bullets into his head.

But the world was not yet done with Sandy Keith. The *Mosel* was towed to another part of the harbor and boarded by rescuers. Walking through the saloon cabins, they heard some moaning and groaning in one of them. They tried to open the cabin door, found it locked, and smashed it down. Inside they found Keith lying on the floor, unconscious and breathing with difficulty, his face bloody. They called for the doctors, who, after a cursory examination in the dim cabin, first thought Keith had been injured in the explosion. There was not much blood since he was suffering from a head wound. Learning that the cabin had been locked from the inside, the doctors searched it and under the couch, found a six-chambered revolver. Two bullets were missing. Now they saw the strange truth: In the midst of the inexplicable horror of the event, this passenger had tried to kill himself. One of the shots had gone upwards into Keith's cheek and lodged in his cortex behind his right eye, paralyzing the left side of his body. His failure was total: Not only had he failed in his plan, but he had even failed in his suicide. With the help of six sailors, the doctors rolled Keith's corpulent body into a blanket, heaved him onto a stretcher with some difficulty, and carried him to the makeshift infirmary in a harbor barrack where the victims of his crime lay moaning, some in their death throes.

Among the wounded were many members of a single family, the ill-fated Etmers, who had come to see their son off to the West Indies, and who were still standing on the dock when the bomb detonated. The mother's arm had been broken. One sister lost her right hand; two others suffered wounds in their hands, faces, and legs. A sister-in-law lost her left foot; a brother-in-law was seriously wounded in the stomach. Six of the Etmers were killed outright. Relatives of other victims were moving about the infirmary, searching desperately for their loves ones or coming to identify their dead.

It was a sad, heartrending business to identify the horrifically disfigured and dismembered corpses. It was the torn remnant of clothing, a briefcase, a ring or some other sign that gave the relatives the painful certainty of their loss. Moving scenes of nameless pain repeated themselves at the hospital. A mother found instead of her anxiously sought daughter, only her fur muff still containing her hands. A father had the head of his son brought into his house. One passenger . . . sought for a long time the remnants of his father, but all he found was a blown off hand which he identified by the ring. That was all he could bring back to his grieving family.

And yet these scenes of stunned horror, many of them taking place around Keith, would not even wring a tear from the utterly self-absorbed perpetrator.

Every day, the doctors and nurses, who had been rushed to the disaster site by train, came to work through the streets of Bremerhaven, filled with broken mirror and glass. Every window near the harbor had been shattered. Doors had been blown off their hinges and broken. The citizens of Bremerhaven walked dejectedly, their faces marked with horror and deep sorrow. The medics watched the town pull together in rescue efforts to aid the wounded and give comfort to two hundred grieving widows and orphans. Those treating Keith had quickly guessed that he was somehow responsible for this misery.

As the doctors tended him, he returned to consciousness. He could no longer feel the left side of his body, his eyesight was blurred and difficult to control, and he felt a searing pain in his cheek where the bullet had entered his head. The doctors immediately demanded to know why he had tried to take his own life. He gave his motive as the realization that he was bankrupt, that he could not survive the disgrace to his family. Dissatisfied and suspicious at the odd coincidences of the case, the doctors urgently attempted to get a further confession. "You are dying," they said, "and will never get a second chance." But Keith tenaciously held to his story. The police came to interrogate him. They plied him with wine and brought witnesses, among them a Bremen insurance agent and one of the clockmakers, Bruns, who came forward to admit their unwitting parts in the crime. But still Keith would not budge. Well versed in criminal psychology, Chief Inspector P. J.

Schnepel asked Keith to think of the fate of his children, a poignant re-
minder that seemed to grab Keith by his soul. He was unsettled enough
to make a partial confession, two days after the catastrophe, but he was
extremely terse, cryptic and evasive, often changing his story, his usual
stew of truth and falsehood.

Never revealing that he was really Sandy Keith, the brewer's son
from Halkirk and Halifax, he told the police that he had been born in
Brooklyn in 1830 of parents who had emigrated from Hamburg and
then moved to Virginia. All lies. He said he had several brothers, that
his family was Protestant, that he had been married in St. Louis and
was father of five children, one dead. All true. He claimed that his real
name was William King Thomson, rather than Thomas, that he was
forced to change his name during the Civil War because of his blockade-running activities. A lie. Unable to suppress his compulsion to brag,
even in his last hours, he said that he had been owner and captain of the
blockade-running ship the *Old Dominion*. A lie: He was the *Old Dominion*'s purchasing agent and only visited the ship when she was lying in
Halifax Harbor. He admitted that he had received a barrel shipped on
the *Rhein* and that he had worked through the broker Skidmore. True,
but he claimed Skidmore was a swindler and the mastermind behind
the plot. Although he kept changing his story about the barrel, waver-
ing between whether its contents were a bomb or only polishing paste,
he kept trying to shift the blame to Skidmore and the "fellows in New
York," implying that he had been their innocent dupe. Although he
often talked of his children, expressing his great fondness for them, he
stated that he felt no remorse and that he was not such a bad man. The
family of Etmers, laying near him, surely had a different opinion.

By day four, Keith had begun desperately trying to yank off his
bandages, hoping he would bleed to death. The doctors held him down
with irons. Fixed to his bed, he begged the doctors to remove the bullets from his head, but they told him the operation would lead to certain death. Hoping for further revelations about the murderer's
accomplices and motives, the doctors and the police were in no hurry
to let him die. They continued to pepper him with questions, a secretary sitting nearby to record his few terse sentences, spoken in child-
like German. Many journalists and curiosity seekers were allowed free
access to Keith as he lay suffering these agonies. Trying to make sense
of such a man and his confused stories, they saw what they wanted to

see. Some found a vulnerable penitent, others a shifty, cold, evasive murderer. One visitor was Charles Mueller, the merchant of human hair who had met Keith on the dock before the explosion. Wondering whether such an amiable man could truly have been a mass murderer, Mueller came to confront him. When he approached the killer's bedside, Keith said, "I wish that I was dead" and closed his eyes. Thinking he detected traces of tears on Keith's face, Mueller admonished him, "It is wrong, sir, to wish that you were dead." Keith repeated, "I wish I was dead." But if Mueller saw something like remorse, a visiting journalist heard only cold consideration in the killer's contradictory confessions and a lurking malevolence previously hidden behind those grayish-blue eyes.

Others too believed that a second, evil nature had suddenly been revealed in the respectable "William King Thomas," that he must have been possessed by a psychological demon. Thus, he became popularly known the "Dynamite Fiend." The German magazine *Die Gartenlaube* positioned its description of the last days of William King Thomas above a serialized novel called *The Doppelgänger.* It is strangely appropriate that Keith—the loving family man whose alter ego was a calculating murderer—ended up in Germany, where the notion of the doppelgänger was first conceived. The fictional doppelgänger (literally "second walker") was a fully embodied alter ego that manifested the repressed, narcissistic, often violent impulses of the primary self: Dr. Jekyll's Mr. Hyde. In Robert Louis Stevenson's brilliant psychological novel, Dr. Jekyll explains his bizarre dual personality: "Henry Jekyll stood at times aghast before the acts of Edward Hyde; but the situation was apart from ordinary laws, and insidiously relaxed the grasp of conscience. It was Hyde, after all, and Hyde alone, that was guilty. Jekyll was no worse; he woke again to his good qualities seemingly unimpaired; he would even make haste, where it was possible, to undo the evil done by Hyde. And thus his conscience slumbered." The history of Sandy Keith, a.k.a. William King Thomas, was resonant with the Hyde-like workings of a hidden self. In a grand, horrific style, his life materialized the great Gothic themes of violence and terror, dark fantasy, technological obsession, compulsive repetition, psychic conflict, and sudden revelation of a demonic inner self.

In the Christian world of nineteenth-century Europe and America, demonic possession was still invoked to explain such criminal madness.

The newspaper reporters saw within Sandy Keith a cunning fiend, a devilish spirit that lurked and suddenly emerged to take control of him. The period's Gothic fiction was preoccupied with how to read a person for signs of a malevolent demon. A flash of lightning, a certain angle of the face, a reflection in the mirror, a glint in the eye could expose an evil personality hidden within the unconscious mind of a friend or loved one. Keith's golden spectacles seemed to hide the trace of his demonic nature, revealed in his narrow gray eyes. In the nineteenth century, the possibility of a shadow self became an obsession of popular literature that often linked it to science. It is Dr. Jekyll's scientific curiosity and his compulsive tinkering in his laboratory that leads to the emergence of the murderous Mr. Hyde. Keith's secret obsession with the new technology's potential for violence and mayhem had at last emerged into full public view.

The public on both sides of the Atlantic were fascinated with the science of the crime, wondering if invention and technological progress were, in fact, evil, unleashing inner demons, making humans ever more capable of new modes of violence. They struggled to understand the complexity of Keith's engineering. The three principal clockmakers all came forward with their stories, which were widely printed. They had friendly arguments over the exact design of the device that exploded at Bremerhaven, and all rued, surprisingly, that they had not designed sturdier models. Otto Martin, who had first introduced Keith to J. J. Fuchs, told the press that if Keith had been clear about the purpose of the clock, "the genius of the master craftsman Fuchs would have been able to take care that the lever would not have been released through a strong shake or blow." A science professor, Dr. Hapke, borrowed Fuch's prototype from the police for a public demonstration, emphasizing the power of the spring, the latent energy of the explosive, and what triggered the accidental blow. The mechanical design and long-range rational planning made it apparent that Thomas was not a deluded lunatic. Rather, he was a coldly deliberate scientific fiend. As the *New York Herald* concluded, "Only a monster could carry such a design into execution, and it is hard to conceive how even a monster could conceive it."

Offsetting this Gothic portrait of the scientific fiend was the smallness and sheer meanness of Keith's motive, the banality of his evil. Keith was not driven by lunacy or revenge, but by a paltry greed: His only object appeared to be money. It was astonishing to think that without any external signs of malice, a seemingly ordinary man had planned to kill hundreds of people just to keep his small family in ease and comfort. Keith's organizational planning and technical skills were appalling in their application and his motives base and utterly heartless. Unaware that the killer had once had an intimate connection with the greedy war profiteering in that city, the editor of the *Montreal Gazette* explained, "Here was a man who in a cool business way, without having ever exhibited any malignity or even unkindness or moroseness towards his fellows, spent months in contriving a plot which was to sweep away a vessel and all onboard in mid-ocean, and leave no trace of the satanic artifact behind." In many ways, newspaper editors saw in Keith an extreme example of the Gilded Age, when profit so often took precedence over people. He seemed to have the violence of an extraordinary monster and the greed of a rather ordinary businessman. As W. C. Church and F. P. Church, the editors of the literary journal *Galaxy*, explained, Keith "went into the destruction of ocean steamers, freighted with hundreds of human beings who were entire strangers to him, as a business, just as he would have gone into selling breadstuffs, or making pianofortes." Furthermore, the Churches wrote, "If most men or many men are capable of such plots the sooner the earth explodes itself the better."

Many felt this apocalyptic dread as they contemplated Keith's crime, which seemed to represent a new, unfathomable side of human nature. In an age without newspaper photographs, the *London Times* correspondent in Bremen spread the story worldwide with his graphic eyewitness descriptions of the scene's aftermath, enough to horrify the most jaded readers: "As in an anatomical dissecting-room, all the individual limbs of the human body might be seen lying about separately in ghastly isolation. Here a head was stuck on a railing, while a hand was seen pointing at space from a windowsill. More horrible, perhaps, than the lacerated limbs whose outward shape was sufficiently preserved to admit of recognition, were the formless masses of flesh strewn in very direction, mixed up with arms and feet." This was a chaotic, disorienting world in which nothing could be recognized, in which nothing made sense. It seemed worse than any war, for war had a certain formal logic, while the Bremerhaven catastrophe was an apocalyptic breakdown of all civilized reason. The reporter pulled at his audience's tender emotions, describing the empty coats, shawls, boots and shoes strewn about in the wreckage: "An infant's shoe was seen, empty, asking for the tiny foot which had tenanted it that morning." It was impossible to read this account without being moved and sickened, without feeling shock at the atrocity. If Keith was capable of such a moral obscenity, than others could be too, making human beings worse than the devil himself.

The famous abolitionist Jane Swisshelm, traveling in Germany at the time, wrote home her analysis that it was Keith's Scots family origins that had driven him to these depths, that he had been raised under a stern parental injunction: "Get money, my son! Get money—honestly if thee can; but get the money!" That Scots ethnic stereotype was not the only one conjured to explain Keith's psychology. Because Keith claimed to have been born in the United States, some newspaper commentators in Germany thought that Keith represented the American national character, with its rough-and-tumble provincialism, stupidity, lack of moral refinement, and unmitigated greed, an analysis that provoked an outcry among Americans at home and abroad. A German immigrant to the United States, Missouri Senator Carl Schurz, made a speech defending the "earnest and manly spirit" of the American people, saying they were "one of the most intelligent races in the world." In Berlin, expatriate Americans held a public meeting on the matter, chaired by Rev. Joseph P. Thompson. Once an editor of the *New Englander* but now a permanent resident of Berlin, this Thompson believed in all nations working for a better civil and social life. He remained an ardent American patriot, but had an equal loyalty to Germany. When the Bremerhaven crime cast doubt on American national pride, Thompson and his like-minded expatriates wrote a public statement that read, "We do not feel called upon to defend American civilization from the charge of a mercenary and materialistic spirit, lacking all idealistic culture, serving as a school of violence and giving but new ingenuity and intensity to crime." Instead, the participants called for cooperation between nations to maintain vigilance against a repeat of steamship bombings, quoting the German Empress Augusta, who said: "Such a crime touches upon humanity, not upon nationality."

There were those in the United States who were not so sure, especially after William King Thomas's true origins were revealed. Still fu-

rious about England's hidden involvement in the Civil War and undoubtedly alerted to the dynamite disaster by his old friend Donn
Piatt, the journalist George Alfred Townsend cast blame back upon
Europe and its support of the Confederacy, stating that Keith's crime
was "to be scored up to the long account of monsters produced in the
imperial scheme of creating a slave republic, an experiment abetted by
England, whose colonial subject he was." Townsend was perhaps the
most astute of all in analyzing Keith's contacts with Confederate terrorists and his former involvement with casual slaughters that most
clearly led to the terrible outcome at Bremerhaven. If it was not precisely Scotland, England, or Canada that was to blame, it was the dis-
integrating ethics and moral chaos of the brutal Civil War that gave
Keith's violent thoughts their full range. Despite the contest of nations
over their responsibility for Keith, the international aspects of his identity—his international business connections and his life in Scotland,
Canada, the United States, and Prussia—remained difficult to resolve.
Perhaps the particular conditions of war, not of any national character,
were to blame for unleashing Sandy Keith's Edward Hyde. The violent
mythologies of the oppressed and displaced Scots had filled him with
the anger and avariciousness; a military outpost had given him a taste
for romantic violence; and the Confederate terrorist campaigns had exposed him to the technology, the ruthlessness, and the callousness required to execute these plots.

However one might explain Keith's character and motivation, most
appalling to everyone was his refusal to engage in any self-reflection, to
apologize publicly and show remorse for his deed. In fiction, characters like Dr. Jekyll are usually tortured by protracted conflict with
their evil second natures, leading to acute self-realization and often
self-destruction. Unlike Keith, Jekyll left a suicide note that revealed
remorse for his hidden murderousness: "No one has ever suffered such
torments, let that suffice; and yet even to these, habit brought—no, not
alleviation—but a certain callousness of soul, a certain acquiescence of
despair; and my punishment might have gone on for years, but for the
last calamity which has now fallen, and which has finally severed me
from my own face and nature." Those who sought justice could only
hope that the Dynamite Fiend suffered similar psychological torments
of his exposed duality. But as he lay dying, if he faced his own despair-

ing and murderous soul, if he feared a final damnation, he refused to give any satisfaction, explaining to his doctors, "I have had ill luck; that's all." Deeply secretive to the end, he remained a riddle, a cipher, a mystery even to his wife who would come in his last hours to beg him for a confession.

THIRTEEN

CECELIA'S JOURNEY

In the Villa Thomas, the panicky Cecelia was feeling slightly cheered by the sun on the frosty snowfields outside her window. It had been a long time coming, after weeks of oppressive cold and gloom. Restless with cabin fever, still feeling her rheumatism deep in her joints, Cecelia was reserving hope that her husband would honor her wish to return to their old apartments in Leipzig, where she could be near her good friends, the Steuarts, who had just dropped by. They had briefly distracted her from dwelling on her desperate financial straits, for this year she did not know how she could buy presents for her children or even afford the Christmas turkey. The children expected the winged Christ child to arrive on Christmas Eve and ring the silver bell, but there would be no skates, no china dolls, no tin soldiers this year. All pretenses were gone. Two days before, she had written to her prodigal husband, "I wish there was no such thing as Christmas!" She feared that any minute the bill collectors would come demanding the debts on the furniture, the bolts of cloth, the new glassware for the table, the wine for entertaining. Instead, the knock on the door came from a boy who delivered an urgent telegram addressed to William Thomas and signed "Thomas": "Wretchedly sick. Come on here. Meet at the Lloyd Agent Bremerhaven."

Confused because of its bizarre address, strange formality, and wording in German instead of their usual English, Cecelia immediately sent a reply to her husband at his hotel, "Are you ill and do you want me to come to you, or who is the dispatch from? Answer immediately almost crazy." But an answer did not come. The Christmas season had brought Cecelia emotional chaos once before, when she and her new husband had been forced to flee the peaceful utopia of Highland. In a state of extreme anxiety, unable to sleep, Cecelia wrote a letter to her husband that night, saying that he would be the death of her:

> write, or telegraph immediately whether I must come or whether it is a mistake. I scarcely know what I am saying—it is in the middle of the night & this letter cannot go before tomorrow morning yet I must write it. Write me just one line & tell me for God's sake the truth, the whole truth. It is unfair never to tell me anything of your movements because in a case of this kind or other where unforeseen circumstances occur a great deal of anguish might be prevented—write and write at once I can not think that you are sick, for I received your letter dated 9th Dec. & you were then when you wrote it apparently in good health!

The next day a detective arrived at her door, saying he had come to take her to Bremen. By this time, Cecelia had heard of the tragedy at the dock, for word was traveling fast, and she thought perhaps her husband had been injured. Without revealing anything much, the detective simply told her that her husband had attempted suicide.

Before boarding the train with the detective, Cecelia telegrammed the Steuarts to ask if they had heard any news of her husband. They had not. She asked Mrs. Steuart to care for the children, and she took only the nine-month-old baby, May, still breastfeeding. All along the way, she saw curiosity seekers who congregated at the depots, trying to catch a glimpse of her, but she did not realize why they were staring. Already, the news was out on the wires that her husband, "William King Thomas" of Dresden, the most devilish murderer of the century, had tried to commit suicide on the *Mosel*. If somehow this information reached her aboard the train, she could not absorb it in her dazed shock. When she arrived in Bremen, another police detective was awaiting her. Still confused, she assumed her husband had sent the detective as a kindness to her. Holding May, she stood on the platform, looking out at a vast throng of people weeping as the long, somber line of forty-three hearses, some bearing only a single limb, moved in procession down the street. Moved by the great grief of the crowd, she wept too.

She was taken to a hotel where she was visited by a Bremen police inspector who revealed the awful story of her husband's crime. Horrified, she asked him to repeat it and he did. Now the interrogation began, for the police could not believe that Cecelia had been oblivious to Keith's activities. How could her husband have traveled, received parcels, met with a clockmaker in their home, and tinkered out in the storage shed at their old apartments in Leipzig without her asking questions? How could she have ignored their dire financial state and not asked her husband exactly what he intended to do about it? And what too, the police wondered, had happened to a parcel, weighing 2.5 kilos, that Keith had sent from Bremen to Dresden on November 27? Cecelia denied ever receiving it. Cecelia's letters to her husband had been found in his pocket, and suggested that she was curious about his plans, relayed information from the banks, and was suffering under the acute pressure of bill collectors. Under intense questioning, she seemed evasive about her husband's activities and acquaintances, though she slipped once and called him "Alexander." That was a critical clue to William King Thomas's real identity. It also showed that Cecelia knew that her husband was living under an assumed name and at least was an accomplice in this deception. At this point, before Cecelia would reveal any more personal information, including her maiden name, she asked to speak to the American consul in Leipzig, her friend and important protector, John Steuart. Now the Bremen investigators began treating Cecelia with kid gloves, claiming that they did not have enough evidence to hold her.

They agreed to let her see her dying husband, but only in the presence of police officers and only if the conversation was completely in German. However, they made her wait an entire day. Taking her familiar role as his comforter, she wrote a letter to the man she had married as "Alexander King Thompson," but with whom she had lived for ten years in Germany as "William":

My good my poor William
I am here with our youngest baby. My heart is broken. May God take care and protect our poor children. If I could shield

you & our poor babies against all harm how I willingly would I give the last drop of my hearts blood! You know how dearly we love you—perhaps their prayers will still save you. They pray every night for their dear darling papa. It was your great love for us, your only joy & your only care in this world, that caused you to take that awful step—let me come to you and talk to you, let me come and look into your good kind face again—that face so full of affection & beaming with pleasure when you look at us & thought us happy. Oh poor poor William no one knows your great goodness, no one can fathom that poor broken heart but your poor unhappy wife. It was to save & shield her & her babies, to give us ease & comfort, that you staked more than your life—

When this letter was read to him, Keith expressed barely any interest in seeing his wife, and asked the doctor to leave him in peace and not to pester him with any more intrusions.

The next morning, after a long medical examination, Keith was declared near death, yet he had moments of lucidity. His wife was led to him, and trembling and breathing with great difficulty he recognized her and reached out a limp hand to her. He was a terrible sight, the left side of his face slack from paralysis, his right eye swollen almost shut. To the acute embarrassment of all the witnesses to this scene, Cecelia said several times, "Doctor, kill him! Kill him!" Then she asked if she could kiss her husband's hand, and began rambling that he must repent for she was afraid that after Judgment Day she would never see him in Nazareth. She was led away just before he died. Even at the end, five days after his terrible deed, Keith did not oblige her. Showing no remorse for his victims, his last words were, "I have been a thick-head. The fellows in New York are guilty."

If Cecelia had been girlish and frivolous before this ordeal, had perhaps even felt partly responsible for driving her husband to commit this desperate crime, she now appeared in a sober cloak of strength and maturity. After Keith's death, she pulled herself out of shock, guided by one purpose: to protect herself, her children, and her family back in St. Louis and Highland. Despite constant hounding by the reporters, who were eager to unravel William King Thomas's mysterious background, she refused to reveal her maiden name. If evidence exists that Cecelia suspected Keith's activities before she left Dresden, it is in the large cache of letters seized by the police at Villa Thomas. The evidence lies not in what is there, but in what is missing. Only two of the letters are from a family member, Fanny, and then signed only, "Your sister." Surely, an energetic letter writer like Cecelia would have received and saved letters from the Parises; from her stepfather John, of whom she was very fond; from her brother Louis, working as a brickmaker in St. Louis; and from her stepbrother Jules, who now lived with his growing family in Highland. Cecelia's mother, Louise, had gone back to her birthplace in Alsace Lorraine after visiting Cecelia in 1873 and later died there. But little sister Blanche was still in France. What had happened to her family correspondence? Had she destroyed it during that long night before she left for Bremen?

Cecelia's celebrity grew, as with the appearance of immense dignity she continued to shield her loved ones. A Bremerhaven journalist, whom she granted a brief interview in her rooms at the Lohr Hotel, found Cecelia to be of stately presence and resolute character, adjectives that would not have applied to her only a week before. Though the German newspapers at first expressed suspicion and anger at Cecelia, and the public gossips speculated that she had ruined her husband with the milliners' bills, she very quickly became a sympathetic heroine, with even more of their pity reserved for her children, who had believed so innocently in their murderous father. The Thompsons' creditors were not so kind. While Cecelia was in Bremerhaven, the Villa Thomas was sealed by order of the court, attached by one of the creditors, and her children thrown out. Cecelia returned to Dresden and gathered up Willie, Blanche, and Klina. She kept up appearances for them, sheltering them from any knowledge of their father's death, much less his horrific deed. For the next few weeks she put her affairs in order, and prepared to sail back to America.

She found a baggage check for a trunk that Keith had left in the Fifth Avenue Hotel, and sent a letter to a friend in Brooklyn, asking him to claim it. Deciding that he had been put in an awkward position and not wishing in any way to be connected to the Bremerhaven disaster, the friend went immediately to the New York police headquarters and, insisting on anonymity, turned over Cecelia's letter. A police officer went to the hotel to search the trunk, scuffed by many journeys. Breaking open the lock, he searched through layers of clothes, until, at the very bottom, he uncovered a ten-foot gutta percha fuse. This was confiscated as evidence, and the rest of Keith's more innocuous effects were turned over to the friend who kept them, waiting for Cecelia to arrive.

Also preparing for another transatlantic crossing were seventy-three deeply shaken survivors of the *Mosel*. All but five of the *Mosel's* passengers had lived, for they were already onboard when the bomb went off. The victims had mostly been dockworkers, sailors, shipping agents, and relatives and friends of passengers who had been bidding goodbye to their loved ones. Keith's original targets, the passengers—mostly merchants, farmers, and tradesmen—for the most part had escaped. The ship chosen to take these survivors to their destination in New York was the *Salier*. It was no comfort to them that the *Salier* had been prevented from embarking from Bremen two months earlier because of a crack in its high-pressure cylinder. Before it sailed, German detectives crawled over the ship, inspecting every barrel, every box, every piece of luggage, listening for mysterious ticking noises and searching carefully for odd mechanisms. Rumors were flying that Keith had placed bombs on every transatlantic ship that was about to sail. Two were said to be on the *Salier* with its passenger list of the already gravely traumatized. Then a dense fog rolled in, delaying the trip for two more days, increasing the passengers' nervousness ten-fold as they imagined the dread fate of the *Deutschland* lying swamped off the English coast, the drowned still floating up on the tide.

When the "all clear" finally came on December 16, the travelers gingerly boarded the *Salier* and it sailed thankfully without incident, arriving in Southampton two days later. There, the survivors were given about £13 each of charitable donations from sympathizers in London, hardly enough to appease their anger at being given nothing at all by the shipping company. They were frightened, they were furious, and they were traumatized, but not as traumatized as the sixty-four survivors from the *Deutschland* wreck who now joined them aboard the *Salier*. A more nervous set of travelers could hardly be imagined. They had come close to the worse disasters the sea had to offer, even one that had heretofore been inconceivable. As they lined up at the gangway, they could see that the dock was heavily patrolled. The German consul was on hand to reassure them of their safety, promising that a detective had once again inspected the cargo. But their ordeal was not yet over. Setting off for New York, the *Salier* encountered a series of thick fogs and crept along with extraordinary caution. Despite the inspections, a skittish reporter in Bremerhaven released yet another story that a bomb was still aboard.

Two weeks later, the *Salier* arrived safely in New York's upper harbor and was greeted by a health officer. It was a fine day for January, with warm southerly winds and clear skies, and the passengers were eager to disembark. But the ship was delayed another several hours while panicky rumors circulated both onboard and on shore among the dozens of expectant friends and relatives leaning over the rails near the Custom House at Castle Garden. They heard that a mysterious letter was being passed from the Lloyd shipping company to the German consul, that plans were being made to inspect the luggage meticulously for explosives, and that secret German detectives were onboard ferreting out clues. It was an agonizing delay. Finally, the *Salier* was released and sailed to Castle Garden, where it put down its gangway. The streaming passengers were greeted as if they had returned from the dead. Lively celebrations were held at several hotels that night, as the survivors told harrowing tales of their ordeal, then broke into New Year's toasts and sang "Prost Neu Jahr" and their favorite patriotic tune, "Die Wacht am Rhein." They would never have another holiday season without thinking of how close they came to death. Two weeks later they would hear that on its return trip to Bremen, the *Salier* had foundered on the Brambles off the Isle of Wight and nearly sank.

On January 19 Cecelia also embarked for America with her four children, taking a second-class berth on the *Wieland*, sailing from Hamburg. She thinly disguised her last name as Thorpe, but it was not enough to conceal her from an enterprising *Herald* reporter who sailed out to the *Wieland* while it lay in quarantine in the gray, rainy New York harbor, two weeks later. The reporter found Cecelia sitting in the saloon, having supper with her children. She was wearing the plain black dress of mourning, complementing her soulful black eyes. With surprise, followed by a great show of dignity, she told her unexpected visitor that she had come to America to escape notoriety and that she did not wish to speak of her painful experience in front of her children. She had carefully protected them: They knew nothing of their father's death or crime. However, she agreed to grant an interview a few weeks later.

She took rooms in a modest boarding house on West 39th Street, keeping a low profile to avoid pesky reporters. However, a Pinkerton Agency detective, hired by the Bremen authorities, traced her whereabouts and rapped at the door. He was told that "Mrs. Thorpe" was ill and could not leave her bed. He sent her a message that she quickly clear up a few mysteries about her husband's many acquaintances in the United States and the strange circumstances of his voyages. She sent a message back: Yes, she would fully cooperate, but she needed a few days to recover from her "tedious voyage." She would be at that location for some time if the detective should need her. But when he returned in a few days, she and the children had gone, leaving no forwarding address.

Still she kept her promise to the *Herald* reporter and met him in her new rooms in the Gramercy Park Hotel for an interview, the only one she would give in America. As a young girl, Cecelia said, she had met her husband in a remote country town in Illinois. She described him as a loving father and a homebody, a quiet man who always kept a certain proud reserve. However, she said, he was given to bouts of delirium, rage, and depression, and was obsessed with the carnage of war and murder. Without mentioning the financial ruin caused by the couple's extravagance, Cecelia told the reporter about her husband's strange disappearances that began in their earliest married days, and detailed the violent mood swings in the last years of his life. She described her dismay at the news of her husband's suicide, her confusion on the trip to Bremerhaven, her interrogation by the police, and her awful visit to her husband's deathbed. Without discussing her own strange behavior there, she told the reporter that she had been led to Keith's side: "His eyes fixed upon her face with a look of recognition and when the doctors inquired if he knew her he pressed her hand tightly and strove, but in vain, to speak. For a few moments Mrs. Thomas was allowed to remain with the dying man, and soon after she was led away he breathed his last." Cecelia worked very hard to maintain sympathy as the innocent young wife who loved her husband and was baffled by his bouts of madness and his final, terrible crime.

During this interview, Cecelia told two lies, one of them significant enough to cast doubt on her character. First, she told the reporter that she had always known her husband as William Thompson. She had, in fact, married him as "Alexander King Thompson," as recorded on their marriage license. Even though the news had been out for weeks that she had revealed the name "Alexander" to the police, Cecelia was still obscuring the past, probably to avoid revealing any more personal details and thus protecting her family. There was good reason for this: Fannie lost her job as a shop girl in St. Louis as soon as the news broke that she was the Dynamite Fiend's sister-in-law. Cecelia's second lie was more serious. She said that she had come to America without means, that wealthy benefactors in Germany had provided money for her travel. Claiming that a wealthy female friend had put her up to it, she ended the interview with a "public appeal for sympathy" because, "exposed to penury after a life of affluence," she needed financial resources "to support the little ones whom she shrinks from intrusting to an eleemosynary institution." However, Cecelia had not arrived in America in a state of poverty. Even though a creditor in Leipzig had attached her possessions, she had managed to escape with a considerable amount of very valuable clothes and jewelry.

A year after she arrived in New York, Cecelia filed a lawsuit in the city's Marine Court against Louisa Randolph, whom she had met during a stay at the Gramercy Park Hotel. According to Cecelia, Randolph presented herself as the immensely charming and cultivated "Louisa Williams," and the two women became fast friends. Having gained Cecelia's trust, "Mrs. Williams" asked to borrow two rings, a watch, and a brooch, all studded with diamonds; a fine leather trunk; and a camel's hair shawl that Cecelia claimed was worth $1,500. When Cecelia asked for return of these possessions, "Mrs. Williams" prevaricated, claiming that she had lent them to her sister. Then "Mrs. Williams" disappeared. Floating from hotel to hotel, Louisa Randolph, a.k.a. "Mrs. Williams," was finally arrested for her theft and thrown into the Ludlow Street Jail. Alleging that she had never used an alias and that Cecelia had overvalued the goods, Randolph was released and filed a counter-suit, claiming that she was one of the few people who had befriended Cecelia and that "the suit against her was evidence of ingratitude." The matter was settled out of court. While this story suggests that Cecelia was as gullible as ever despite her long trials with a deceptive husband, it shows how rich she still was. With calculation and foresight, she had protected her valuables, secreting them away before she had even left for Bremen.

Who was Cecelia Thompson, née Paris? Innocent girl, dignified widow, protective mother, gullible mark, or canny swindler herself? Like her husband, Cecelia had based her adult identity on a false premise, that she was the genteel, well-born wife of a prosperous businessman. They had shared this carefully constructed life together for ten years. Even though she knew it to be false, and that she was really the illegitimate child of a milliner, she continued to live out this fantasy, for this was the reputed age of great transformations, when ragged urchins could become robber barons. Like her husband, she could not give up this identity, and she would even reduce herself to begging under the guise of nobly soliciting charity rather than hock the diamonds that marked her status. They were her social capital. From her letters in those confused days leading up to the Bremerhaven catastrophe, it does not seem that she knew of her husband's plans, but she shared with him a proud obsession with appearances that would lead to their downfall. Craving both privacy and her old life as an elegant lady, she now found herself exiled from good society. After the incident with Louisa Randolph, Cecelia and her children changed their names again and disappeared forever from public view.

FOURTEEN

EXIT DYNAMITE FIEND

When Chief Inspector P. J. Schnepel heard the final rattle of William King Thomas, he had been left with two great mysteries: who the Dynamite Fiend really was and whether he had accomplices. The most notorious criminal of the century was dead, but this did not relieve Schnepel of the burden of an investigation. Keith, after all, had claimed that "the fellows" in New York had organized the monstrous plot, suggesting that he was an innocent dupe in a sophisticated international conspiracy. In the excitement of the disaster, Schnepel was receiving paranoid rumors of satanic agreements between ordinary swindlers and anarchist insurgents to bomb passenger ships, satisfying both greed and political anger in one terrible blow. The transatlantic ghost ship, *City of Boston*, was much on the chief inspector's mind as he wondered whether other ships would soon disappear, victims of other diabolical figures, Keith's secret accomplices lurking in the ports.

The most compelling rumor came from a letter sent to the *London Times* a little over a week after the Bremerhaven catastrophe. Written by the anonymous "Warhawk," it warned of elaborate conspiracies by secret societies to blow up passenger ships sailing from European ports. Claiming that he was an initiate of these secret societies, Warhawk authoritatively declared that in March 1873 he had been informed that mysterious conspirers were planning to spirit infernal machines onto ships, sink them, and collect the insurance money. In June of that year, Warhawk had written to the *Times* and the *London Spectator* warning of these conspiracies, giving details of various instruments that might be used to scuttle ships. Warhawk knew of the coal bomb and of a machine called a "rat," equipped with an automatic screw that could surreptitiously bore a large hole into a ship's keel. The timing of Warhawk's first letter nearly coincided with Keith's first approaches to Fuchs, the clockmaker. Now, two years later, Warhawk claimed that Keith was part of a wider criminal conspiracy, and that if Warhawk's earlier warnings had been heeded, then the Bremerhaven tragedy would never have taken place.

The *Times* editor, John Delane, who generally spent more time at his club than in his office, was taken in by Warhawk's "exceptional information" and believed him to be authentic even though his tales seemed to come from an "imaginary world of sanguinary fiction and sensational romance." When Delane read the gruesome reports of his Bremen correspondent, he felt that civilization had become so morally numb that any scenario was possible. Like many others, he shook his head at the depravity of human nature, and he was in an especially susceptible mood for Warhawk's tales. Furthermore, he had verification from the French legation's military attaché, Baron de Grancey, that Warhawk had once warned him of conspirators in Bourdeaux and Marseilles. Delane ran Warhawk's story, and the next day editorialized: "A not very timid imagination might almost picture to itself guns in every hedge-row, infernal machines on every ship, poison in every cup of kindness, and murder in every grasp of friendship." A traveler on a ship, Delane warned, could never step aboard without knowing that "his days may indeed be numbered with mathematical precision." Widely reprinted and discussed, Warhawk's story caused an international sensation, for it supported a widespread suspicion that Keith had accomplices still lurking in the ports. Expressing shock at this "new perversion of human instincts," the *New York Times* cautioned: "Justice demands that Thompson's accomplices shall be hunted down and relentlessly punished." And the *Herald* worried that "the mid-ocean is a new field for the exploits of a new species of criminal." Alarmed by the story, Schnepel commissioned Scotland Yard to find and interview Warhawk.

Scotland Yard's Superintendent, Frederick Williamson, and his assistant, Ruiners, tracked Warhawk down on London's Duchess Street.

Warhawk, revealed to be "Colonel" Fraser Palmer, surrounded himself with an aura of intrigue and mystery, intimating to the detectives that he knew all about the plot behind the Bremerhaven explosion. He told them that he had once acquired a model of an infernal machine much like Keith's but had handed it over to the German consul in Paris. As Palmer bragged about his important political connections and secret associations, Williamson grew more and more skeptical of his story, concluding that he was an attention-craving fantasist whose plots existed only in his fertile imagination. He was, in fact, yet another poseur, a well-known gadfly who preyed on the paranoid gullibility of diplomats across the breadth of an uneasy Europe, warning them of impending assassinations and other vast conspiracies. Williamson reported back to Schnepel that he was "convinced that Palmer is an imposter, and totally incapable of giving any information whatever." In a twist of fate, a dynamite bomb would destroy Williamson's office ten years later, sent by an international network of Irish insurgents who threatened to "blow him off his stool." He would survive both the attack and the embarrassment of weak intelligence at the insecure offices of Scotland Yard.

Despite the exposure of Warhawk as a fraud, the problems of accomplices and Keith's mysterious past had not been solved. Schnepel and his detectives had been combing through dozens of other false rumors, comparing mug shots of known criminals, taking depositions from Keith's acquaintances, and hunting down clockmakers, coopers, hotel clerks, porters, insurance salesmen, and dynamite manufacturers, including Alfred Nobel, who lived in Hamburg and disavowed supplying the explosives. Everyone involved in the making and transport of the bomb turned out to be innocent dupes, and could give little insight into Keith's secret criminal life. Even the Dynamite Fiend's old friends in Leipzig and Dresden, including Consul John Steuart, had no answers, for their old friend seemed as mysterious to them as he was to the police. Nor were they especially cooperative with Schnepel's quest, for they were carefully guarding their own respectability and had no desire to be implicated in the machinations of the Dynamite Fiend. Though Schnepel could trace the path of the bomb through Leipzig to Bremen to New York and back, he was finding little satisfaction in tracing the history behind "William King Thomas." For one brief moment he thought he had discovered a valuable clue when the Basel police reported that ten years before, in December 1866, they had arrested and extradited an Englishman with the alias "Thompson," who, in collusion with the captain, had tried to scuttle two ships by drilling holes in their hulls in order to collect £24,000 insurance. With his full beard and moustache, this Thompson looked remarkably like Keith, but it was yet another false lead.

Schnepel's pursuit of Keith's accomplices was given a strange edge by the public debates, which exercised the best legal minds, over whether Keith had actually committed a crime other than the illegal transport of explosives. After all, the bomb had gone off by accident, and Keith had not intended to kill the victims on the dock. If Keith had lived, could he have been tried merely on the vague intention to bomb a ship? If so, wasn't this a pre-crime scenario, second-guessing whether Keith would have acted or not? Perhaps on the way to Southampton he might have changed his mind. After all, a man who simply carried a loaded gun in his pocket was not yet guilty of murder. Yet it was the massive scale of the crime that demanded justice. Concurring with several German legal experts, the distinguished British judge James Fitzjames Stephen inferred that under both French and German law, "the wickedest act of modern times was not a crime at all." Yet under the superior English homicide laws, he explained, Keith would have been guilty, since they included acts of negligence and unintended consequences in the commission of a crime. Another barrister, Leopold Goldberg, argued that the spirit of German penal law included murderous acts by a perpetrator who, "in the execution of his design, by mistake kills another person than the one he intended to kill." It was a bizarre wrinkle in the case that if Keith had lived, he might have been exonerated with the help of a skillful lawyer. If accomplices were found, were they guilty of a crime?

These considerations did not stop Schnepel, for the 135 orphans, 45 widows, and 20 hopelessly maimed victims cried out for justice and had no patience for the niceties of law. They demanded to know why they suffered and who was capable of subjecting them to such a terrible fate. The police inspector's community had been severely traumatized, not only the immediate victims, but those left to pick up the gruesome debris: pages blown from the notebook of a dead man, a human finger found lying next to a townswoman's chicken coop, a leg discovered in a coal bin. The harbor had to be dredged to collect the human body parts floating in it. The long process of identifying the fragments of the dead was ongoing as the town tried to piece together its shattered spirit. No legal debate could encompass the horror of these events or the depravity of the mind that wrought them. Furthermore, Schnepel felt the scrutiny of an international public that wanted to know whether more travelers would perish in widespread conspiracies.

Schnepel had been working backward, tracing the elements of the bomb back to their origins, but he eventually came to a dead end when the *Rhein* sailed to New York, carrying Keith's infamous barrel of dynamite. Knowing that the answers lay somewhere across the sea, Schnepel turned for help to the "eye that never sleeps": the Pinkerton Detective Agency. The United States government had only a few secret service agents who were mostly busy tracking down counterfeiters, and so foreign governments often privately contracted the Pinkerton Agency to carry out their investigations.

That the Thomas case should fall onto Allan Pinkerton's desk had a certain irony because Pinkerton was everything Sandy Keith had aspired to be: the owner of a prosperous business, a genuine secret agent, the respected friend of politicians and diplomats, and a Scotsman who made good. Born in Glasgow, Pinkerton had almost ended up settling in Canada himself in 1842, but in a strange twist of fate, the emigrant ship on which he and his wife were sailing ran aground near its destination: Halifax. The young couple lost nearly all their possessions, and as a final blow, Pinkerton's wife had had her wedding ring forcibly removed by some of the perennial Nova Scotian scavengers who sailed out to prey upon shipwreck victims. Sandy was a boy of fifteen when Pinkerton and his new bride passed through Halifax on their way west to Montreal. Put off Canada by their ordeal, the Pinkertons decided to move instead to Chicago, where Allan began life in the New World as a cooper in Lill's Brewery. Like Sandy's uncle, Pinkerton was extremely ambitious and rose above his humble lot in the brewery, first to run his own cooperage and then to become involved in local law enforcement, eventually forming his own private detective agency.

On the other side of the Civil War from Sandy Keith—the winning side—Pinkerton was charged with forming the country's first secret service to ferret out Confederate spies in Washington. He had once successfully played one of Sandy's favorite roles—the rich Southern gentleman—in order to attain information about troop movements in Memphis. The war had been good to Pinkerton, delivering him wealth, an extremely successful career, and extravagant tales of dangerous assassins and lady spies that he was only too eager to tell, with the help of his ghostwriter. When a craniologist examined the bumps on Pinkerton's head, he told him, "You are one of the best of bargain-drivers and shrewdest of men (great, both in making money and taking good care of it), are none too hopeful or venturesome, and have succeeded splendidly, not so much by speculation as by real hard work and sagacity." The two Scotsmen, the hard-working Pinkerton and the speculative Keith, had strangely parallel lives, with one rising to the greatest honor and respectability while the other descended into disgrace and villainy.

By the time of the Bremerhaven catastrophe, Pinkerton had settled in Onaraga, Illinois, on a densely forested estate that he called "the Larches," not far from Keith's old haunts in St. Louis and Highland. Though his health was failing, he rose every morning at 4:30 for a brisk walk and a cold bath. When he was not tormenting Jesse and Frank James, the Molly McGuires, and other enemies of the robber barons, Pinkerton entertained special guests in his Snuggery, a small hideaway on this grand property, decorated with paintings of the Civil War and a mural of events from Scottish history. He nostalgically imagined himself as a noble Celt transplanted to the prosperous New World, very much like Keith's uncle Alexander, the powerful and wealthy Scot whom Keith had so envied.

Though Keith had come within his orbit on more than one occasion, Pinkerton did not recognize his man. Holding only the slim, false clues that "William King Thomas" had been born in Brooklyn with the surname "Alexander," was the captain of the *Old Dominion,* and had an accomplice named Skidmore, Pinkerton deployed his detectives, including his sons, Robert and William. It was a mark of the high importance of the case that the tough, bulldog Pinkerton sons, born to the profession and known for their ability to mingle with the criminal elements, did much of the work.

The investigation commenced in New York, where Robert Pinkerton ran the Eastern office under the demanding and imperious eye of his father. Bob, as his friends knew him, was a big, burly man who loved to combine work and pleasure at the horse races. He was fresh off his big success busting a gang of swindlers who had robbed the

Bank of England, the institution affectionately known as the Old Lady of Threadneedle Street. The culprits were caught trying to ship $220,920 worth of bonds under some old clothes in a chest on the transatlantic steamer *Thuringia*. One of the swindlers, George Bidwell, went on the run, and managed to disguise himself as an Irish nationalist, a Russian, a professor, and a deaf and dumb man before he was arrested in Edinburgh. William Pinkerton had succeeded in tracking down another elegant railroad bond forger, Stephen Raymond, who, wearing a high silk hat, represented himself in London as a member of the New York Stock Exchange. These cases had proven the skill of the Pinkertons at international investigations, especially those involving swindlers, frauds, and masters of disguise. For the Bremerhaven case, Bob was aided by Benjamin Franklin (no relation to the Founding Father), the head of Pinkerton's Philadelphia office: an obvious choice, since Franklin had knowledge of German police operations. In his younger days on the Philadelphia detective force, Franklin had arrested the forger I. P. Singer, the first criminal in the United States to be extradited to Germany.

Bob Pinkerton enlisted his most experienced operatives to do the more tedious legwork on the case of the Dynamite Fiend. They were experts at tracking swindlers, forgers, robbers, abducted children, and cheating spouses. Paid $8.00 a day plus first-class traveling expenses, the "false beard" men combed through city directories, dead letters, bank records, shipping and customhouse receipts, and hotel registers, tracking Thomas and his infamous barrel from their arrival in port. With Thomas's mug shot and his signature in hand, they interviewed confused hotel clerks and reluctant bankers who feared being part of any investigation. They investigated passengers and crew who had recently sailed with Thomas, whom they all remembered as "the fat man." But they adamantly insisted on their own innocence, nervously wondering if they too had been his targets.

Believing that Thomas's true name was William King Alexander, the detectives hunted down everyone in town with the last name Alexander. An especially likely connection seemed to be F. A. Alexander and Sons, owners of a steamship line between New York and Havana, but they strenuously denied any connection and none of their clerks could identify Keith's photograph. Some folks in Brooklyn reported that they had known a Captain Alexander, formerly of the New

York to Galveston steamship line, and one of his former neighbors said that she always suspected he had poisoned his wife before sailing off to unknown shores. None of these Alexanders turned out to have anything to do with Keith.

The detectives also looked for accomplices, interviewing anyone who might have had contact with Thomas, trying to find any signs of nefarious doings. Bob Pinkerton received a letter that read, "I think you will get a clue to the terrible explosion of dynamite by arresting D. H. Bearkley, 119 Nassau St., N.Y. Signed, A German." Pinkerton ran an ad in the papers asking "A German" to come forward, but he or she never did. A foreman for a cooper shop in New York contacted the Pinkerton office with his intriguing story of selling two men an extra-strong cask to be used for dynamite experiments. One of these men had "a very tallow complexion, black hair and eyes and a 'hang dog' expression," while the other looked exactly like the Dynamite Fiend, stout, with golden spectacles. An unemployed machinist, James Boyle, told the Pinkertons his tale of overhearing conversations in an elegant saloon between an angry Englishman and a stout, red-faced German.

> GERMAN: When the next steamer comes, we'll have money enough.
> ENGLISHMAN: Yes, when the next steamer comes, we may be boxed.
> GERMAN: You know what is in Liverpool.
> ENGLISHMAN: Yes, they are at it there and will be after us here. I
>   want money to go to Canada.

This was an eerily suggestive conversation indeed, and seemed to fit right in with Warhawk's conspiracy theories. The Pinkertons paid Boyle a few dollars to keep an eye on the saloon for the return of these gentlemen, along with their companion, a mysterious Englishwoman who carried a satchel full of letters. But all of these leads turned out to be red herrings.

Bob Pinkerton then turned the investigation to Edward Skidmore, whom Keith had accused of being the criminal mastermind who had duped him into the insurance plot. One of Pinkerton's men first reconnoitered Skidmore's house and spoke to Skidmore's wife, alleging that he was looking for a friend he'd made on a transatlantic crossing. The wife declared that her husband had never been overseas. Reputedly possessed of an uncanny understanding of criminal psychology, Bob

Pinkerton went personally to the customhouse to interview Skidmore, finding him to be nothing but an ordinary respectable bureaucrat. The mild-mannered Skidmore protested that not only had he never traveled to Europe, as Keith had alleged, but had never traveled beyond Sandy Hook, the outermost barrier of New York's harbor. Furthermore, he had always kept diligently to his desk at the Custom House. Pinkerton instantly concluded that Skidmore was hardly a criminal mastermind. Nor could any other of the "fellows in New York" be found. Still, it seemed doubtful that one man could have conceived and implemented such a complicated scheme, and despite an utter lack of evidence, detectives on both sides of the Atlantic remained reluctant to accept that the Dynamite Fiend had acted alone.

In the flurry of investigative activity and sensational newspaper interviews of passengers who had sailed with Keith, New York customs inspectors searched their own warehouses for clues. They became curious about the worn treasure box he had left behind after the voyage of the *Celtic*. Keith had consistently claimed it was full of gold coins, but now the possibility that it held more deadly contents worried city officials. On an unusually warm day of a January thaw, they gathered at the pier to find out whether they had been holding one of Keith's hair-trigger bombs in their customhouse. They gingerly picked up the box, carried it out to the dock, and gave it to the pier's cooper for the risky business of opening it. It turned out to be three nested boxes. The cooper first removed the wooden outer box, covered with oilcloth. He then carefully pried off the metal straps and popped the French nails that sealed the second box, made of steel. The lid had a mysterious hole the size of a thumb. Inside, there were bits of paper, straw envelopes for holding small pharmaceutical bottles, two twenty-five pound bags of birdshot, and a wooden box, ten by four by eight inches, securely wrapped with paper and twine. Standing at a distance, the witnesses tensed, sure that this third box contained explosives. The cooper carefully removed the four screws that held the lid and pried it off. There was collective relief. As empty of worth as Keith himself, the box contained nothing but two more bags of birdshot. The evidence was taken into the custody of the New York police superintendent, where it joined the submarine fuse that had been found in Keith's abandoned suitcase at the Fifth Avenue Hotel.

The evidence in New York was not adding up to much in the quest for William King Thomas, or William King Thompson, or William

King Alexander, nor could any trace of him be found in New Orleans, where he claimed to have been married. And so the Pinkerton investigation turned to his alleged captainship of the blockade-runner the *Old Dominion*. Excited folks around the Southern ports remembered that a William Henry Thompson had once captained the *Old Dominion*, running between Wilmington and the Bahamas, and had made a fortune as one of the most daring blockade-runners of the war. Perhaps he was another inspiration for Keith's alias, but here too, the gumshoes seemed to hit a brick wall. One of them, the seasoned detective William Loader, traveled to Petersburg, Virginia, home of the *Old Dominion*. Loader went first to the town's clubhouse and talked to the old folks who had a long memory of everyone who had ever lived and worked in town. They couldn't remember any Thomas or Alexander, but one of them thought that Keith's photograph strongly resembled a notorious gambler from Richmond, Judge George Stevens. Knowing that Keith had once revealed to one of his fellow passengers that his mother was a Sutherland, Loader tracked the only Virginia Sutherlands down on their farm, but they expressed only extreme surprise that they could be in any way linked to the fiend. They were positive he was no relation.

Loader then interviewed the managers and agents of the Petersburg Steamship Company, owners of the *Old Dominion*. Unlike many other informants, they were very eager to talk since they wished to disassociate themselves from the rumors that they had ever employed the Dynamite Fiend. They all disavowed that William King Thomas was William Henry Thompson, or had ever been a crew member, much less captain, of the *Old Dominion*. However, when shown Keith's *carte de visite*, many of them had a suspicion that they had seen the man somewhere before, in Bermuda or Halifax. But they couldn't put their finger on him nor could they remember his name. Loader asked for a list of the *Old Dominion*'s pilots, but were told they were "very ignorant men, and very reticent in regard to anything relating to running the blockade." Most of the old blockade-runners were hardened by imprisonment after the war and now maintained a stony silence around memories they would rather take to their deaths. In fact, one of the agents, Captain J. M. West, strongly doubted the Dynamite Fiend's deathbed claim to have piloted the *Old Dominion* because none of the crew "would, on a deathbed, and after such a lapse of time, make such an assertion." Still, one of the company's pilots, Richard Doscher, agreed to an interview, and he too remembered seeing Keith in Halifax and Bermuda, where he had been "a sort of speculator in cotton and block-ade goods." These were tantalizing hints that the detectives were get-ting closer to their man, especially since the investigation into Keith's association with the *City of Boston* was also taking them toward Halifax, where one James Thomas had shipped three boxes of furs onboard that ill-fated ship.

Then came the big break in the case. Rumors were already rife in St. Louis that the city had once harbored the bomber. Only a week after the explosion, the managing clerk of the Southern Hotel, Wilson, sauntered into the newspaper offices of the *St. Louis Republican* and the *St. Louis Globe Democrat,* claiming to know the real identity of William King Thomas and offering to write up a story. From the description of the fiend, he and his fellow employees remembered one Alexander King Thompson, a fat, pleasant, blondish man who had often stayed at the Southern and who was particularly memorable because he ap-peared to be on the lam and had such huge wads of cash. They also re-membered that he was an associate of the Frenchman, now two years dead, and that the two liked to spin entertaining tales of their block-ade-running adventures. The clerk recalled that Alexander King Thompson "had considerable dash in his bearing at times, but would not confine himself to strict veracity if he thought it would be to his ad-vantage to depart from it."

At this point, the evidence that Alexander King Thompson was the Dynamite Fiend still seemed slender and completely coincidental. Ru-mors were flying across the United States regarding Keith's mysterious identity. A newspaper editor in small Indiana town was sure that he was a former resident known as "Dynamite Johnson." In Richmond, Virginia, many citizens were convinced that he was the Englishman Henry Thomas, who had arrived there in 1874 with his beautiful wife and a child whom his suspicious neighbors believed to be Charlie Ross, a famous kidnap victim. Posing as an "analytical and synthetic chemist," Thomas had set up the Canton Oil Color Works, employing young women to fill beautifully labeled bottles with tinted water that he called "aniline dye" and pack them in elaborately decorated boxes. He forged a number of invoices and took out insurance on his stock, claiming it was worth $36,000. He then set fire to his buildings, endan-gering his female employees, and collected the insurance before it was

discovered that he was a swindler. Henry Thomas not only had an in-
triguingly similar name, but a modus operandi that echoed the ruthless
behavior of William King Thomas. Henry Thomas seemed a more
likely candidate than St. Louis's competing Alexander King Thompson, at least on the surface. But the dates did not add up.

Suspicions that the Dynamite Fiend had once lived in St. Louis
gained momentum. Wilson's story had jolted memories of Keith's old
associates, including Detective John Eagan, who now offered his version of the events of 1865, the year the war ended and the nervous
stranger came to town. Featuring himself as a central player, Eagan recounted Luther Smoot's arrival in Baltimore and the daring pursuit
and midnight arrest of Alexander King Thompson. Eagan still had the
suspect's *carte de visite*. It was imprinted "Halifax, Nova Scotia."

When Eagan's story broke, a reporter in Washington, D.C.
tracked down Luther Smoot, who was still embroiled in arguments
with the government over compensation for his Norris locomotive engines. He was an irritable man, made more irritable by having his name
associated with the Bremerhaven bomber and even worse with blockade running, a revelation that might damage his decade-long claims
dispute. Agreeing to an interview with the reporter, Smoot insisted on
being referred to only as "the creditor." He did not tell nearly what he
knew, including Alexander King Thompson's real name, Sandy Keith.
Instead, he was mostly interested in disputing key details of Eagan's
story, namely that Eagan had accompanied him to Highland for Keith's
arrest. Bursting with his own self-importance, Smoot did not appreci-
ate Eagan's version, which placed the detective in the principal role.
Smoot declared that it was he, himself, who, holding his pistol ready,
had confronted Keith at the Weber House.

Reading of these intriguing encounters, the citizens of St. Louis
were still not entirely sure that the city had ever harbored the Dynamite Fiend. However, in February, Allan Pinkerton finally arrived in
town. He had come on the advice of his son, Bob, who had hired an informant in St. Louis to investigate hotel registers for the name
"William King Thomas" or any other of Keith's aliases. Instead, following the stories about Alexander King Thompson in the local newspapers, the informant interviewed Detective John Eagan, who showed
him Thompson's *carte de visite*. The informant was struck by the resem-
blance to the Dynamite Fiend, writing to Bob Pinkerton that it was "a

splendid likeness, though there seems to me to be a marked difference in the lapse of 10 or 11 years between this picture and the one you sent me . . . many who have examined both confessed that they are one and the same person." Furthermore, the informant obtained Alexander King Thompson's signature from the register of the Southern Hotel, looking very much like the Dynamite Fiend's handwriting, and a marriage license with the telling name of his spouse, Cecelia. He interviewed one of Keith's old friends, Brydon, who revealed that the Dynamite Fiend was from Halifax and that his uncle was a well-known brewer in that city. "The proper or real name of this person," the informant wrote, "is Alexander Keith." That was enough for Allan Pinkerton to travel personally to St. Louis and announce to the papers that he was on the case there. In the competition for who owned the Dynamite Fiend, his presence was evidence that the city had won that dubious distinction.

Allan Pinkerton called his son, William, known among his many friends as Willie, who ran the agency's Western operations, down from Chicago and ordered him to Highland, Illinois, to interview its citizens. It was to be one of the more peaceful investigations of Willie's life, since he was chasing a dead man. He took the all-night train from Chicago to St. Louis, arriving by stage in Highland at 6:30 in the morning. There he was cordially greeted by the notary public, John Menz, who had presided over the marriage of Alexander King Thompson and Cecelia Paris. Cecelia, Menz gossiped to Willie, did not get along with her mother and had been born out of wedlock. Menz was happy to take the detective around town to meet Cecelia and Keith's old acquaintances, though there were not many left after the recent wreck of the *Schiller*. They went to the house of the milliners, where Margaretha Meyer said that Cecelia had been like a daughter to her and that she had been deeply hurt when Cecelia stopped writing. She gave Willie a photo of the young Cecelia Paris that he deemed a "splendid likeness" of Mrs. Cecelia Thompson, wife of the Dynamite Fiend. The notary and the detective then went on to the house of the miller, Charles Sebyt, who was having flashbacks of his several eerie encounters with his mysterious old friend. He said sadly of him, "He has told me so many stories of his life that I cannot tell what's truth and what's falsehood." Julius Hammer, who taught Keith his first German sentences; Jacob Weber, the owner of Keith's favorite hotel; and Jacob

Suppiger, the brother of Keith's old friend, all recognized the photograph of William King Thomas as the memorable stranger who had once passed through their quiet town. William Pinkerton left town the next morning and went on to St. Louis to interview Cecelia's father, John Paris, who denied any connection to the Dynamite Fiend and slammed the door in the detective's face. Paris would never utter publicly a word about the whole affair. The attitude of the folks who once knew Keith was summed up by the *Edwardsville Intelligencer*: "Born in Germany, raised and depraved in Brooklyn, partly reformed in St. Louis, mortally ruined again abroad. Exit dynamite fiend."

While William Pinkerton was confirming Keith's connections to Highland, Bob Pinkerton's man, William Loader, had been floating somewhat aimlessly around the Southern ports, trying to hunt down blockade-runners who were mostly interested in avoiding him. In Wilmington, Loader received a telegram from Bob ordering him to investigate with the new information from St. Louis. Loader now had a real name, Sandy Keith, and armed with a photograph he went to speak to Wilkes Morris who, when he was twenty-five, had worked as the State of North Carolina's supply clerk. Morris had spent time dickering and dealing in Halifax, and he was just the kind of adventurous, ambitious young man who would end up partying at the Halifax Hotel. Now co-owner of an auctioneering firm, Morris gazed with certainty upon the photograph Loader showed him. Morris recognized Sandy Keith well enough, the "Confederate Consul" who had deceived and hoodwinked them all. He told Loader of others who would be most willing to confirm that the Sandy Keith and the Dynamite Fiend were one and the same.

Loader had now stumbled across a network of Keith's disgruntled former victims. Unlike the disillusioned pilots, most of these men had landed on their feet after the war and ran successful businesses. They were all willing to talk about Sandy Keith and his cheating ways. One of them was James Sprunt, the sixteen-year-old boy who had served as purser on the *Lilian* and who been cheated of $1,600 precious dollars by his alleged friend, Sandy Keith. Sprunt was now in his mid-twenties, still unmarried, living at home, and running a highly successful cotton business with his father. He was one of the most ambitious young men of Wilmington, and would eventually acquire a very considerable wealth and a palatial estate. When Loader showed him the photograph, he thought he recognized the face, and when Loader prompted him with the name, Sprunt swore that yes, it was none other than Sandy Keith. Sprunt willingly participated in Loader's investigations around Wilmington, introducing him to various parties who told many tales of Sandy Keith's swindles and cheating ways. But despite Sprunt's cooperation, he was not very proud of his former friendship with Sandy Keith. Later, he became a well-known writer of local Wilmington history, recounting romantic stories of Confederate ships and sailors, including his own nostalgic adventures with his blockade-running chums. But he never told the history of Sandy Keith or his association with him.

It was inevitable that Loader should arrive finally in Baltimore at the office of Luther Smoot, who had figured with such grave consequences in the life of Sandy Keith. Loader met Smoot on the evening of February 16, 1876. Smoot regaled him with the story of his grand pursuit of his nemesis, bragging about his friendship with General William Tecumseh Sherman. He insisted on tarring John Eagan's name, complaining that Eagan had insisted on $1,000 up front before he would help Smoot. But Smoot did not tell Loader the motivation behind his anger with Sandy Keith: the Norris locomotive engines. This he kept to himself, saying only that Keith had absconded with $25,000 of his money. Instead, Smoot cut the detective off before any embarrassing questions might arise, saying that he could say no more until he was certain that Keith was William King Thomas. In the end, he would never say another word about it.

With all their detectives' final reports in, the Pinkertons were now satisfied that they had found the true identity of William King Thompson, and sent their report to Schnepel, with an invoice for $642.42. From the many who had identified him, Schnepel was satisfied that Sandy Keith from Halifax was the Dynamite Fiend. There was even compelling physical evidence: Both Sandy Keith and William King Thomas had the same ragged scars on their left hands and the same forearm tattoos, the "A" or "K" that Keith had once shown Julius Hammer during his German lessons in Highland. Furthermore, the Pinkertons had found absolutely no evidence of accomplices in any of Keith's travels, and Schnepel could now alleviate those fears in his second public report, released in March 1876 to the press worldwide. The *New York Herald*, which had closely followed the case for months, said of it, "The annals of crime contain few stories so interesting or so terrible." Schnepel had one last loose end to wrap up: the case of the lost *City of Boston*. He wrote to Halifax and received word that the James Thomas, who had shipped furs on that ship was a legitimate businessman who had not even insured his wares. Schnepel laid the *City of Boston* to rest, declaring in July that the thoroughly wicked Sandy Keith was innocent at least of that crime.

Strangely, the investigation barely reached Halifax, beyond a few letters home from the German consul there reporting on Sandy Keith's background. Haligonians had reacted with a profound silence to the news that they had nurtured a viper in their midst. A single editorial appeared in the *Morning Chronicle* countering the official report from Bremen. The writer insisted that William King Thomas was not Alexander Keith, Jr., and that the connection was based only on the "faintest of evidence" designed for "a sensation-seeking American public." Upon being shown photographs of William King Thomas, "those who knew Keith most intimately," the writer argued, "are satisfied that the dynamite fiend was not Alexander Keith, Jr." In fact, Keith's friends and family allegedly believed him to have been dead for nine or ten years, and "if he had been alive up to December last, he would have been heard from and recognized often."

Halifax closed protectively around the Keiths and refused to entertain the possibility that a member of the family, despite his faults, would have been capable of the crime of the century. Sandy Keith's relatives were living quietly as well-established citizens: Two of his brothers ran successful businesses and were busy raising children; four of his spinster sisters were still living in the old family home on Morris Street. His uncle, Alexander Keith, had died, leaving behind his brewery for his children to run; his image was so imposing that well over a hundred years later Haligonians would still recognize his face and celebrate his legacy. Occasionally, some writer on local history would get the false impression that the paterfamilias Alexander Keith had been somehow involved in a few daring antics during the American Civil War, an ironic case of mistaken identity that would have pleased neither uncle nor nephew. By then, the Civil War days of Halifax were considered quaint memories of exciting times, and no one much wanted to face the dire truth of terror and greed embodied in Sandy Keith. And so Sandy Keith was forgotten in Halifax, a town that never really wanted to remember him in the first place.

By the summer of 1876, the Dynamite Fiend was gone from the news and purged from collective memory. There were no more editorials about the depravity of human nature or the certainty that more bombings would surely follow. The port authorities deemed unnecessary the rigid inspections of passenger luggage called for by the papers. Though legislation was passed in England, Germany, and the United States regulating the transport of explosives, authorities never seriously entertained the more extreme measure suggested: of placing cargo and passengers on separate ships. The reports were complete, the evidence all gathered, the conclusions solidified. Travelers could now experience a certain peace knowing that the Dynamite Fiend had been declared a human anomaly. No more bombers prowled the ships, making jolly with their fellow travelers while murder and mayhem churned in their brains. Or did they?

FIFTEEN

THE INSPIRATION

A young man who had spent two years studying abroad, thought nothing of stepping up the gangway of a transatlantic ship bound for home, in the summer of 1876, only five months after the Bremerhaven catastrophe. Accompanied by his English tutor, he sailed without incident into New York harbor and left a box for storage in the same customs house where Keith had once left his infamous treasure chest. When the student received a declaration form at his hotel, he hastily filled it out, but did not list the contents of his box, as required. He left the form on a hotel table for the concierge. A passing stranger found the form irresistible, and in the empty space for the contents wrote, "I hereby swear that the box containing the dynamite fixtures arranged for the purposes of blowing up the present administration was carefully placed under the White House on Sunday night, the 28th. It is so arranged that it will explode on the night of the 30th of May, at 11:30 o'clock." The wag added that he hoped the apparatus would "perform its work successfully."

The unsuspecting student took his tutor for a tour around New York, while his declaration form was causing great agitation at the customs house. Having barely recovered from the search for Alexander Keith, Jr. and his nefarious devices, the customs officials were all too familiar with dynamite apparatuses that might be hidden in satchels, barrels, and boxes. Two detectives were sent to find the student and curtail his devilish plot to destroy Ulysses S. Grant. They tracked the student down at Barnum's hippodrome, where an angry confrontation ensued as the hapless student protested his innocence, adamantly refusing to cooperate. The student was finally released after he had called a lawyer who pointed out the discrepancies in the handwriting on the form. By this time, a thorough search had been made of the White House. A plot to blow up the President was not new; the Lincoln assassination conspirators had once planned to pack gunpowder in a hallway near the War Department, an echo of the famous Gunpowder Plot of 1605, when Catholic conspirators had tried to place explosives in the cellar in the House of Lords. What was new was the concept of a clock attached to dynamite, a much more portable weapon, since it would have taken hundreds of pounds of gunpowder to achieve the same effect.

The massive international press coverage of the Bremerhaven explosion, including elaborate descriptions of the bomb, had introduced a novel idea. Like all great public criminals, Keith inspired not only practical jokers preying on the anxieties of the day, but real imitators: swindlers and political conspirators who saw a practical use for both his device and his modus operandi. Police detectives and transport officials across the world had reason to fear a new species of criminal that was largely created by the newspapers, for it was the newspapers that had sensationalized Keith's story, giving it the mysteries of a diabolical science. The awesome power of the dynamite bomb, its ability to terrorize, and the secrecy with which it could be deployed, all attracted an educated, literate class of murderers and schemers.

For instance, there was Charles Schantz, an English language teacher in Frankfort-on-the-Main who read the news and became obsessed with Sandy Keith. Schantz was known as an industrious, honest, friendly man from a wealthy, respectable family in Vienna. He had immigrated to the United States, at one time running a soda-bottling manufactory in St. Louis before returning home to Germany in 1875. In his secret life, Schantz fantasized that he was a burglar, practicing with a complete set of safe-cracking tools, including picks, chisels, and acids, keeping his fascinations hidden in his bedroom. The Bremerhaven catastrophe gave him delusions of a much more satisfactory crime that could catapult him to worldwide fame, at least in his imagination.

Leaving a bold paper trail, he wrote to the clockmaker, J. J. Fuchs, a few months after the Bremerhaven disaster and ordered a model of Keith's device. Despite his role in the catastrophe, Fuchs enjoyed his new popularity and was not averse to making a little profit from Keith's admirers. Nor did he bother contacting authorities if anyone showed an unusual interest. He sent Schantz the model, which Schantz kept alongside the tools in his bedroom. Schantz excitedly wrote letters to every explosives manufacturer he could find, asking for samples of nitroglycerine, dynamite, and other products to be used in his experimentation. None of these manufacturers noted his requests as unusual. He wrote to the owner of a wax museum in Berlin and obtained a talisman: Keith's death mask, cast in plaster. Schantz not only had a practical interest in the clockwork device, but a deep drive to contemplate the likeness of his obsession, Sandy Keith.

None of this would have been revealed had Schantz not brought himself to the attention of the police through his inquisitiveness. He had never become proficient at the use of his state-of-the-art burglar's tools. So, claiming to have lost the key to his iron safe, he talked a safe manufacturer into sending a workman to his house to open it. What Schantz really wanted to do was closely observe an expert at work and learn his methods. When the locksmith discovered that the safe had been purposely tampered with, he grew suspicious and notified the police. Schantz was picked up and detained, but the police could find no evidence to hold him. Thus, Schantz's Walter Mitty-ish criminal career was ended before it began. Schantz still had the emotional satisfaction of seeing his rather paltry life splashed across the newspapers of America and Europe, where he was called a "dangerous character" and potential heir of the Dynamite Fiend.

Schantz and other scientifically minded criminals were highly intrigued by Keith's use of dynamite, only discovering the potential of this powerful new technology through newspaper accounts after the Bremerhaven disaster. In Germany, just after the catastrophe, readers were surprised to learn that lying off Hamburg in the frozen River Elbe were three ships loaded with one thousand boxes of dynamite. These were taken off and buried. Citizens in Minden insisted that all dynamite be removed from a local construction site. These stories emphasized the excitement and terror that dynamite could now provoke in communities after such a spectacular catastrophe. A widely reprinted article, "What is Dynamite?," originally from the *Mil-waukee Daily Wisconsin,* suggested, "it may be interesting to our readers to know what is this fearful substance which has so unsuspectedly [*sic*] caused such a destruction of human life." Dynamite, the writer as-sured, was "the safest of all explosives," but that certain anomalous conditions had caused the luggage to explode on the Bremerhaven docks. Given that a mere bump to a barrel full of the stuff had caused the most horrific explosion, dynamite seemed a dangerous, even dia-bolical substance. The editor of the *New York Times,* Louis Jennings, wrote with a certain wry humor that soon trains, steamships, and ho-tels would be regularly blown up while customs officials would become extinct. "The time will come," he wrote, "when enormous quantities of dynamite will be dispersed over the earth and will suddenly explode, with the result of erasing mankind from existence."

Because of potential damage to their sales, the dynamite companies began a public relations campaign to prove the safety of their product to worried communities. In the wake of revelation that the city had harbored the Dynamite Fiend, citizens of St. Louis, for example, were surprised and alarmed to learn that 30,000 pounds of dynamite were stored in the Lowell magazine outside of town. Thus, Fred Julian, a salesman for the Atlantic Giant Powder Company and tireless pro-moter of dynamite, came to appease the fears of the public. He invited a few official guests from St. Louis to board his horse-drawn carriage, transporting them out to the Lowell magazine.

The witnesses were shocked to observe him enter the magazine with a smoking cigar between his teeth and begin throwing boxes of dynamite around with reckless disregard for his own life. He then threw one twenty-five pound box out the door, as the reporter for the *Globe Democrat* reared back, seeing the exploding luggage of the *Mosel* before his eyes. Julian led them all to a ridge over the riverbank where he threw the box over, dashing it against the stones at the bottom. He leapt down onto the bank, picked up a pickaxe, and began wildly strik-ing the sticks of dynamite that had flown out of the box. He gathered the pieces up and made a great pile that he set on fire; it burned with such intensity that the beleaguered spectators above had to stand at a good distance from the heat. Still the dynamite did not explode.

Finally, Julian took a small piece of dynamite out of his pocket, and attached it to a percussion cap. He lit it, lodged it in the gravel, and hastily scrambled up the bank. The dynamite went off with tremendous force, throwing dirt up into the brisk northerly winds and filling the air with a sharp smell, reminiscent of cloves. Suffering from nervous exhaustion but thoroughly convinced of dynamite's safety, the spectators boarded Julian's carriage, riding calmly next to fifty pounds of the explosive. They "wended their way back to town, thinking of how the people would shy off if they knew what was on board, and how little cause for alarm there really was."

There were unexpected consequences to these public relations. Though they were intended to appease fearful consumers, some heard another message: Dynamite was immensely powerful, capable of horrible mayhem in the wrong hands, but highly portable and utterly safe. Combined with a timed detonator, dynamite made the perfect weapon for bombers who required secrecy. The brilliance of Keith's device had occurred to some devious inventors, more ruthless and determined than Schantz, who took up the challenge of perfecting it. They acquired dynamite, poured over the descriptions and the diagrams in the newspapers, and built models of Keith's infernal machine.

Less than a year after the Bremerhaven catastrophe, one of these inventors was ready to try out his device. He carefully placed it in a Saratoga trunk, surrounded by hay and straw. At three in the afternoon on a Wednesday in November, he lugged the cumbersome trunk to the busy Philadelphia train station and had it placed in the baggage car of the express train to New York. Most of the travelers milling about the station had been on holiday to see the Centennial Exhibit, and they boarded the train toting their souvenir porcelain ashtrays and paperweights, happily oblivious to the menace amid their luggage. Fear of a bomber was probably not on their minds. Only a week before, a coal train had smashed into another Centennial excursion train, crushing three cars like an accordion and killing and injuring dozens of passengers. Such accidents often happened, but none of the passengers had any reason to believe that they were traveling with dynamite.

The express left the station and rolled along peacefully for about seventy miles when suddenly the passengers heard a sound like a loud gunshot in front of them. The entire baggage car burst into flame. The train ground to a halt while the fire spread rapidly, endangering the other cars. The passengers crowded out of the train and stood at a safe distance while the crew managed to douse the flames. Lying amidst the wet, smoking luggage, a strange machine was found, a clock attached to a small pistol. It was bent and twisted, but investigators could see that the clock was meant to run for a certain number of hours before releasing the trigger of the pistol, discharging a shot that they guessed would detonate an explosive like dynamite. It was a bizarre device and a baffling crime: No one ever knew whether the bomber had purposely targeted the train or whether his bomb had gone off accidentally, like Keith's. The press recognized the parallels, and heralded the disaster as another dynamite plot.

It is likely that the maker of the device was George Holgate, a Philadelphia metalsmith who would achieve infamy over the next decade as one of the most inventive, prolific bombmakers of his time. Holgate was a lowland Scot who once ran a bomb-making factory in London, disguised as a paint shop. He immigrated to the United States for his health, settling in Philadelphia, and there claimed to be an associate of James McClintock, inventor of the Confederate submarine *Pioneer*. He continued to apply his fertile ingenuity to making bombs, constructing them in the cellar of his house on Juniper Street, a few blocks from the ports on the Delaware River. Like Keith, he was a man of independent commercial enterprise and technical expertise, and possessed a certain callousness toward violence.

Charging anywhere from $5 to $400, he pedaled his devices mostly in New York, carrying prototypes and designs in a satchel, seeking out known revolutionaries who might be interested in such weapons. He was driven entirely by profit; he once told a Philadelphia reporter, "I no more ask a man when he buys [a bomb] whether he proposes to blow up a Czar or set fire to a palace anymore than a gunsmith asks his customers whether they are about to commit a murder or a match merchant asks if his purchaser is about to become an incendiary. I make the machines for those who want them." His wares included a cheap hand grenade, a bomb concealed in a satchel that had a fuse running through its keyhole, and a hat bomb comprised of dynamite pressed between two sheets of brass sewn into the crown with a fuse running around the brim. His "Little Exterminator" operated through a delicate watch mechanism that moved a tiny saw, releasing a chemical that smelled like cayenne pepper, killing anyone within one hundred feet. Holgate was clearly inspired by the time bomb intended for concealment on ships: Several of his prototypes were versions of it. The

"Ticker," for example, was a clockwork bomb that could be hidden in an ordinary tin can, placed in a barrel of lard, tobacco, or flour.

One of Holgate's customers was Jeremiah O'Donovan Rossa, a well-known Irish revolutionary patriot whose family had been dispossessed of its lands in Cork. Rossa had been exiled to the United States after a six-year imprisonment in British dungeons for his radical political activities, where he and his prison mates were tortured, locked in solitary confinement for months, and forced to eat their meals on their knees like animals. He nurtured a bitter, passionate hatred of the British oppressor, and fantasized constantly about revenge as he plied his legitimate trade as the owner of a fifth-rate hotel and a subagent for steamship tickets. Plotting with like-minded Fenian revolutionaries in his organization, the United Irishmen, Rossa often thought about blowing up British ships, and claimed to have destroyed the H.M.S. *Doterel,* a British war ship that exploded in April 1876 in the Strait of Magellan. One hundred and forty-seven seamen had been killed by burns and flying debris. Though many British officials were not sure of the cause, the explosion was ruled an accident precipitated by the buildup of coal gas. Rossa repeatedly claimed that his men had used a clockwork bomb to destroy the ship. Whether his tale was fanciful or not, it was undoubtedly inspired by the Dynamite Fiend, who had introduced the idea of such a bomb to an international reading public only a few months earlier.

Clockwork bombs and dynamite had already long been in Rossa's mind when, in the winter of 1880, Holgate paid a visit to him in his disheveled hotel office. Under the green flag and harp of Erin, Rossa's rooms were a busy place, usually harboring a few disgruntled exiles who loyally served their hero. There, the war chieftains who advocated the use of dynamite held many long meetings, thickened with tobacco smoke, to plot the utter destruction of the British by any means possible. Holgate introduced them to his case of curious wares, and after several interviews, Rossa commissioned Holgate to make a prototype of a clockwork bomb. Somewhere out in the woods near Fishkill, in the Catskill Mountains, Holgate demonstrated the power of his device, including his hand-mixed nitro-explosives. Rossa was so impressed that he ordered twenty on the spot, paid for by his "skirmishing fund," collected from his many supporters across the country. The bombs were to be shipped to England and used to blow up

British government offices and monuments, for the United Irishmen had an overreaching plot to "give Liverpool to flames and reduce London to disaster." They were entranced with "denny-o-mite," seeing it as the ultimate secret weapon for terrorizing "the modern Sodom, the British metropolis, and slay her Philistines."

On July 25, the Cunard liner *Malta*, sailed into Liverpool harbor, arriving from Boston. Standing at the dock were customs officials, who had been alerted by informants. They immediately boarded the ship and pulled off six barrels, listed on the cargo manifest as full of cement. The barrels were each marked with a black cross, shipped by the fictitious Phoenix Manufactory Company, and consigned to the equally fictitious "John Lawson" and "John Evans." In each of these barrels was a bomb with a charge of eleven cartridges of weak, homemade dynamite attached to a clockwork mechanism. A few days later the *Bavaria*, of the Leyland Line, arrived with six more bombs confiscated by waiting officials. The devices had all been made by George Holgate.

It was custom at the time for police departments to publicly display evidence, especially in big cases, and the Liverpool constabulary featured one of the bombs for reporters and other curiosity seekers. One observer described it as beautifully designed: "The machine is enclosed in an oblong case, of zinc, in which it occupies the upper portion. There is a clockwork arrangement which, upon being set running about six hours, causes a lever to descend upon a tube bearing a cap and communicating with the lower half of the case. The tube is filled with explosive material which, upon being fired, sets off a detonating cap placed in the middle of the dynamite compound in the bottom of the case." The device very closely emulated Sandy Keith's bomb, though another witness thought it had "none of the nicety and finish." An experiment by the eminent British explosives expert, Colonel Vivian Majendie, showed that the explosive was powerful enough to pulverize granite. Holgate had packed his bombs carefully so that an accident like the Bremerhaven explosion would not take place. He had surrounded the explosive with cement, and left the clockwork mechanism detached. But these precautions were lost in an international panic.

The news of passengers once again unwittingly traveling over ticking time bombs caused a sensation on both sides of the Atlantic. The Berlin papers demanded to know why European countries should continue doing business with the United States. The British foreign office forcefully urged the U.S. government to suppress Irish revolutionaries by shutting down their radical newspapers. And summer travelers once again felt the premonition of imminent doom. A telegram from a private citizen to Secretary of State James Blaine captures the public alarm: "On behalf of myself and other American citizens about to cross the Atlantic, I appeal to you not to wait formal complaint by the British government before investigating and punishing the illegal & inhuman shipment on passenger steamers of infernal machines liable to explode on shipboard & destroy many valuable lives." An editor in Bristol, Pennsylvania, remembered the hair-trigger effects of the Bremerhaven bomb: "The pleasures of the ocean voyage, will not be enhanced by the thought that somewhere in the cargo of a steamship, may be stored one of these diabolical instruments of death and destruction, which the slightest concussion might cause to explode." Another, in Fort Wayne, Indiana, threw up his hands: "Heaven only knows where it will end."

Blame immediately fell on Rossa, who was always the point man for any alarm involving the Fenians. Rossa was well known as a braggart. He liked to toy with gullible reporters, often inflating the power of his organization. But the discovery of the barrels, revealing the United Irishmen's ineptness and lack of discretion, was an embarrassment. Rumors alleged that Rossa's handbills had been found alongside the dynamite, provoking him to issue a public statement: "How absurd! If we sent such [machines] more caution would have been used. My printed circulars would not be inclosed as an advertisement, and, moreover, if such were sent by the skirmishing fund they would not be sent to blow up steamers leaving our port and carrying some of our dearest friends."

The truth was that Rossa had been duped, and duped badly by an unexpected spy. His weakness was his blind belief in the technology of clockworks and dynamite and his fantasies of causing a great catastrophe that would bring Britain to its knees. As a bomb maker who frequently dealt with delusional men enamored of power, Holgate understood this weakness, and all along he planned to exploit it, for it was he who first approached the British consul in Philadelphia, as early as October 1880, asking for "sufficient encouragement": $200 a month to turn British spy and agent provocateur. And so he had spun an elaborate hoax, drawing from the notorious Dynamite Fiend an idea that he knew would be graphically recognizable to his clients: technologically complicated dynamite bombs, innocuously disguised in shipping barrels placed on passenger trains and ships, catalyzing international terror and panic.

In the debacle, Rossa and the United Irishmen lost much of their credibility, but this only inspired them further to prove they were more than a great cry and little wool. Over the next five years, the United Irishmen and the more secretive Chicago-based organization Clan na Gael, managed to inflict a few feeble blows on the British empire, bombings that caused more panic than actual damage. The most alarming of these were simultaneous attacks on London train stations. In October 1883, two bombs went off in tunnels on London's Metropolitan and District Lines. One of them damaged a gas main and the explosion roared through three third class coaches in the rear of a train, injuring seventy-two people. A few months later, in February 1884, a bomb went off in Victoria Station, injuring two men and destroying the cloakroom, the ticket office, and the ladies waiting room. A subsequent search turned up bombs in the cloakrooms at Paddington, Ludgate Hill, and Charing Cross. The unexploded bomb found in luggage left at Charing Cross consisted of an alarm clock wired to the trigger of a small Remington pistol, which would have detonated percussion caps studding forty cakes of Atlas dynamite. Most of the devices had turned out to be duds because of small flaws in their mechanisms.

Despite their failures, the Fenians are now widely regarded as the originators of modern terrorism, along with Russia's *Narodnaya Volya*. This group consisted of radical students, many of them studying medicine, who had also been inspired by the Dynamite Fiend's explosive crime. They were obsessed with assassinating Czar Alexander II, who ran a dreaded secret police force known for terror and torture. When the members of *Narodnaya Volya* read of Keith's dynamite bomb, they began their own exploration of nitro-explosives and timed detonators. Enlisting unwitting watchmakers and opticians, the group experimented with infernal machines, producing clockwork- and electrically-detonated bombs in malodorous household dynamite factories, transporting them across treacherously rutted roads. Their first attempt was to lay bombs on the rails to destroy the Czar's train, a disappointing failure. In April 1880, they targeted the Winter Palace, disguising a dynamite bomb in the cellar under the dining room. When it went off, it threw up the floorboards, splintered the furniture, and blew out windows and gaslights in the neighborhood, casting the scene into darkness. The plotters had gotten their timing wrong, and the Czar and his guests had not yet entered the dining hall. Instead, eleven of the Czar's Finnish guards were killed. "The dynamite used," reported the *New York Times*, "was inclosed in an iron box, and exploded by a system of clock-work similar to that employed by the man Thomas at Bremen some few years ago." The news excited fantasist Colonel Fraser Palmer, a.k.a. Warhawk, so much that in October he sent his own warning that three secret conspirators were traveling to Glasgow to place clockwork bombs on the Czar's pleasure yacht *Livadia*. A thorough search ensued, including the removal of all the coal on the ship and an inspection of the hull by divers. None of these precautions saved the Czar, who, a few months later, died at the hands of students whose instruments were dynamite bombs. The paranoia that ensued over radicals armed with dynamite would last for decades, resulting in the severely repressive measures known as the "red scare."

Keith was not responsible for the political passion and rage of these violent political groups, but he played a role in showing them a means of action. The origins of his own violence lay deep in terror, in conspiratorial organizations devoted to achieving their purpose by any means necessary. The terrorist activities of the Confederates were fundamentally conservative. Their aim was to preserve their lands from what they perceived as the invasion of the Yankee aggressor. But the new terrorist organizations were devoted to creative destruction, the annihilation of old lives, old institutions, old civilizations, to make way for the new. The dynamite bomb was the ideal weapon to display this radical energy. An explosion was a spectacularly visible way to announce great change, the apocalyptic advent of revolutionary transformation. Even in Keith's small world, he conceived the explosion as a way of suddenly renewing his faltering life. His motivations were banal and self-serving, but in his narrow imagination were the apocalyptic cycles of destruction and resurrection that would inspire others to turn to dynamite.

EPILOGUE

At anniversaries of the Bremerhaven catastrophe, it is tradition to end with the fate of Sandy Keith's head. Long after Keith's body had been tossed unceremoniously into a pauper's grave, his decapitated head remained above the surface, in a bottle, an object of public fascination. The great interest in Keith's head shows how baffled people were by the psychology of the man. Almost every description of him by those who encountered him in his last days spoke of the mysteries that lay behind his golden spectacles. What dark and terrible thoughts churned underneath his disguises, his deceptions, his aliases, and his bogus stories? Even to his own wife, he revealed almost nothing of himself; he never really confessed, and every explanation of his motives was only ever a guess. The answers lay buried somewhere in his mysterious head.

After his death, photographs of Keith's head circulated widely, provoking newspapers to warn that unscrupulous sellers were offering bogus images that were not "William King Thomas" at all. Immediately after the catastrophe in Bremerhaven, American tourists in Germany for the holiday season snapped up postcards showing the dual personalities of "Thomas, der Mörder." On the left side of the card, in a bright oval, was a broad-shouldered, well-dressed, prosperous man in a vest and greatcoat, his expression calm and determined, his face flooded with light, a fine example of the renowned photographic art of Dresden. On the right side, in a dark oval, was the hydrocephalic head of a dead man, lips slightly parted, whiskers black and greasy, face slackened. The two visages were turned towards each other, like life and death, good and evil twins. Between them in the background, the ghostly name "Thomson" rose up over a lighthouse and the bright star of a great explosion. In the stalls of the vendors, there were no commemorative photographs of the victims or of the vast train of mourners at the funeral in Bremerhaven. What souvenir hunters demanded was Keith's head.

The fascination began at the moment of Keith's death. One of the onlookers, who hovered around Keith's deathbed waiting for his last breath, was Louis Castan, proprietor of a wax museum, the Panopticum, in Berlin. Taking notes and sketching, Castan carefully observed Keith's expressions and his coloring, for there was no better way to make a wax figure than from direct observation. Almost as soon as the death rattle was heard, Castan approached the body and covered Keith's slackened face first with oil and then with wet plaster. The process of getting a cast took about fifteen minutes. Back at his workshop, with the help of a photograph, he corrected the mold because plaster has a tendency to make the subject's eyelids and face muscles sag. He then poured flesh-colored wax into the mold, and when the wax nearest the surface hardened, poured out the rest of it. Carefully removed from the mold, the face was pale and hairless. With a needle, Castan applied reddish-brown human hair for the head, eyebrows, eyelashes, beard, and moustache, painstakingly poking in each hair individually. With a spatula and a blunt needle, he reproduced crow's feet around the eyes, the wrinkles that seasoned the face of a forty-eight-year-old man. He covered the lips with pinkish wax, and then pressed a small tool made of up fine needles into the "skin" to make pores. Carefully touching up the face with paint to look life-life, he made sure it still showed the paralysis caused by the bullet.

He then placed the death's head in his museum's Chamber of Horrors, which lay on the second floor of a building in the down-market side of a shopping arcade. Even in death, Keith had lost his chance at better real estate. Castan was an excellent portraitist, and visitors admired his handiwork, contemplating the head with great curiosity. A *New York Herald* reporter wrote, "From the mask it is easy to perceive how Alexander alias Thomas shot himself in the head, the ball remaining under the left eye. The face of Thomas, bearing a prominent English physiognomy is tolerably large. The features betray nothing indicative of deep villany—they even express a certain mildness, marked with great energy, and the rounded forehead betokens intelligence." In an age steeped in the false science of race, it was popularly believed that Anglo-Saxons would not ordinarily be given to vicious crimes. The typical criminal type was a dark and swarthy foreign type, or, if white, had congenital abnormalities revealed in a Neanderthal forehead, sharp features, small eyes, pointed ears, a thrusting chin, a mangy beard, and a curled upper lip with visible teeth ready to bite. In other words, a criminal did not resemble an ideal Northern European, and Sandy Keith did. Even in death, he looked like a prosperous burgher, with a sanguine temperament, about to bestow a gift. Was this a new, heretofore unknown criminal type?

The coroner certainly pondered this issue as he examined the bumps on Sandy Keith's head, for he had received official permission to have it removed from Keith's body shortly after death. With a phrenological map of the anterior, lateral, and posterior portions of the human skull in view, he felt for the propensities, emotions, and faculties that made up this baffling criminal mastermind. Around the temples, cold to the touch and rigid with rigor mortis, the doctor searched for the organs of appetite, knowing Keith's was prodigious. His hands carefully probed the forehead for signs of intelligence, the broad well-developed bone speaking to him of the ability to reason. He moved across the supposed organs of morality and aesthetics over the top of the cranium, expecting to find these portions flat and undeveloped. He then ran his fingers behind the ears, where he hoped to find well-developed markers of greed, deception, secretiveness, and destructiveness. If he believed in these physical inheritances, that the shape of the skull determined the behavior of the murderer, he knew that he was in danger of giving up religious faith in free will. If the shape of a man's skull made him a criminal, then he had had no choice in his murderous deeds and was therefore blameless. He was driven by a set of inherited traits beyond his control, and therefore morality had nothing to do with his misdeeds. This was hardly a viable philosophical position for a student of human behavior, especially a Christian one, and phrenologists and their critics were deeply vexed by this dilemma. Whether the coroner found features that fit the scientific view of the physiology of a fiend, he kept it to himself. He placed the head in a large glass jar, weighting it down until it could absorb a preservative of glycerine, alcohol, salt, and potassium chloride, a solution that was said to protect the soft tissues and prevent their discoloration. Then he gave the head to a local museum of natural history.

Later the head was moved again to the Bremen police building, where it lay for many years on a shelf, provoking the idle curiosity of visitors with its gruesome history. Floating in alcohol, the head witnessed the end of the nineteenth century and the first half of the twentieth, as brutal slaughters were made ever more possible by technological progress. Increasingly powerful explosive weapons with complicated mechanisms could now be dropped remotely from planes on innocent civilians. Removed from the scene of mayhem and grief, the bomber pilots experienced the human suffering they caused only from a great distance. With Keith's desire for technological power, his unwillingness to personally witness the consequences of his violence, and his determination to sacrifice the innocent, he would have understood the new infernal machines. As petty were his motives, Sandy Keith was a harbinger of his age.

Thus, it seemed a fitting end that Keith's head should meet its fate during World War II, during an Allied bombing of the Bremen harbor. According to local legend, a bomb fell on the police museum, shattering the jar and dumping its gruesome contents into the wreckage. There the head became mixed with the dismembered fragments of the bombing victims, and during the cleanup, was taken away and buried with other unidentified human appendages. Keith, so concerned with his image, had finally descended into total anonymity.

WORKS CITED

This is a work of narrative nonfiction, but not a work of pure imagination. I have taken very few liberties with the historical record. What is written here is based on the best evidence, and can be verified through many sources. When primary sources were discrepant, I made my best guess as to which seemed more accurate. I have sometimes extrapolated the states of consciousness and thoughts of my historical characters, but only when I perceived broad patterns of their behavior that led me to these conclusions. My interpretations are based on an understanding of my characters' psychological patterns and the social worlds in which they moved. I was also greatly aided by my reading of nineteenth-century travel writing and authors like Mark Twain, Charles Dickens, and Henry James, who observed their times better than any detective or newspaper reporter. While no work of history can be said to be absolutely true, I have strived for accuracy throughout. One of my goals has been to offset more blindly romantic portraits of the past, to emphasize the humanity of historical figures, especially those of nineteenth-century terrorists and criminals.

PRIMARY SOURCES

The most important documents on Keith's life are the various police reports and case documentation in the Bremen State Archive (Bremen *Staatsarchiv*) in Germany, filed under the name *Dynamitattentat des Amerikaners Alexander Keith alias William King Thomas gegen den Lloyd Dampfer, "Mosel" am 11 dez. 1875*. The files include Cecelia Thompson's and Alexander Keith's personal letters; Keith's suicide note; family photographs, bank statements, and sales receipts; transcripts of the police interrogations of Keith; and the records of the investigations by the Bremen and Dresden police, Scotland Yard, and the Pinkertons. There are many false leads and blind alleys in these papers but eventually the truth begins to emerge. The Pinkerton report, authored by Robert A. Pinkerton (January 11, 1876), provides a narrative of Keith's life, especially his movements in the United States, and gives a new glimpse into the chains of financial connections among Confederate blockade-runners in Halifax and Wilmington. Many details throughout the book come from the interviews with Keith's former associates and acquaintances included in the report. There is no question, after viewing these documents, that Alexander

Keith, Jr., and William King Thomas are the same man. The Bremerhaven City Archive contains documents related to local news coverage of the "Thomas-Katastrophe," both at the time of the disaster and at anniversaries.

I also relied on databases with full text-search capabilities to enrich my understanding of the period. Especially useful for local history was the Historical Newspapers (1786–2000) database at ancestry.com, a website of MyFamily.com, Inc. Invaluable for general nineteenth-century history were the Historical *New York Times* and the American Periodical Series available through Proquest; Nineteenth Century Books, Nineteenth Century Periodicals, and other American Memory collections through the Library of Congress; Historical Newspapers (including the index for the *London Times*) through History Online; and the Making of America database provided by the University of Michigan. I also consulted online versions of the U.S. Censuses for 1850, 1860, and 1870, and 1880 (St. Louis, Missouri, and Madison County, Illinois) at ancestry.com, and the Canadian census for 1881 at familysearch.org, a website of the Church of Jesus Christ of Latter-Day Saints.

In Scotland, I conducted genealogical research on the Keith family at the General Register Office (GRO) of Scotland, Edinburgh, and the North Highland Archive in Wick, where I viewed maps, landholdings, censuses for the region, and the *John O'Groats Journal.* Unfortunately, few records, including any censuses, existed before 1841, making the record quite spotty. For dates and places of the Keith family in Scotland, I consulted Proclamations of Banns & Marriages and Births & Baptisms, Parish of Reay, Old Parochial Register, GRO. Limited versions of these records are available online, for a fee, at http://www.scotlandspeople.gov.uk. The first (1791–1799) and second (1834–1845) Statistical Accounts of Scotland, available in the North Highland Archive, provided invaluable glimpses of life in Caithness from clergy members of the time.

In Halifax, I visited the Provincial Archives of Nova Scotia, where various documents related to the Keith family reside. Most of these documents have to do with the Hon. Alexander Keith and his Masonic activities, but the archive also holds information on the membership of the Chebucto Greys, Keith's official petition for the return of his pork, the aldermen's report on the explosion of the powder magazine, and full runs of local newspapers for this period, including coverage of the Sutherland/Smith arson case. Evidence of Keith's culpability for the powder magazine explosion came later, and can be found in the Pinkerton report and a letter from C. A. Creighton, German Consul to Halifax (June 1876) among the *Dynamitattentat* papers in the Bremen State Archive. There is no way of knowing with absolute certainty that Keith committed this crime, since neither he nor anyone else was ever convicted in court, but memories were long in Halifax among those who believed he was responsible. Many of the houses in old Halifax, including Keith Hall, are marked with plaques that give the name and date of the original occupant, making for an extremely useful historical tour of the city.

The history of Confederate secret operations in Canada is complex and difficult to interpret, as are the histories of all secret organizations. Most historians agree that assassination plots, raids across the border, and other schemes were disorganized efforts, by and large, whose effects were often inflated in

the Northern press. Nevertheless, there was an informal network of saboteurs, daredevils, and assasination plotters whose machinations will never be
fully known. The involvement of the highest level of the Confederate government in terrorist plotting in Canada has been highly disputed for over a century, although there is growing evidence that Jefferson Davis and other
Confederate leaders in Richmond knew of many of these activities even if they
did not direct them. My concern has been with one player in these events,
who probably had more involvement than I have represented here. Many
records were lost, and the vast majority of former Confederate secret service
agents kept a silence they took to their graves.

Mortimer Melville Jackson's correspondence with the War Department
regarding Keith can be found in the Despatches from United States Counsels
in Halifax, 1833–1906 (T–469, Roll 10) in the National Archives and Records
Administration (NARA). Also helpful are the documents from the political
disputes between Great Britain and the United States, collected in *Correspondence Concerning Claims Against Great Britain*, Vol. II (Washington, D.C.: Philip
& Solomons, 1869). These include first-hand accounts of the second *Chesapeake* affair. Brain and the *Chesapeake* pirates, including newspaper clippings
about them, can also be found in the Despatches from United States Counsuls
in Halifax and Quebec.

The Confederate currency caper was covered in the *New York Times* (January 4, 1864) and in the personal accounts of War Department telegraph officer David Homer Bates, who names Alexander Keith, Jr. Further particulars
of the New York ring can be found in the Lamar correspondence, captured on
a blockade-runner by the U.S. Navy and reprinted in the *New York Times*
(June 16, 1864). More of Charles Lafayette Lamar's letters were reprinted in
"A Slave-Trader's Letter Book," *North American Review* 143 (1886): 447–463.

Keith's involvement in the Luke Blackburn's yellow fever plot was revealed by Godfrey Hyams in a deposition to the Police Court in Toronto
(reprinted in the *New York Times*, May 26, 1865) and at the Lincoln assassination trial. Hyams mentioned Keith's role in Halifax, but does not say that
Keith was with him on the journey to the United States. However, Luther
Smoot, interviewed by Pinkerton detectives after the Bremerhaven disaster,
places Keith in Philadelphia in July 1864, at the same time Hyams was there.
Hyams's testimony about the yellow-fever plot was corroborated by reports
from Bermuda and by a statement from one of the shippers chosen by Hyams
to handle the trunks. Although the yellow-fever plot has been treated with
skepticism, largely because of corruption in the Lincoln assassination trial,
many historians (see especially Steers, 46–54) believe that the evidence is persuasive enough that it did indeed occur.

The story of Patrick Martin is largely based on George P. Kane's account
to journalist George Whitehead Townsend in *The Daily Graphic* and Martin's
friend James W. A. Wright's article in the *Overland*. These were written ten
years after the fact, but Townsend, especially, was a conscientious, well-
known journalist and therefore a credible source. Despatches from United
States Consuls in Quebec, 1861–1906 (NARA, T–482, Roll 2) verify the loss
of the *Marie Victoria* and the salvage of Booth's costumes. There are, of course,
other possible interpretations of these events. The loss of the ships indeed

might have been entirely accidental, though in any event the wrecks appear to have benefited Keith, and I have chosen to believe Kane's story to Townsend. Two original versions of John Maxwell's bombing of the City Point depot exist, one in *War of the Rebellion: A Compilation of the Official Records of the Union and Confederate Armies,* Series 1, Vol. 42, Part 1 (Washington: GPO, 1892); the other in Morris Schaff's eyewitness account from the *Civil War Papers of the State of Massachusetts,* Vol. 2 (1900), reprinted in Stern, 230–235.

Luther Smoot's trials with the locomotive engines are documented in his claims petition, which can be found in NARA, RG 46, Records of the U.S. Senate, Forty-fourth Congress, Committee on Claims, Petitions and Memorial File (SEN 43A-H4). Unfortunately, some of the attachments, including the statement of William Almon, have been lost. In the Pinkerton report Smoot briefly describes his meeting with Mary Clifton and other informants mention Keith's relationship to her. Much of my interpretation of Mary's story comes from an article in the *St. Louis Republican* (February 21, 1876) after the Bremerhaven explosion, written by a correspondent in Halifax. I have based my version of Smoot's pursuit and Keith's arrest mostly on the Eagan version in the *St. Louis Republican* (December 31, 1875).

My interpretation of Keith's movements through ships and hotels comes from the Bremen police's first report (released February 18, 1876) and second report (released March 30, 1876) and the Pinkerton report, all in the Bremen State Archive's *Dynamitattentat* files. A lengthy summary of the Bremen police's first report appeared in the *New York Herald* (February 19, 1876, 2). Colonel Donn Piatt's story of his frightening trip with Keith onboard the *Celtic* first appeared in his newspaper, *Washington Capitol,* and was widely reprinted in other papers. The Pinkerton report and stories in the *New York Herald* (January 6, 1876; January 17, 1876) give many details about the incident on the *Celtic,* including interviews with the ship's staff. Though Keith's plans for the *Celtic* cannot be known with certainty, his history and the circumstantial evidence add up to a compelling argument that he had planned to bomb the ship. My knowledge of the travelers on these ships was aided by a review of the *Passenger Lists of Vessels Arriving at New York, 1820–1897* (NARA, M–237), including those of the *Celtic,* the *Salier,* and the *Republic.*

Bremen's *Weser-Zeitung* carried the most extensive stories on the tragedy that affected the city so personally. The most poignant story, from an eyewitness, appeared in *Die Gartenlaube* (No. 2, 1876). From its correspondent in Bremen, the *London Times* provided the best English-language news of disaster and investigation, and in its letters column offered an energetic debate over the legal implications of the crime. Consular correspondence concerning the effect of the crime on relations between Germany and the United States can be found in Despatches from U.S. Ministers to German States and Germany, 1799–1906, NARA, M44, Roll 28. These papers include copies and translations of articles from German newspapers condemning America for producing a mass murderer like Keith. The *St. Louis Republican* has the credit for breaking the story of the connection between Alexander Keith, Jr. and William King Thomas, based on information from an employee at the Southern Hotel. The *New York Herald* provided full coverage of activities at the New York docks, including interviews with the *Celtic's* personnel and survivors of the *Deutschland*

and the *Mosel*. The Nova Scotia newspapers remained almost completely and eerily silent.

Details of the Pinkerton investigation come from two sources: the Pinkerton Detective Agency Papers at the Library of Congress and the Pinkerton report and invoice in the Bremen State Archive. The former includes Allan Pinkerton's phrenology report, his letters to his sons and employees during this period, and the agency's time books that document the names and movements of the detectives, including their investigation of the "explosion at Bremerhaven," commissioned by Salomon and Burke (Time Book, Vol. 1, 1873–1877).

The stories of the hapless student and George Schantz come from *New York Times* coverage. The train bomb was covered in many newspapers, including the *Elyria Constitution* (November 9, 1876). The story of George Holgate and the infernal machines is based on reports in the *New York Times* and on the Fenian Brotherhood Papers in the Public Records Office in London, especially Vol. 26. Holgate's bargain with the British government is evident in a letter from Consul George Crump to British foreign secretary Earl Granville (October 29, 1880). Further particulars can be found in the reports of A. L. Drummond and D. H. Gilkinson, NARA, RG 87, Daily Reports of U.S. Secret Service Agents, 1875–1936.

NOTES

ABBREVIATIONS

BSA: Bremen State Archive, *Dynamitattentat des Amerikaners Alexander Keith* files.
BCA: Bremerhaven City Archive
PANS: Provincial Archives of Nova Scotia
NARA: U.S. National Archives and Records Administration
PRO: Public Records Office, London

INTRODUCTION

2   Fritz Zumann: *Sedalia Daily Democrat*, February 2, 1876, 1.
3   "most diabolical": *Times*, December 18, 1875, 9.
4   "dynamite fiend": See for example *New York Times*, January 29, 1876, 8; *New York Herald*, February 3, 1876, 8; *Decatur Daily Republican*, December 17, 1875, 2; *Burlington Hawkeye*, December 16, 1875, 1; *Atlanta Constitution*, January 9, 1876, 2; W. C. Church and F. P. Church, "Nebulae," *Galaxy*, February 1876, 289; *Berliner Fremdenblatt*, December 18, 1875, translated in NARA, M44, Roll 28, Despatches from U.S. Ministers to German States and Germany, 1799–1906, No. 233, enclosure 2.

CHAPTER 1

8   "By God": Halifax City Council, *The Report of the Committee of Alderman Respecting the Recent Explosion of the Gunpowder Magazine at Halifax* (Halifax: Mourning Journal, 1857), 34.
9   "very slovenly state of things": Halifax City Council, *Report*, 12.
9   "prominent banker": Pinkerton report, BSA, Q.9.k.3.b, Nr. 5, 275; C. A. Creighton, German consul to Halifax, Letter, June 6, 1876, BSA, Q.9.k.3.b, Nr. 5, 287.
11   "industrious, temperate": Finlay Cook, "Parish of Reay," *New Statistical Account of Scotland*, Vol. 15 (Edinburgh: Blackwood, 1845), 68.

11   tacksmen: Eric Richards, *The Highland Clearances: People, Landlords and Rural Turmoil* (Edinburgh: Birlinn, 2000), 36–44.

12   the ministers railed: John Munro, "Parish of Halkirk," *The New Statistical Account of Scotland*, Vol. 15 (Caithness: Blackwood, 1845), 68–82.

12   "great big Rum shop": Judith Fingard, *The Dark Side of Life in Victorian Halifax* (Nova Scotia: Pottersfield, 1991), 26.

13   "Mount, ye gallants free!": James Taylor, *The Great Historic Families of Scotland*, Vol. 1, 2nd ed. (1889; Baltimore, MD: Genealogical, 1995), 98–125.

13   Big Keith: James Traill Calder, *Sketch of the Civil and Traditional History of Caithness from the Tenth Century* (Wick: Raw, 1887). Available online at Caithness Community Web Site http://www.caithness.org/caithness/castles/historyofcaithness, December 21, 2004.

15   an amusing story: *John O'Groats*, May 4, 1838, 3.

15   "Poyais": David Sinclair, *The Land That Never Was: Sir Gregor Macgregor and the Most Audacious Fraud in History* (Cambridge, MA: Da Capo, 2004).

16   "The undersigned": Advertisement, *Morning Chronicle*, April 1, 1851.

18   John McDougall: Pinkerton report, BSA, 131–135.

19   "infernal machine": *Novascotian*, April 30, 1834, 2.

20   Chebucto Grays, Victoria Rifles: *St. Louis Republican*, February 21, 1876, 5; Greg Marquis, *In Armageddon's Shadow: The Civil War and Canada's Maritime Provinces* (Montreal: McGill-Queen's University Press, 2000), 64–65.

20   "brawny firm race": George Augustus Sala, *Daily Telegraph*, December 15, 1863, 5.

21   "long line of uplifted bayonets": Kinahan Cornwallis, *Royalty in the New World; or, the Prince of Wales in America* (New York: Doolady, 1860), 43.

21   *Great Eastern*: *St. Louis Republican*, February 21, 1876, 5; Stephen Fox, *Transatlantic: Samuel Cunard, Isambard Brunel, and the Great Atlantic Steamships* (New York: HarperCollins, 2003), 155–167.

22   "triumphal cars": Charles Dickens, *American Notes: and the Uncommercial Traveler* (Philadelphia: Peterson, n.d.), 45.

CHAPTER 2

23   five thousand troops: Thomas H. Raddall, *Halifax: Warden of the North* (Montreal: McClelland & Stewart, 1971), 192.

24   One version he gave of his life: Pinkerton report, BSA, 126–127.

24   Alexander Keith ... did not sympathize with the Confederacy: Pinkerton report, BSA, 92.

25   "The people generally are very friendly": "Bohemian," *New York Times*, September 29, 1864, 1.

25–26 The first blockade-runner they fitted out: *St. Louis Republican*, February 21, 1876, 5.

26   jewel-encrusted sword: James Sprunt, *Derelicts* (Wilmington: Lord Baltimore, 1920), 53.

26   seventy-five dollars a month: James Morris Morgan, *Recollections of a Rebel Reefer* (New York: Houghton Mifflin, 1917), 101.

27   "The only vulnerable part": "Captain Roberts" [Augustus Charles Hobart-Hampden], *Never Caught* (London: John Camden Hotten, 1867), 49.

27   "an ordinarily brave man": James Sprunt, *Chronicles of the Cape Fear River: 1660–1916* (1916; Wilmington: Broadfoot, 1992), 451.

27   "a course, ill-bred vulgarian": J[ohn] Wilkinson, *The Narrative of a Blockade-Runner* (New York: Sheldon, 1877), 177.

28   "Confederate Consul": Wilkinson, *Blockade-Runner,* pg. 177; Pinkerton Report, BSA, 91.

28   Boykin: Pinkerton report, BSA, 91.

28   They romantically named their plantations: Celeste Ray, *Highland Heritage: Scottish Americans in the American South* (Chapel Hill: University of North Carolina Press, 2001), 188–189.

29   "As a boy": Sprunt, *Chronicles,* ix.

29   "dear Dixie Land": Sprunt, *Chronicles,* 392.

29   Keith so earned Sprunt's trust: Pinkerton report, BSA, 93.

29   "rosy and robust Nova Scotia girl": *St. Louis Republican,* February 21, 1876, 5.

30   "a hotel chambermaid": Mark Twain, *A Tramp Abroad,* ed. Jim Manis (1881; Hazelton, PA: Penn State Electronic Classics Series, 2000), 63–64.

31   Zarvona Thomas: John Thomas Scharf, *Chronicles of Baltimore* (Baltimore, MD: Turnbull, 1874), 613–614; William A. Tidwell, *Come Retribution: The Confederate Secret Service and the Assassination of Lincoln* (Jackson: University Press of Mississippi, 1988), 330; George Alfred Townsend, "Thomassen," *Daily Graphic,* March 22, 1876, 1.

31–32 raid on Johnson's Island: Tidwell, *Come Retribution,* 180–181.

32   "He is a great scamp": Marquis, *Armageddon's Shadow,* 135–136.

35   "No! No!": *Morning Journal,* January 13, 1864, 1.

CHAPTER 3

40    $3 million: James Grant Wilson and John Fiske, eds., "Mortimer Melville Jackson," *Appletons' Cyclopædia of American Biography,* Vol. 3 (New York: Appleton, 1888), 390.

40   Keith was the hub: M. M. Jackson to Frederick Seward, letter, August 20, 1864, Despatches from United States Consuls in Halifax, 1833–1906, NARA, T–469, Roll 10.

41   "he thinks her virtuous": *New York Times,* June 16, 1864, 1.

41   Coded letter: David Homer Bates, "A Rebel Cipher Despatch: One Which Did Not Reach Judah P. Benjamin," *Harper's* 97 (1898): 108.

42   "Sacred Three": David Homer Bates, *Lincoln in the Telegraph Office: Recollections of the United States Military Telegraph Corps During the Civil War* (New York: Century, 1907), 72.

43 "Willis is here": Bates, "Rebel Cipher," 108.

44 *Pulaski:* Rebecca J. McLeod, "Wreck of the *Pulaski*," ed. Mary De-Lashmit. Available online at Eleanor Colson, Lamar Family Genealogy http://members.aol.com/eleanorcol/WreckPulaski.html, December 22, 2004.

45 "You are aware": Charles Lafayette Lamar, "A Slave-Trader's Letter Book," *North American Review* 143 (1886): APS Online, 459; see also Thomas Henderson Wells, *The Slave Ship* Wanderer (Athens: University of Georgia Press, 1967).

45 "There are devilish few rebels": *New York Times,* January 16, 1864, 1.

46 "As the risks increase": *New York Times,* January 16, 1864, 1.

46 "With Mexico": *New York Times,* January 16, 1864, 1.

47 Blackburn had made his reputation: Nancy Disher Baird, *Luke Pryor Blackburn, Physician, Governor, Reformer* (Lexington: University Press of Kentucky, 1979), 1–35.

50 "the expedition," "the working men of Manchester": Benn Pitman, ed., *The Assassination of President Lincoln and the Trial of the Conspirators* (New York: Moore, Wilstach & Baldwin, 1865), 54–56; *New York Times,* May 26, 1865, 5.

51 "cajolery of those who knew," "powerful conspiracy": Mason Philip Smith, *Confederates Downeast: Confederate Operations In and Around Maine* (Portland: Provincial, 1985), 33, 39.

52 "it was generally concluded": Bates, "Rebel Cipher," 109.

CHAPTER 4

54 William Russell: Anthony Godfrey, *Pony Express National Historic Trail,* Historic Resource Study, U. S. Department of the Interior, National Park Service, 1994, available online at http://www.nps.gov/poex/hrs/hrs2b.htm, December 22, 2004.

54 scam: United States Congress, House, Select Committee on the Fraudulent Abstraction of Bonds from the Interior Department, *Abstracted Indian Trust Bonds,* Report 78 (Washington: 1861).

54 "Money is insane": Henry Ward Beecher, *Freedom and War* (Boston: Ticknor, 1863), 36.

55 "most profitable business": Luther Smoot, Claims Petition, NARA, RG 46, Records of the U.S. Senate, Forty-fourth Congress, Committee on Claims, Petitions and Memorial File (SEN 43A-H4).

55 supervised construction of 200-foot Sir Walter Scott monument: Pat Lotz, *Banker, Builder, Blockade Runner: A Victorian Embezzler and His Circle* (Kentville, Nova Scotia: Gaspereau, 2002), 154.

56 "American locomotives in England": "Fresh Gleanings," *American Literary Magazine* (October 1847): APS Online, 235. See also "Our Manufactures," *United States Magazine of Science, Art, Manufactures, Agriculture, Commerce and Trade* (October 1855): APS Online, 151.

56–57 Two more gullible investors: Pinkerton report, BSA, 103; Lotz, *Banker,* 197–210.

58   "little Confederates," "African aristocracy": Georgiana Gholson
      Walker, *The Private Journal of Georgiana Gholson Walker, 1862–1876*,
      ed. Dwight Franklin Henderson, *Confederate Centennial Studies* 25
      (1963): 41, 50.

58   Walker was shocked: Pinkerton report, BSA, 95.

58   "great pecuniary loss": Alexander Keith, Jr., petition, PANS, RG
      5, Series G, Misc. A, Vol. 4, #188.

59   Rose O'Neal Greenhow: Walker, *Private Journal*, 113–114.

59   "with much kindness and attention": Walker, *Private Journal*, 114.

60   Booth visited Martin: Tidwell, *Come Retribution*, 329–331.

60   "purely humane and patriotic": Samuel Bland Arnold, *Memoirs of a
      Lincoln Conspirator*, ed. Michael W. Kaufmann (Bowie, MD: Her-
      itage, 1995), 133–137.

61   *Caledonia:* Pinkerton Report, BSA, 96; Lotz, *Banker*, 171.

62   "wizard of the saddle": Bennett Henderson Young, *Confederate Wiz-
      ards of the Saddle* (Kennesaw, GA: Continental, 1958); John W.
      Headley, *Confederate Operations in Canada and New York* (New York:
      Neale, 1906), 259.

63   "genial, whole-souled, and brave": J. W. A. Wright, "Mysterious
      Fate of Blockade Runners," *Overland Monthly and Out West Magazine*
      7 (1886): APS Online, 298.

63   "bad fellow": Townsend, "Thomassen," 1.

64   "an ordinary candle box," "party of ladies": Morris Schaff, "Explo-
      sion at City Point," in ed. Philip Van Doren Stern, *Secret Missions of
      the Civil War* (Chicago: Rand McNally, 1959), 235.

64   "From the top of the bluff": Schaff, "Explosion," 232. See also Ella
      S. Rayburn, "Sabotage at City Point," *Civil War Times Illustrated* 22,
      2 (1983): 28–33.

64–65 Thomas Courtenay: Thomas Thatcher, "Thomas Courtenay/coal
      torpedoes," personal email, September 15, 2003; Thomas Thatcher,
      "The plot thickens," personal email, September 16, 2003.

65   "destructionists": William A. Tidwell, *April '65: Confederate Covert Ac-
      tion in the American Civil War* (Kent, OH: Kent State University
      Press, 1995), 32.

65   as many as sixty steamboats: Edward Steers, Jr., "Terror: 1860s
      Style," *North & South* 5 (2002): 16.

65   Godfrey Hyams: *New York Times*, April 23, 1865, 1; *New York Times*,
      April 29, 1865, 1.

CHAPTER 5

67   "That's Taylor's saloon": Horatio Alger, Jr., *Ragged Dick or Street Life
      in New York*, ed. Carl Bode (New York: Penguin, 1985), 26.

68   "Drink a glass of wine with me": *St. Louis Republican*, February 21,
      1876, 5.

69   He had arranged to ship thirty bales of cotton: Pinkerton report,
      BSA, 92.

69   "First, Men are valued": Edward B. Lytton, *The Dramatic Works of the Right Hon. Lord Lytton* (Freeport: Books for Libraries, 1972), 305, 407.

70   A few furious men: Pinkerton Report, BSA, pp. 78, 96.

72   "Chicago amuses": "The City of St. Louis," *Atlantic Monthly* (June 1867): 655.

72   "grimacing in astonishment": Dickens, *American Notes*, 209.

72   "Some fiend": *Missouri Republican*, December 12, 1864, reprinted in G. E. Rule, "Hell and Maria," 2001. Available online at Civil War St. Louis   http://www.civilwarstlouis.com/boatburners/steamermaria. htm, December 22, 2004.

73   "My favorite cure": Theodore Dreiser, *Newspaper Days*, ed. T. D. Nostwich (Philadelphia: University of Pennsylvania Press, 1991), NetLibrary, 275.

74   "the sharpest play": Gordon Samples, *Lust for Fame: The Stage Career of John Wilkes Booth* (Jefferson, NC: McFarland, 1982), 150.

74   At his own expense: William Gurley, letter, June 3, 1865, Despatches from the United States Consuls in Quebec, 1861–1906, NARA, T482, Roll 2.

75   The trunks . . . were eventually auctioned off: Samples, *Lust for Fame*, 173–174.

75   An enterprising detective: *Leipzige Zeitung*, January 8, 1876, 66.

CHAPTER 6

77–78   Camp Jackson: Louis S. Gerteis, *Civil War St. Louis* (Lawrence: University of Kansas Press, 2001), 97–125.

78   Keith was on his way to Camp Jackson: Pinkerton report, BSA, 118–119.

78   Francis X. Jones: Smith, *Confederates Downeast*, 31.

78   "I have loved the prairie": Carl Sandburg, "Prairie," in *Complete Poems* (New York: Harcourt, Brace, 1950), 79.

79   "Notwithstanding that the birds": Cornwallis, *Prince of Wales*, 167.

79   "no aesthetic appreciation": Joseph Suppiger, Salomon Koepfli, and Kaspar Koepfli, *Journey to New Switzerland: Travel Account of the Koepfli and Suppiger Family to St. Louis and the Founding of New Switzerland in the State of Illinois*, trans. Raymond J. Spahn, ed. John C. Abbott (Carbondale, IL: Southern Illinois University Press, 1987), 196.

79   A barber and a hosteler: W. T. Norton, *Centennial History of Madison County, Illinois* (Chicago: Lewis, 1912), 551.

79   "sufficient onto itself": Mark Twain, "The Man That Corrupted Hadleyburg," in *The Man That Corrupted Hadleyburg and Other Essays and Stories* (New York: Harper & Brothers, 1901), 12.

81   "Oh, that is all right": Pinkerton report, BSA, 123.

82   Keith told Hammer: Pinkerton report, BSA, 126–128.

83   a large family in Alsace Lorraine: Norton, *Centennial History*, 905.

83 milliners practiced a strict social hierarchy: Wendy Gamber, *The Female Economy: The Millinery and Dressmaking Trades, 1860–1930* (Urbana: University of Illinois Press, 1997), 178.

83–84 "the pleasure seekers," "sequestered," "English-looking gentleman": *New York Herald*, February 21, 1876, 6.

84 "short and merry life": Pinkerton report, BSA, 125.

84 "your most obedient sarvant": Cecelia Thomas to William Thomas, letter, December 3, 1875, BSA, Q.9.k.3.b, Nr. 2, 1c.

85 "Refined and recherché: John H. Claiborne, qtd. in Dwight Franklin, Introduction, Walker, *Private Journal*, 11.

86 "astonishing effect of the explosion": *War of the Rebellion, A Compilation of the Official Records of the Union and Confederate Armies* (Washington: GPO, 1892), Series I, Vol. 40, Part I, 788–789.

86 "a restless old snoozer": *St. Louis Republican*, January 10, 1876, 8.

CHAPTER 7

89 "Oh, they'll buy you fine trinkets": J. H. Collins, *The Unconstant Lover* (New York: J. Andrews, n.d.); *America Singing: Nineteenth-Century Song Sheets*, American Memory, Library of Congress, memory.loc.gov, December 22, 2004.

89–90 "The calamity": Josiah Gorgas, *The Journals of Josiah Gorgas, 1857–1878*, ed. Sarah Woolfolk Wiggins (Tuscaloosa: University of Alabama Press, 1995), 167.

90 "Is it an emergency?" "little eyes like a pig's": *St. Louis Republican*, December 31, 1876, 8.

91 "outrage on humanity": David L. Phillips to Abraham Lincoln, letter, October 29, 1860, American Lincoln Papers, Series 1, General Correspondence, 1833–1916, Library of Congress.

92 "My god": *St. Louis Republican*, January 28, 1876, 8.

92 William Tecumseh Sherman: Pinkerton report, BSA, 105–108.

93–94 "Ruinous loss," "English agent": Smoot, Claims Petition, NARA.

CHAPTER 8

98 "the aroma of huge estates": *Atlanta Constitution*, August 12, 1876, 1.

98 700 Americans: James Leonard Corning, "American Life in Dresden," *Saturday Evening Post*, March 19, 1870, APS Online, 4.

98 "once one commences to move": "Miscellany," *Appleton's Journal of Literature, Science and Art* (November 16, 1872): APS Online, 558.

99 The Thompsons' circle: The couple's social activities are documented in Cecelia's letters in BSA, Q.9.k.3.b, Nr. 2. Their travels are described in the Bremen police's second official report on the dynamite explosion, March 26, 1876, BSA, Q.9.k.3.b, Nr. 6.

99 "Mother Earth": *New York Times*, March 2, 1882, 2.

100 "He was small in stature": T[heodore] A[ugustus] Barry and B[enjamin] A[da] Patten, *Men and Memories of San Francisco, in the "Spring of '50"* (San Francisco: Bancroft, 1873), 41.

101   Typical of his stories: *Atlanta Constitution,* January 9, 1876, 2.
101   "exquisite": *San Francisco Daily Morning Call,* September 7, 1864, in ed. Edgar M. Branch, *Clemens at the Call* (Berkeley: University of California Press, 1969), 103.
102   "entreé into delightful circles": "Miscellany," 558.
103   Florie told a sordid story: *New York Times,* December 19, 1883, 8; *New York Times,* December 20, 1883, 8; *New York Times,* December 22, 1883, 8; *New York Times,* December 22, 1884, 8; "Gotham's Latest Scandal," *National Police Gazette,* February 16, 1884, APS Online, 3.
103   "petty tyranny": *New York Times,* May 10, 1884, 8.
104   "My own darling": Newspaper clipping, BSA, Q.9.k.3.b, Nr.2.
104   The Keith Highland clan: Taylor, *Great Historic Families,* 120–122.
104   "would lose control of himself," "seemed to gloat," "Poor fellows": *New York Herald,* February 21, 1876, 6.
105   Charles Sebyt, George Lentz: Pinkerton report, BSA, 120.
106   *City of Boston: New York Times,* January 1, 1876, 1; Pinkerton report, 31, 64; Correspondence between W. Inman and Marine Department, London, BSA, Q.9.k.3.b, Nr. 3, 116.
106   ghost ship: Elinor De Wire, "Phantom Ships and Spectral Crews," *Trailer Boats* 24 (1995): 88.
106   a small smuggling business: Pinkerton report, BSA, 20–22.
106   "they burned through the money": The couple's lavish spending is documented in extensive sales receipts and bank records in BSA, Q.9.k.3.b, Nr.2.
107   "as a man and a Mason": Warren Gould to W. K. Thomas, 1872, BSA, Q.9.k.3.b, Nr.2.
108   Cecelia owed $1,429: *New York Herald,* January 11, 1876, 6.
108   "Ladies, what is capital": "Political Economy for Ladies," *Saturday Evening Post,* June 12, 1875, APS Online, 8. See also Gamber, *Female Economy,* 103–123.
108–109   Madame Louise: Pinkerton Report, BSA, 116.
109   "a strange wild look," "with a passionate earnestness": *New York Herald,* February 21, 1876, 6.
109   Charles Seybt: Pinkerton Report, BSA, 120.
109   "According to the nanny": *Atlanta Constitution,* August 12, 1876, 1; Bremen police, second official report, BSA.

CHAPTER 9

111   "with the clear color": *Die Gartenlaube* (Bremen), No. 1 (1876): 19.
112   "talented imagination": *Die Gartenlaube,* No. 1 (1876): 19.
113   Teadro Wiskoff: Bremen police, second official report, BSA.
113   Ignas Rhind: *New York Herald,* January 17, 1876, 3; Bremen police, second official report, BSA.
114–115   "a dark-haired, devilishly handsome": A photograph of Garcie is in the photograph file, BSA, Q.9.k.3.b, Nr. 2.
115   Hotel de Pologne: Bremen police, second official report, BSA.

116 Fuchs was amazed to see Keith again: *New York Herald,* January 17, 1876, 3; Bremen police, second official report, BSA. Fuchs's drawing of his clockwork appeared in the *Illustrierten Zeitung* (Leipzig), clipping, BSA, Q.9.k.3.b, Nr. 5, 199a.

116–117 he went back to Krebs in March: Bremen police, second official report, BSA.

117 he packed the explosives into zinc boxes: *Times,* December 22, 1875, 8.

117–118 *Schiller:* Joseph E. Suppiger, "Suppiger/Menz genealogy," personal email, March 10, 2002; Richard Barber and "The Commodore," *Tresco Times — The Last Piece of England* (Devon: Halsgrove, 2002); Keith Austin, *The Victorian Titanic: The Loss of the S. S. Schiller in 1875* (Devon: Halsgrove, 2001).

119 "The *Honest Endeavor*": "Marine Disasters in 1853," *Debow's Review* 16 (1854): 528.

119 Winslow Homer: "The Wreck of the Atlantic — Cast Up by the Sea," illustration, *Harper's Weekly,* April 26, 1874, 345.

119 "The loss of the steam-ship *Atlantic*": *New York Times,* April 12, 1873, 1.

120 "You will please effect insurance," "We shall be glad to know": Bremen police, second official report, BSA.

120 Fred Boultbee: Pinkerton report, BSA, 47–49.

121 "he was always very neat": Pinkerton report, BSA, 23–24.

121 purported to the customs officials: Pinkerton report, BSA, 5.

121 Edward Skidmore, L. B. Foster: Pinkerton report, BSA, 5.

122 "anxious that some parties": Pinkerton report, BSA, 33.

122 "We beg you to take note": Baring Brothers to William Thomas, letter, September 27, 1875, Q.9.k.3.b, Nr. 2, 11.

122 "betokened natural sense": *New York Herald,* January 12, 1876, 3.

122 Keith talked another bank: Brown Brothers to William K. Thomas, letter, December 7, 1875, BSA, Q.9.k.3.b, Nr. 3, 97d.

122 He returned to Brothers Krebs: Bremen police, second official report, BSA.

CHAPTER 10

123 "oceans of kisses": Cecelia to "My dearest best of Manies," Letter, October 4, 1875, BSA, Q.9.k.3.b, Nr. 2, 1a.

124 20,000 ships from all parts of the world: William H. Rideing, "England's Great Sea-Port," *Harper's New Monthly,* January 1879, 164.

124 "There is not a brick in your town": Rideing, "England's Great Sea-Port," 163.

125 "I trust you have been well": Cecelia Thomas to William Thomas, letter, October 4, 1875, BSA, Q.9.k.3.b, Nr. 2, 1a.

125 "fears of some dreadful accident": *New York Herald,* February 21, 1876, 6.

126 He approached the S. S. *Republic,* Stern & Son: Bremen police, second official report, BSA; W. Ruiners, sergeant, and F. Williamson,

superintendent of the Metropolitan Police Office, Scotland Yard, official report, January 7, 1876, BSA, Q.9.k.3.b, Nr. 5, 216; *New York Times*, January 1, 1876, 1.

127 the purser assured him: *New York Times*, January 5, 1876, 8.

127 "Cave of the Wind": William Henry Perrin and J. H. Battle, *History of Logan County and Ohio* (Chicago: Baskin, 1880), 583–585.

127 "Inebriated Excellency": Charles Grant Miller, *Don Piatt, His Work and His Ways* (Cincinnati: Clarke, 1893), 243.

127 "the Ink Fiend": Miller, *Don Piatt*, 249, 307.

128 "a very agreeable man": *St Louis Daily Globe-Democrat*, March 3, 1876, 3.

128–129 "a fire in hiding": Dickens, *American Notes*, 33.

129 "It must be very rough": *St Louis Daily Globe-Democrat*, March 3, 1876, 3.

129 Keith . . . was in for a shock: Bremen police, second official report, BSA.

129 strange and surreptitious doings: *St. Louis Globe-Democrat*, January 8, 1876, 2.

130 Keith maintained his gregarious persona: *St. Louis Globe-Democrat*, January 8, 1876, 2.

130 "What do you do that for, sir": *St Louis Daily Globe-Democrat*, March 3, 1876, 3.

131 "Rations for three on one plate": Pinkerton Report, BSA, 24.

131–132 He participated in a little amateur dramatics: *St Louis Daily Globe-Democrat*, March 3, 1876, 3.

132 "It is when crime": *St Louis Daily Globe-Democrat*, March 3, 1876, 3.

133 Keith still had one of the mystery treasure boxes: *New York Herald*, January 6, 1876, 8; *New York Times*, January 5, 1876, 8.

133 He wired Cecelia: William to Cecelia, telegram, October 26, 1875, BSA, Q.9.k.3.b, Nr. 3, 78b.

134 "Oh, how I longed for this moment!": *New York Herald*, February 21, 1876, 6.

134 "I do not want to grieve you": *New York Herald*, February 21, 1876, 6.

CHAPTER 11

135 $25 million: Charles A. Dana, ed., *Meyer's Universum*, Vol. 1 (New York, Meyer, 1852), 168.

135 "a very comfortable room": William to Cecelia, letter, December 6, 1875, BSA, Q.9.k.3.b, Nr. 3, 24.

135 he took breaks from his work for lunch: Thomas's room receipt, Hotel Stadt Bremen, December 9, 1875, BSA, Q.9.k.3.b, Nr. 2, 1p.

136 Friedrich Bruns: Friedrich Bruns recounted Thomas's visit to him in a pamphlet in which he also corrected Fuchs's drawing of the clockwork (see note above): *Das Uhrwerk Des Thomas in natürlicher Grösse Kurz vor der Explosion in Bremerhaven reparirt und nach dem Gedächtniss auf das Gehaueste gezeichnet und beschrieben von Friedr.*

Bruns, Uhrmacher in Bremen (Bremen: Hensius, 1876). This rare pamphlet is available in the British Public Library. See also Bremen police, second official report, BSA.

136–138 *Deutschland: Times,* December 7, 1875; *Times,* December 9, 1875, 5; *Times,* December 11, 1875, 7; *Times,* December 13, 1875, 10; Sean Street, *The Wreck of the Deutschland* (London: Souvenir, 1992).

137 "the bravest girl of the century": *Daily Free Press* (Manitoba), January 14, 1876, 2.

138 "The people who were saved": William Thomas to Cecelia Thomas, letter, December 11, 1875, BSA, Q.9.k.3.b, Nr. 3, 24.

138 "My darling Pett": William to Cecelia, letter, no date, BSA, Q.9.k.3.b, Nr. 3, 24.

139 "a dirty old beast": Cecelia Thomas to William Thomas, letter, December 1, 1875, BSA, Q.9.k.3.b, Nr. 2, 1b; *New York Times,* November 13, 1875, 5; *New York Times,* November 14, 1875, 7.

139 "You must not be afraid": William Thomas to Cecelia Thomas, letter, no date, BSA, Q.9.k.3.b, Nr. 3, 24.

139 "Keep your mind at ease": William Thomas to Cecelia Thomas, letter, December 6, 1875, BSA, Q.9.k.3.b, Nr. 3, 24.

139–140 "it proves," "the servants": Cecelia Thomas to William Thomas, letter, December 9, 1875, BSA, Q.9.k.3.b, Nr. 2, 1d.

140 "I want to know positively": Cecelia Thomas to William Thomas, letter, no date, BSA, Q.9.k.3.b, Nr. 2, 1f.

141 "Now do be patient": William Thomas to Cecelia Thomas, letter, December 9, 1875, BSA, Q.9.k.3.b, Nr. 3, 24.

141 "if the devil": William Thomas to Cecelia Thomas, letter, December 9, 1875, BSA, Q.9.k.3.b, Nr. 3, 24.

141 Kafesch and Stossky, barrel of supposed caviar: Bremen police, second official report, BSA.

CHAPTER 12

143 "I have had a troublesome work": William Thomas to Cecelia Thomas, letter, December 11, 1875, BSA, Q.9.k.3.b, Nr. 3, 24.

144 The passengers felt a need for conversation: *Die Gartenlaube* No. 2 (1876): 36.

145 "Excuse me": *St. Louis Daily Globe-Democrat,* January 5, 1876, 2.

145 "Do I look anything like a criminal?": *New York Herald,* January 11, 1876, 6.

146 "I covered up the nakedness": *St. Louis Daily Globe-Democrat,* January 5, 1876, 2.

146–147 "a monstrous field of corpses": *Die Gartenlaube* No. 2 (1876), 36.

147 "God bless you and my darling children": William Thomas to Cecelia Thomas, letter, BSA, Q.9.k.3.b, Nr. 2, 1g.

147 "To the Captain of the Steamer Mosel": Letter, December 11, 1875, BSA, Q.9.k.3.b, Nr. 2, 1h.

148 Etmers: *Die Gartenlaube* No. 2 (1876): 36.

149   "it was a sad, heart-rending business": *Die Gartenlaube* No. 2
      (1876): 37.
149   "You are dying": *Die Gartenlaube* No. 2 (1876): 37.
150   a partial confession: Interrogation of William Thomas by the mag-
      istrate, December 12, 1875, BSA, Q.9.k.3.b, Nr. 1, 26; Interroga-
      tion of William Thomas by P. J. Schnepel, December 13, 1875,
      BSA, Q.9.k.3.b, Nr. 1, 27.
151   "I wish that I was dead": *St. Louis Daily Globe-Democrat,* January 5,
      1876, 2.
151   "Henry Jekyll stood at times aghast": Robert Louis Stevenson, *The
      Strange Case of Dr. Jekyll and Mr. Hyde,* ed. Jenni Calder (1886; New
      York: Penguin, 1979), 87.
152   "the genius of the master craftsman Fuchs": *Die Gartenlaube* No. 1
      (1876): 19.
152   Dr. Hapke: *New York Herald,* January 17, 1876, 3. See also "The
      Thompson Infernal Machine," *Appleton's Journal of Literature, Sci-
      ence, and Art,* March 4, 1876, 317; "Infernal Machines," *Scientific
      American,* January 29, 1876, 64; "New Device in Infernal Machin-
      ery," *Manufacturer and Builder,* March 1876, 60–61.
152   "only a monster": *New York Herald,* February 19, 1876, 4.
153   "Here was a man": *Montreal Gazette,* January 18, 1876, 3. For other
      examples, see *Times,* December 18, 1875, 9; "Is Insurance a Bene-
      fit," *Scientific American,* January 8, 1876, 17; *Berliner Fremdenblatt,*
      December 18, 1875, trans. NARA, M44, Roll 28, Despatches from
      U.S. Ministers to German States and Germany, 1799–1906, No.
      233, enclosure 2.
153   "went into the destruction of ocean steamers": W. C. Church and F.
      P. Church, "Nebulae," 289.
153   "As in an anatomical dissection room": *Times,* December 22, 1875, 8.
154   "Get money": *Atlanta Constitution,* August 12, 1876, 1.
154   "earnest and manly spirit": *New York Herald,* January 17, 1876, 3.
154   "We do not feel called upon": *New York Herald,* January 17, 1876, 3.
      See also Nicholas Fish, U.S. Consul in Berlin, to Secretary of
      State, Letter, December 30, 1875, NARA, M44, Roll 28,
      Despatches from U.S. Ministers to German States and Germany,
      1799–1906, No. 233.
155   "to be scored up to the long account of monsters": Townsend,
      "Thomassen," 1. On the German side, the editor of *Germania* (De-
      cember 22, 1878, 4) also blamed Keith's involvement in a blood-
      thirsty war, as well as his decadent living.
155   "No one has ever suffered such tortures": Stevenson, *Dr. Jekyll,* 96.
156   "I have had ill-luck": *Times,* December 22, 1875, 8.

CHAPTER 13

157   "I wish there was no such thing as Christmas": Cecelia Thomas to
      William Thomas, letter, December 9, 1875, BSA, Q.9.k.3.b, Nr. 2,
      1d.

157 "Wretchedly sick": Cecelia Thomas to William Thomas, letter, December 11, 1875, BSA, Q.9.k.3.b, Nr. 2, 1e.

158 "Are you ill": Cecelia Thomas to William Thomas, telegram, December 11, 1875, BSA, Q.9.k.3.b, Nr. 3, 50.

158 "Write, or telegraph immediately": Cecelia Thomas to William Thomas, letter, December 11, 1875, BSA, Q.9.k.3.b, Nr. 2, 1e.

158 a detective arrived at her door: *New York Herald,* February 21, 1876, 6.

159 "My good my poor William": Cecelia Thomas to William Thomas, letter, no date, BSA, Q.9.k.3.b, Nr. 1, 189.

160 "Doctor, kill him!": *Die Gartenlaube* No. 2 (1876): 37; description of Thomas's death, BSA, Q.9.k.3.b, Nr. 1, 189.

160 "I have been a thick-head": Bremen police, second official report, BSA; *New York Herald,* February 19, 1876, 2.

161 resolute character: *Das Thomas-Verbrechen in Bremerhaven* (1875; Bremerhaven: Provincial-Zeitung, 1925), 25, BCA.

161 "She found a baggage check": *New York Times,* January 16, 1876, 12.

162 *Salier: New York Times,* December 20, 1875, 1; *New York Times,* January 3, 1876, 8; *New York Times,* January 4, 1876, 9; *New York Times,* January 18, 1876, 1.

163 "Prost Neu Jahr": *New York Herald,* February 3, 1876, 8.

163 an enterprising *Herald* reporter: *New York Herald,* February 21, 1876, 6; *Montreal Gazette,* February 10, 1876, 3.

164 Pinkerton Agency detective: Pinkerton report, BSA, 80–81. Cecelia's voyage home under the name "Thorpe" is confirmed by the Hamburg Passenger Lists, Family History Library, Church of Jesus Christ of Latter-Day Saints, Roll 0472909, Bd. 33, 1876.

164 "His eyes fixed upon her face," "public appeal for sympathy": *New York Herald,* February 21, 1876, 6.

165 Fannie lost her job: *St. Louis Republican,* February 17, 1876, 8.

165 Louisa Randolph: *New York Times,* January 11, 1877, 8

165 "the suit against her: *New York Times,* January 12, 1877, 3.

CHAPTER 14

167 "Warhawk": *Times,* January 6, 1876, 7; *Times,* June 10, 1873, 10; *New York Herald,* January 10, 1876, 8; W. Ruiners and F. Williamson, Scotland Yard, official report, BSA.

168 "exceptional information," "a not very timid imagination": *Times,* January 7, 1876, 9.

168 international sensation: The *Times* article was widely reprinted. For example, see *Berliner Fremdenblatt,* January 12, 1876; *New York Times,* January 4, 1876, 9; *New York Times,* January 21, 1876, 4; *New York Herald,* January 10, 1876, 8.

168 "perversion of human instincts": *New York Times,* December 17, 1875, 1.

168 "the mid-ocean": *New York Herald,* February 19, 1876, 4.

169 "convinced that Palmer is an imposter": W. Ruiners and F. Williamson, Scotland Yard, official report, BSA.

169 "blow him off his stool": Metropolitan Police, Scotland Yard, "The Fenians and the IRA," MPS Historical Timeline, available online at http://www.met.police.uk/ history/fenians.htm, December 22, 2004.

169 Alfred Nobel: BSA, Q.9.k.3.b, Nr. 1, 116; Nr. 5, 159b, 167a.

169 John Steuart: Though he was the Thompson's closest friend, Steuart was only briefly questioned: BSA, Q.9.k.3.b, Nr. 5, 175.

170 Englishman named Thompson: BSA, Q.9.k.3.b, Nr. 5, 218.

170 the public debates: In the last week of December 1875 and first week of January 1876, the *London Times* ran numerous letters from lawyers who commented on the legal aspects of the crime. For a summary of the German point-of-view, see the *Berliner Fremdenblatt*, December 30, 1875, translated in NARA, M44, Roll 28, Despatches from U.S. Ministers to German States and Germany, 1799–1906, No. 233, enclosure 9.

170 "the wickedest act": *Times*, December 24, 1875, 10.

170 "in the execution of his design": *Times*, December 24, 1875, 10.

170 135 orphans, 45 widows, and 20 hopelessly maimed victims: Georg Bessell, *Geschichte Bremerhavens* (Bremerhaven: Morisse, 1927), 489.

170 the gruesome debris: *Times*, December 22, 1875, 8.

171 Allan Pinkerton: Sigmund A. Lavine, *Allan Pinkerton—America's First Private Eye* (New York: Dodd, Mead, 1963). Further biographical information about Robert, William, and Allan Pinkerton can be found in the Family Director's File, 1854–1990, Pinkerton's National Detective Agency Records, Manuscript Division, Library of Congress, Washington, D.C.

172 "You are one of the best": O[rson] S[quire] Fowler, Phrenological Description, 1874, Box 4, Folder 7, Pinkerton's National Detective Agency Records.

173 "the fat man": Pinkerton report, BSA, 50, 99.

173 Captain Alexander: Pinkerton report, BSA, 73–74.

174 "I think you will get a clue": Pinkerton report, BSA, 68.

174 "a very tallow complexion": Pinkerton report, 103–104.

174 "when the next steamer comes": Pinkerton report, BSA, 16–17.

174–175 Skidmore: Pinkerton report, BSA, 70–71.

175 "the worn treasure box": *New York Herald*, January 5, 1876, 10.

176 *Old Dominion:* Pinkerton report, BSA, 52–55, 64–66.

176 "very ignorant men": Pinkerton report, BSA, 78.

176 "would, on a deathbed": Pinkerton report, BSA, 66.

177 "a sort of speculator": Pinkerton report, BSA, 82.

177 "had considerable dash": Pinkerton report, BSA, 131.

177 "Dynamite Johnson": *Sedalia Democrat*, February 8, 1876, 2.

177 "analytical and synthetic chemist": *Burlington Hawkeye*, December 30, 1875, 8.

178 Eagan: *St. Louis Republican*, December 31, 1876, 8.

178 "the creditor": *St. Louis Republican*, January 28, 1876, 8; *St. Louis Republican*, January 29, 1876, 3.

178   Allan Pinkerton arrived: *St. Louis Republican*, February 17, 1876, 8.

178–179   "a splendid likeness": Pinkerton report, BSA, 88.

179   John Menz: Pinkerton report, BSA, 114.

179   "He has told me so many stories": *St. Louis Republican*, January 1, 1876, 5. For more of Highland's reaction, see *Highland Union*, December 24, 1875, 2.

180   John Paris: Pinkerton report, BSA, 130.

180   "Born in Germany": *Edwardsville Intelligencer*, March 8, 1876, 2.

180   Wilkes Morris: Pinkerton report, BSA, 91–92.

180   James Sprunt: Pinkerton report, BSA, 93–94.

181   Luther Smoot: Pinkerton report, BSA, 107–110.

181   same forearm tattoos: *St. Louis Republican*, January 28, 1976.

181   "the annals of crime": *New York Herald*, February 4, 1876, 4.

182   "faintest of evidence": Halifax *Morning Chronicle*, April 6, 1876, clipping, BSA, Q.9.k.3.b, Nr. 5, 286.

182   leaving behind his brewery: Peter L. McCreath, *The Life and Times of Alexander Keith, Nova Scotia's Brewmaster* (Tantallon, Nova Scotia: Four East, 2001), 73.

182   Alexander Keith had somehow been involved: The informal legend became entrenched by Keith's first biographer, Reginald Harris, in *Hon. Alexander Keith: Ruler of the Craft in Nova Scotia, 1839–1873* (Halifax: Grand Lodge of Nova Scotia, 1957), 4.

183   rigid inspections, legislation: The history of international explosives laws is too complex to cover here, but the Bremerhaven disaster did contribute to public discussions over the need for such legislation. The *New York Times* immediately called for shipping regulations, and its position was supported by George M. Mowbray, well-known head of a large nitroglycerine manufactory: *New York Times*, December 14, 1875, 4; Letter to the editor, *New York Times*, December 23, 1875, 4. Within weeks, legislation was introduced in the U.S. House of Representatives to regulate transport of explosives on ships: *New York Times*, February 12, 1876, 1.

CHAPTER 15

185   "I hereby swear": *Atlanta Constitution*, June 8, 1876, 1.

186   Charles Schantz: *New York Times*, December 3, 1876, 2.

188   "What is Dynamite?": *Decatur Daily Republican*, December 22, 1875, 6.

188   "The time will come": *New York Times*, May 11, 1876, 6.

188–189   Fred Julian: *St Louis Daily Globe-Democrat*, January 12, 1876, 3.

190   "another dynamite plot": *Elyria Constitution*, November 9, 1876, 1.

190   Charging anywhere from $5 to $400: *Chicago Tribune*, February 23, 1885, 6.

190   "I no more ask a man": *Philadelphia Record*, March 17, 1883, 1; *Philadelphia Record*, March 25, 1883, 4.

191   *Doterel*: *New York Times*, June 15, 1881, 1; July 2, 1881; *New York Times*, July 1, 1881, 2; *New York Times*, October 26, 1881, 4.

192   "give Liverpool to flames": "The Hostiles," *Irish World*, May 28, 1881, 5.

192   "the modern Sodom": P. M. McGill, *The Irish Avenger or Dynamite Evangelist* (Washington, D.C.: Globe Printing, 1881).

192   The Cunard liner *Malta:* Details of the official investigations of the bombs found on the *Malta* and the *Bavaria* can be found in the volumes for the years 1881–1882, Fenian Brotherhood papers, PRO; NARA, Despatches from U.S. Ministers to Great Britain, M 30, Roll 138; and A. L. Drummond and D. H. Gilkinson, NARA, RG 87, Daily Reports of U.S. Secret Service Agents, 1875–1936.

192   "the machine is enclosed": "Who Sent the Machines?," *Philadelphia Times,* July 28, 1881, 1.

193   "On behalf of myself": James Alson to James Blaine, telegram, July 27, 1881, NARA, Miscellaneous Letters of the Dept. of State, M 179, Roll 591.

193   "pleasure of an ocean voyage": *Bucks County Gazette,* August 4, 1881, 2.

193   "Heaven only knows": *Fort Wayne Daily Gazette,* August 11, 1881, 4.

193   "How absurd!": *New York Times,* July 27, 1881, 2.

193   "sufficient encouragement": George Crump, British consul at Philadelphia, to Earl Granville, letter, October 29, 1880, PRO, Fenian Brotherhood papers, Vol. 26. Francis Kelly, a Philadelphia police officer who helped investigate the infernal machines for the State Department, concluded that the plot was a hoax: George W. Walling, *Recollections of a New York Chief of Police* (1887; Montclair, NJ: Patterson Smith, 1972), 570–571.

194   over the next five years: Kenneth R. M. Short, *The Dynamite War: Irish American Bombers in Victorian Britain* (Dublin: Gill & Macmillan, 1979).

194   originators of modern terrorism: See, for example, Lindsay Clutterbuck, "The Progenitors of Terrorism: Russian Revolutionaries or Extreme Irish Republicans," *Terrorism and Political Violence* 16 (2004): 154–282; Bruce Hoffman, *Inside Terrorism* (New York: Columbia University Press, 1998), 171; Andrew Sinclair, *An Anatomy of Terror: A History of Terrorism* (Oxford: Macmillan, 2003), 175–179.

195   "the dynamite used": *New York Times,* March 4, 1880, 2.

195   Warhawk, *Livadia:* New York Times, May 24, 1885, 11. Warhawk disappeared soon after and was arrested in Turkey for conspiring to assassinate the Grand Vizier: *New York Times,* June 7, 1881, 1.

EPILOGUE

197   "his decapitated head": Coroner to Bremerhaven registrar's office, Letter, December 20, 1875, BSA, Q.9.k.3.b, Nr. 1, 186.

198   "From the mask": *New York Herald,* January 11, 1876, 6.

200   According to local legend: "Untat eines Biedermannes," *Kurier Am Sonntag* (Bremen), December 11, 1988, BCA.

SELECTED BIBLIOGRAPHY

Alger, Horatio, Jr. *Ragged Dick or Street Life in New York.* Ed. Carl Bode. New York: Penguin, 1985.

Antonucci, Michael. "Code-Crackers." Supplement. Spies and Missions: A History of American Espionage. *Military History* (2002): 26–32.

Arnold, Samuel Bland. *Memoirs of a Lincoln Conspirator.* Ed. Michael W. Kauffman. Bowie, Maryland: Heritage, 1995.

Austin, Keith. *The Victorian Titanic: The Loss of the S. S.* Schiller *in 1875.* Devon: Halsgrove, 2001.

Baird, Nancy Disher. *Luke Pryor Blackburn, Physician, Governor, Reformer.* Lexington: University Press of Kentucky, 1979.

Barber, Richard, and "The Commodore." *Tresco Times — The Last Piece of England.* Devon: Halsgrove, 2002.

Bates, David Homer. *Lincoln in the Telegraph Office: Recollections of the United States Military Telegraph Corps During the Civil War.* New York: Century, 1907: 72–76.

———. "A Rebel Cipher Despatch: One Which Did Not Reach Judah P. Benjamin." *Harper's* 97 (1898): 105–09.

Beecher, Henry Ward. *Freedom and War.* Boston: Ticknor, 1863.

Bessell, Georg. *Geschichte Bremerhavens.* Bremerhaven: Verlag, 1927.

Brinnin, John Malcolm. *The Sway of the Grand Saloon: A Social History of the North Atlantic.* New York: Delacorte, 1971.

Brandt, Nat. *The Man Who Tried to Burn New York.* Syracuse, NY: Syracuse University Press, 1986.

Browning, Robert M. *From Cape Charles to Cape Fear: The North Atlantic Blockading Squadron During the Civil War.* Tuscaloosa: University of Alabama Press, 1993.

Bruns, Friedrich. *Das Uhrwerk Des Thomas in natürlicher Grösse Kurz vor der Explosion in Bremerhaven reparirt und nach dem Gedächtniss auf das Gehaueste gezeichnet und beschrieben von Friedr. Bruns, Uhrmacher in Bremen.* Bremen: Hensius, 1876.

Calder, James Traill. *Sketch of the Civil and Traditional History of Caithness from the Tenth Century.* Wick: Raw, 1887. Available online at Caithness Community Web Site. http://www.caithness.org/caithness/castles/ historyofcaithness December 21, 2004.

"Captain Roberts" [Augustus Charles Hobart-Hampden], *Never Caught: Personal Adventures Connected with Twelve Successful Trips in Blockade-Running During the American Civil War.* London: John Camden Hotten, 1867.

Clutterbuck, Lindsay. "The Progenitors of Terrorism: Russian Revolutionaries or Extreme Irish Republicans." *Terrorism and Political Violence* 16 (2004). 154–181.

Coats, Betty Spindler, and Raymond Jurgen Spahn, Eds. *The Swiss on the Looking Glass Prairie: A Century and a Half, 1831–1981*. Edwardsville, IL: Southern Illinois University Foundation, 1983.

Cornwallis, Kinahan. *Royalty in the New World; or, The Prince of Wales in America*. New York: Doolady, 1860.

Coughlin, Thomas Lamar. *Those Southern Lamars: The Stories of Five Illustrious Lamars*. Xlibris, 2000.

Dickens, Charles. *American Notes: and the Uncommercial Traveler*. Philadelphia: Peterson, n.d.

Dreiser, Theodore. *Newspaper Days*. Ed. T. D. Nostwich. Philadelphia: University of Pennsylvania Press, 1991.

Fingard, Judith. *The Dark Side of Life in Victorian Halifax*. Nova Scotia: Pottersfield, 1991.

Fox, Stephen. *Transatlantic: Samuel Cunard, Isambel Brunard, and the Great Atlantic Steamships*. New York: HarperCollins, 2003.

Gamber, Wendy. *The Female Economy: The Millinery and Dressmaking Trades, 1860–1930*. Urbana: University of Illinois Press, 1997.

Gerteis, Louis S. *Civil War St. Louis*. Lawrence: University of Kansas Press, 2001.

Gray, Clayton. *Conspiracy in Canada*. Montreal: L'Atelier, 1957.

Guttridge, Leonard F. and Ray A. Neff. *Dark Union: The Secret Web of Profiteers, Politicians, and Booth Conspirators that Led to Lincoln's Death*. Hoboken, NJ: Wiley, 2003.

Harland-Jacobs, Jessica. "'Hands Across the Sea': the Masonic Network, British Imperialism, and the North Atlantic World." *Geographical Review* 89 (1999): 237–53.

Harris, Reginald V. *Hon. Alexander Keith: Ruler of the Craft in Nova Scotia 1839–73*. Grand Lodge of Nova Scotia, 1957.

Hay, David, and Joan Hay. *The Last of the Confederate Privateers*. Edinburgh: Paul Harris, 1977.

Headley, John William. *Confederate Operations in Canada and New York*. New York: Neale, 1906.

Heritage Trust of Nova Scotia, *Founded Upon a Rock: Historic Buildings of Halifax and Vicinity Standing in 1867*. Halifax: Heritage Trust, 1967.

Hoffman, Bruce. *Inside Terrorism*. New York: Columbia University Press, 1998.

Horan, James D. *Confederate Agent: A Discovery in History*. New York: Crown, 1854.

Hunt, Cornelius E. *The Shenandoah, or the Last Confederate Cruiser*. New York: Carleton, 1867.

Jones, Francis I. W. "A Hot Southern Town: Confederate Sympathizers During the American Civil War." *Journal of the Royal Nova Scotia Historical Society* 2 (1999): 52–69.

———. "This Fraudulent Trade: Confederate Blockade-Running from Halifax During the Civil War." *Northern Mariner/La Marin du Nord* 9.4 (1999): 35–46.

Lamar, Charles Lafayette. "A Slave-Trader's Letter Book." *North American Review* 143 (1886): APS Online, 447–462.

Lavine, Sigmund A. *Allan Pinkerton—America's First Private Eye.* New York: Dodd, Mead, 1963.

Lewis, Lloyd. *The Assassination of Lincoln: History and Myth.* Lincoln: University of Nebraska Press, 1994.

Lotz, Pat. *Banker, Builder, Blockade Runner: A Victorian Embezzler and His Circle.* Kentville: NS: Gaspereau, 2002.

Lytton, Edward B. *The Dramatic Works of the Right Hon. Lord Lytton.* Freeport: Books for Libraries, 1972.

Mackay, James. *Allen Pinkerton: The Eye Who Never Sleeps.* London: Mainstream, 1996.

Mcreath, Peter L. *The Life & Times of Alexander Keith, Nova Scotia's Brewmaster.* Tantallon, Nova Scotia: Four East, 2001.

Marquis, Greg. *In Armageddon's Shadow: The Civil War and Canada's Maritime Provinces.* Montreal: McGill-Queen's University Press, 1998.

McLeod, Rebecca J. "Wreck of the *Pulaski.*" Ed. Mary DeLashmit. Available online at Eleanor Colson. Lamar Family Genealogy. http://members.aol.com/eleanorcol/WreckPulaski.html December 22, 2004.

Meyer, Douglas K. *Making the Heartland Quilt: A Geographical History of Settlement and Migration in Early-Nineteenth-Century Illinois.* Carbondale: Southern Illinois University Press, 2000.

Miller, Charles Grant. *Don Piatt, His Work and His Ways.* Cincinnati: Clarke, 1893.

Milton, David Hepburn. *Lincoln's Spymaster: Thomas Haines Dudley and the Liverpool Network.* Mechanicsburg, PA: Stackpole, 2003.

Morgan, James Morris. *Recollections of a Rebel Reefer.* New York: Houghton Mifflin, 1917.

Morn, Frank. *The Eye That Never Sleeps: A History of the Pinkerton National Detective Agency.* Bloomington: Indiana University Press, 1982.

Moss, Michael, and John Hume. *The Making of Scotch Whisky: A History of the Scotch Whisky Distilling Industry.* Edinburgh: James & James, 1981.

"New Device in Infernal Machinery." *Manufacturer and Builder.* March 1876, 60–61.

Norton, W. T., Ed. *Centennial History of Madison County, Illinois.* Chicago: Lewis, 1912.

Pitman, Benn, ed. *The Assassination of President Lincoln and the Trial of the Conspirators.* New York: Moore, Wilstach & Baldwin, 1865.

Raddall, Thomas H. *Halifax: Warden of the North.* Montreal: McClelland and Stewart, 1971.

Ray, Celeste. *Highland Heritage: Scottish Americans in the American South.* Chapel Hill: University of North Carolina Press, 2001.

Rayburn, Ella S. "Sabotage at City Point." *Civil War Times Illustrated* 22.2 (1983): 28–33.

Report of the Committee of Aldermen Respecting the Recent Explosion of the Gunpowder Magazine at Halifax. Halifax, Nova Scotia: Morning Journal Office, 1857.

Richards, Eric. *The Highland Clearances: People, Landlords and Rural Turmoil.* Edinburgh: Birlinn, 2000.

Rule, D. H. "The Boat Burners." Civil War Saint Louis. 2003. December 23, 2004. http://www.civilwarstlouis.com/boatburners/index.htm.

Rule, G. E. *Hell and Maria.* Civil War Saint Louis. 2001. December 23, 2004. http://www.civilwarstlouis.com/boatburners/steamermaria.htm.

Samples, Gordon. *Lust for Fame: The Stage Career of John Wilkes Booth.* Jefferson, NC: McFarland, 1982.

Schweizer, Max. *A Portrait of New Switzerland, 1831–1900.* Zug, Switzerland: Zürcher Books, 1979.

Short, K. R. M. *The Dynamite War: Irish-American Bombers in Victorian Britain.* Dublin: Gill & Macmillan, 1979.

Sinclair, Andrew. *An Anatomy of Terror: A History of Terrorism.* Oxford: Macmillan, 2003.

Sinclair, David. *The Land That Never Was: Sir Gregor Macgregor and the Most Audacious Fraud in History.* Cambridge, MA: Da Capo, 2004.

Smith, Mason Philip. *Confederates Downeast: Confederate Operations In and Around Maine.* Portland, ME: Provincial, 1985.

Smoot, L[uther] R[ice]. *Report of Col. L. R. Smoot, Quartermaster General of Virginia, Relative to the Virginia State Line.* Richmond, 1863.

Spencer, A. P. *Centennial History of Highland, Illinois, 1837–1937.* Highland, Illinois: Highland Historical Society, 1978.

Sprunt, James. *Chronicles of the Cape Fear River, 1660–1916.* Raleigh: Edward & Broughton, 1916.

———. *Derelicts.* Wilmington: Lord Baltimore, 1920.

Steers, Edward, Jr. *Blood on the Moon: The Assassination of Abraham Lincoln.* Lexington: University Press of Kentucky, 2001.

———. "Terror: 1860s Style." *North & South* 5 (2002): 12–18.

Stern, Philip Van Doren, Ed. *Secret Missions of the Civil War.* Chicago: Rand McNally, 1959.

Stevenson, Robert Louis. *The Strange Case of Dr. Jeckyll and Mr. Hyde.* 1886; New York: Scribner's, 1888.

Still, William N., Jr., John M. Taylor, and Norman C. Delaney. *Raiders and Blockaders: The American Civil War Afloat.* London: Brassey's, 1998.

Street, Sean. *The Wreck of the Deutschland.* London: Souvenir, 1992.

Suppiger, Joseph, Salomon Koepfli, and Kaspar Koepfli. *Journey to New Switzerland: Travel Account of the Koepfli and Suppiger Family to St. Louis and the Founding of New Switzerland in the State of Illinois.* Trans. Raymond J. Spahn. Ed. John C. Abbott. Carbondale: Southern Illinois University Press, 1987.

Taylor, James. *The Great Historic Families of Scotland.* London: J. S. Virtue, 1889.

Taylor, Thomas E. *Running the Blockade: A Personal Narrative of Adventures, Risks, and Escapes During the American Civil War.* London: John Murray, 1896.

Thatcher, Thomas. *Thomas Edgeworth Courtenay.* 2000. http://home.rochester.rr.com/thatchertree/tec.htm. March 27, 2004.

"The Thompson Infernal Machine." *Appleton's Journal of Literature, Science, and Art.* March 4, 1876, 317.

Tidwell, William A. *April '65: Confederate Covert Action in the American Civil War.* Kent, OH: Kent State University Press, 1995.

————. *Come Retribution: The Confederate Secret Service and the Assassination of Lincoln*. Jackson: University Press of Mississippi, 1988.

Townsend, George Alfred. "Thomassen." *Daily Graphic*. March 22, 1876, 171, 174.

Twain, Mark. "The Man That Corrupted Hadleyburg." *The Man That Corrupted Hadleyburg and Other Essays and Stories*. New York: Harper & Brothers, 1901.

————. *A Tramp Abroad*. Ed. Jim Manis. 1881; Hazelton, PA: Penn State Electronic Classics Series, 2000.

U.S. Senate, *Correspondence Concerning Aims Against Great Britain, Vol. IV*, Washington, D.C.: GPO, 1869.

Vandiver, Frank Everson. *Confederate Blockade Running Through Bermuda, 1861–1865: Letters and Cargo Manifests*. Ed. John Tory Bourne and Smith Stansbury. Austin: University of Texas Press, 1947.

Walker, Georgiana Gholson. *The Private Journal of Georgiana Gholson Walker, 1862–1876*. Ed. Dwight Franklin Henderson. *Confederate Centennial Studies* 25 (1963).

Wells, Thomas Henderson. *The Slave Ship* Wanderer. Athens: University of Georgia Press, 1967.

Wilkinson, J. *The Narrative of a Blockade Runner.* New York: Sheldon, 1877.

Wise, Stephen R. *Lifeline of the Confederacy: Blockade Running During the Civil War.* Columbia: University of South Carolina Press, 1988.

Wright, J. W. A. "Mysterious Fate of Blockade Runners." *Overland Monthly and Out West Magazine* 7 (1886): 298–303.

Young, Bennett Henderson. *Confederate Wizards of the Saddle*. Kennesaw, GA: Continental, 1958.

ACKNOWLEDGMENTS

I owe a special debt to the many archivists and librarians who helped with my research, including Gail Inglis at the North Highland Archive, Kathy Kessels at the Louis Latzer Memorial Public Library in Highland, Garry Shutlak and Philip Hartling at the Nova Scotia Archives, Uwe Jürgensen at the Bremerhaven City Archive, Adolf Hofmeister and the extremely helpful and patient staff at the Bremen State Archive, and William H. Davis at the National Archives and Records Administration. The interlibrary loan staff at Michigan State University went far beyond the call of duty. Various people provided invaluable genealogical information and local history. I am especially indebted to Thomas Thatcher, who provided exceptional information on his ancestor, Thomas Courtenay. Roy Worstell, Joseph Suppiger, Jeff Menz, James Zeller, Donald Roussin, Jr., and Kevin Kious, gracefully shared their knowledge of Highland and its families. Mark Roseman generously took time from his own work to help me navigate German archives and translate innumerable documents. Paul Travers and my son, Noah Blon, read versions of the manuscript and offered invaluable comments. My editor Brendan O'Malley wisely reigned in some of my narrative excesses, asked the right questions for clarity, and helped me capture the language and spirit of the time. I also owe a debt to those who encouraged me. Bruce Nunn, through the help of Pat Lotz, gave me a great chance to talk about my work on CBC–Nova Scotia radio. I am ever grateful to my agent, Ted Weinstein, for his faith in this project. Through the intense year of writing, I have treasured the emotional support of my favorite women: my daughter, Lissa Blon; my dearest friend, the gifted writer Maria Bruno; and my mother, Ruth Larabee, to whom this volume is dedicated.

INDEX

49773